PLAYING WITH HISTORY

Why do we feel the need to perform music in an historically informed style, and is this need related to wider cultural concerns? In
the most ambitious study of the topic to date, John Butt sums up recent debates on the nature of the early music movement and historically informed performance, calling upon a seemingly inexhaustible
fund of ideas gleaned from historical musicology, analytic philosophy, literary theory, historiography and theories of modernism and
postmodernism. He develops the critical views of both supporters
and detractors of the movement, while claiming ultimately that it
has more intellectual and artistic potential than its detractors may
have assumed. He also asks whether the phenomenon of historically
informed performance reflects changes in the culture of western
music and how it, in turn, may have influenced that culture, particularly in regard to such issues as the status of the composer, the
work, intentionality and notation.

JOHN BUTT is the Gardiner Professor of Music at the University of
Glasgow, having previously been a lecturer in music at the University of Cambridge and Fellow of King's College, and University Organist and Associate Professor of Music at the University of
California, at Berkeley. He is the author of *Bach Interpretation* (1990),
Bach: Mass in B Minor (1991), *Music Education and the Art of Performance
in the German Baroque* (1994), and editor of *The Cambridge Companion to
Bach* (1997), all published by Cambridge University Press. He is also
a highly acclaimed harpsichordist and organist and has recorded
ten CDs for Harmonia Mundi, France.

CAMBRIDGE MUSICAL TEXTS AND MONOGRAPHS
General editors: John Butt and Laurence Dreyfus

This series has as its centres of interest the history of performance and the
history of instruments. It includes annotated translations of authentic
historical texts on music and monographs on various aspects of historical
performance and instrument history.

MUSICAL PERFORMANCE AND RECEPTION
General editors: John Butt and Laurence Dreyfus

This series continues the aim of Cambridge Musical Texts and Monographs to publish books centred on the history of musical instruments and the history of performance, but broadens the focus to include musical reception in relation to performance and as a reflection of period expectations and practices.

Published

John Butt
Playing with History: The Historical Approach to Musical Performance

Forthcoming

James Garratt
Palestrina and the German Romantic Imagination: Interpreting Historicism in Nineteenth-Century Music

Daniel Leech-Wilkinson
The Modern Invention of Medieval Music: Scholarship, Ideology, Performance

Michael Musgrave and Bernard Sherman (eds)
Performing Brahms: Early Evidence of Performance Style

PLAYING WITH HISTORY

The Historical Approach to Musical Performance

JOHN BUTT

CAMBRIDGE
UNIVERSITY PRESS

PUBLISHED BY THE PRESS SYNDICATE OF THE UNIVERSITY OF CAMBRIDGE
The Pitt Building, Trumpington Street, Cambridge, United Kingdom

CAMBRIDGE UNIVERSITY PRESS
The Edinburgh Building, Cambridge CB2 2RU, UK
40 West 20th Street, New York NY 10011-4211, USA
477 Williamstown Road, Port Melbourne, VIC 3207, Australia
Ruiz de Alarcón 13, 28014 Madrid, Spain
Dock House, The Waterfront, Cape Town 8001, South Africa

http://www.cambridge.org

First published 2002
Reprinted 2004

Printed in the United Kingdom at the University Press, Cambridge

Typeface Baskerville Monotype 11/12.5 pt.   *System* LATEX 2$_\varepsilon$ [TB]

A catalogue record for this book is available from the British Library

Library of Congress cataloguing in publication data
Butt, John.
Playing with history: the historical approach to musical performance / John Butt.
p.   cm.
Includes bibliographical references and indexes.
ISBN 0 521 81352 2 (hardback) – ISBN 0 521 01358 5 (paperback)
1. Performance practice (Music)   2. Music – History and criticism.   I. Title.
ML457 B92 2002 781.4'311 – dc21   2001043656

ISBN 0 521 81352 2 hardback
ISBN 0 521 01358 5 paperback

Contents

vii

Preface

We want to serve history only to the extent that history serves life.
Nietzsche[1]

History has one great strength over the things a Waldzell tutor feels to be worthy of his interest: it deals with reality. Abstractions are fine, but I think people also have to breathe air and eat bread.
Hermann Hesse, *The Glass Bead Game*[2]

Perhaps every work of scholarship and criticism contains a trace of autobiography, and this could hardly be truer of the present case. Much of my career has been taken up with both performance and scholarship and thus inevitably with the constant mediation between them. Moreover, much of the performance and much of the scholarship has related directly to the issue of 'historically informed performance' (henceforth HIP) and the debates about this concept have become particularly vigorous during the very course of my career.

When I began a dissertation on performance practice issues in Bach during the early 1980s at the University of Cambridge, the order of things seemed quite clear in the context of that faculty. Composition stood at the top of the hierarchy and performance (which had barely a place in the curriculum) at the bottom; scholarship in performance stood marginally above performance itself so long as it involved rigorous, scientific and historical methods. I could claw my way a rung or two higher by working on a Great Composer and by tying in some of the results with musical analysis (the most respected discipline below composition proper). What seemed obvious to me was that historical performance was fundamentally anathema to the modernist regime; it was something to be seen – more often than not – as a rather bemusing throwback to nineteenth-century antiquarianism. If HIP did share anything with modernism it was in its counter-cultural credentials, its distance from a supposedly conservative mainstream. Particularly fascinating was the fact that a huge industry connected to the revival of early music and HIP was blossoming just down the road in London. Yet this represented the activities of surprisingly small groups of people who seemed to have enjoyed virtually no consistent or institutional training in history or historical performance. The movement was dominated by a handful of scholar–performers directing versatile vocalists and instrumentalists who learned the historical styles and techniques more or less 'on the job'.

Moving to California in 1989, many of my impressions and assumptions were completely overturned. Here many universities and conservatories did, in fact, teach historical performance on a far more institutionalised basis than in Britain, yet the professional success of the movement was considerably slimmer; indeed many of the best American artists had moved abroad. Instrument building could be of an extraordinarily high standard and there was much public enthusiasm for early music and HIP, particularly as a counter-cultural movement. Most inspiring of all was the critical work of new colleagues such as Joseph Kerman and Richard Taruskin, both of whom had been connected with the movement in one way or another and both of whom looked critically at common assumptions regarding both historical performance and historical research *per se*. They called into even greater question the concept of the academic composer at the head of the musical food chain. Most striking – and jarring, given my own experiences – was Taruskin's association of HIP with modernism. Had I not just moved from an environment in which modernism had seemed the very antithesis of HIP, in which members of the early music movement often placed themselves in direct opposition to the culture of progress and the relentless advance of 'technique'? Another issue was Taruskin's belief that research into performance practice is categorically distinct from performance and that good scholarship does not necessarily result in good performance. Yet I felt that my development as a performer had definitely benefited from my research as a graduate student (and beyond); indeed it would be impossible for me to perform the way I do now without the benefit of that experience. But, taking his view on board, it was clear that the relationship was not direct – with each new discovery neatly paralleling a new way of performing – but that the very action of historical thinking, 'playing with history' as it were, informed my entire attitude towards performance.

This experience of crossing cultures, crossing disciplines of performance and scholarship and, increasingly, experiencing the critical turn in musicology itself, has led directly to the questions formulated in this book. Given the diversity of impressions and opinions, what actually is Historically Informed Performance? Or rather, what conceptions of western music does it seem to confirm, alter or develop? How, in turn, might it reflect changes in our cultural conceptions of music? Why has it happened on such a scale during the last few decades and how does it fit into contemporary culture? Here there is no room for a comprehensive history of the movement or advice on how to 'do' historical performance – there is plenty of that elsewhere – rather I write from a position of bafflement in the face of the cross-currents I have experienced, and by examining my own motives and preferences. It clearly follows from the ongoing debate about HIP, as the first chapter shows, and could hardly have been written without the precedents set by previous writers. I endeavour to adopt and develop the critical stances of such writings although, perhaps inevitably, my ultimate goal is to provide a defence for the movement; it has been debunked enough already. Much of what I write is done in the – perhaps erroneous – belief that HIP is an essential part of contemporary culture and that, however great its shortcomings, it contributes to the continued survival and flourishing of western music.

The study begins with a review of important stages in the HIP debate as a way of drawing out threads and topics that inform the remainder of the study. The debate is traced from the seminal work of Adorno in 1950 through to important articles by Laurence Dreyfus and Robert Morgan in the 1980s. A large part of the discussion is dedicated to the books by Richard Taruskin and Peter Kivy: Taruskin's study represents a fascinating critique of the movement from within the increasingly rich and polyglot discipline of critical musicology while Kivy's represents the supremely abstract discourse of analytical philosophy. The two could hardly be more different although some of their resulting opinions are strikingly similar. They perhaps represent the two poles of the discourse on HIP, the one rich in its rhetorical flair and diverse cultural perspectives, the other seemingly logical and precise. Such is the success and sheer force of Taruskin's writing (published as a whole in 1995) that many within musicology and music criticism in general have perceived that the debate over HIP is effectively closed, that there is nothing more to say, and, indeed, that the movement as a whole is running out of steam (like modernism itself).[3] I attempt here to show that Taruskin's work – far from closing the debate – is really the work that has most made future debate possible and has entirely reformulated the issues concerned with the discussion of HIP.

The next three chapters examine how HIP relates to three important parameters in our traditional conception of western music: the work, the composer and the intermediary role of notation. How does HIP relate to the view of musical works as somehow universal and portable from one historical context to another? Does it actually effect a change in our preconceptions of works? I suggest that HIP gained much of its prestige by capitalising on existing attitudes to the integrity of musical works, yet – in its admission of history and the concept of contingency – it has actually served to loosen the concept of the essential musical work. The relation of HIP to the concept of a composer and his intentions has endured particular critical approbation within the early music debate. Chapter 3 puts the question in a new way: instead of inquiring into the composer's intentions in order to discern a correct performance, this study suggests that HIP can actually enable us to form a different concept of the composer and his intentions, namely, how his encounter with the media and practices of performance fed into the very act of composition in the first place. In other words, performance might be a useful parameter in understanding how a piece of music came to be created and notated. Performance could then be seen as much a part of the past, as of the future, of a newly finished piece. As chapter 2 also suggests, the boundary between work and performance thus becomes much looser when the issue of historical performance is raised. The last chapter in this sequence examines the idea of notation as a recipe for performance, one we commonly presume to have developed progressively over the years. Consideration of HIP allows us to reformulate this function of notation by suggesting many other ways in which notation may relate (or not) to performance, the composer and the 'work', however these are to be understood. This study thus consolidates some of the points about work and author formulated in the previous two chapters.

Having discussed what I consider to be the significance of HIP in refining or developing our conceptions of music, the final part of the book attempts to place the movement within the wider cultural context. Chapter 5 examines HIP from the perspective of modernism and post-modernism. Clearly there is hardly the room here to define either of these concepts in any way that can begin to be adequate. I try to isolate those aspects that might relate most closely to musical performance and history, in the belief that HIP has to fit somewhere within the debate on modernity, that there is no such thing as a purely isolated cultural phenomenon and that even the most naive antiquarianism must relate – if only by negation – to larger cultural movements over the last century or so.

The final chapter takes a closer look at a particular phenomenon related to the modernism/postmodernism debate, namely the culture of 'Heritage' and preservationism that has so characterised the final decades of the twentieth century. Perhaps the coincidence of this with the overwhelming commercial success of HIP is too obvious to have deserved much comment in the recent debates. Or, more likely, Heritage has generally been considered an amateurish and populist form of history and thus not serious enough to be part of the academic discourse on musical performance. But the connection between the two seems unmistakable and the Heritage industry must surely provide much of the context in which it has become fashionable to invest considerable financial resources in performances 'on original instruments' just as one does in 'period' furnishings, houses and drama.

I cannot claim to be able to explain all that happens, or might happen, within the world of HIP. Rather I try to present a more theoretical conception of HIP by standing back from the immediate day-to-day concerns of the movement. In this way I hope at least to show how the movement has more intellectual and artistic potential than its detractors might have assumed. I make liberal use of various philosophical and cultural forms of 'theory', but in a relatively practical, ad hoc, way that, I suppose, betrays both my English empirical disposition and my untutored status in so many of the disciplines I co-opt. But, hopefully, the combination of approaches and the peculiarities of my experience will shed some new light on what Lydia Goehr describes as HIP's potential to help 'us overcome that deep-rooted desire to hold the most dangerous of beliefs, that we have at any time got our practices absolutely right'.[4]

Acknowledgements

Some portions of the following chapters have already been published in earlier versions. Chapter 1 (and small sections of chapter 3) draw on reviews I have written of Richard Taruskin's *Text and Act* and Peter Kivy's *Authenticities*. I am grateful to Oxford University Press for permission to reprint material from 'Acting up a Text: The Scholarship of Performance and the Performance of Scholarship', *EM*, 24 (1996), pp. 323–32, and to the *American Musicological Society* for permission to reprint material from my review of Kivy's *Authenticities*, in *JAMS*, 53 (2000), pp. 402–11.[5] Chapter 4 is an expanded and revised version of my article 'Performance on Paper: Rewriting the Story of Notational Progress', *Actualizing Absence: The Pastness of Performance*, ed. Mark Franko and Annette Richards (Hanover, NH, 2000), pp. 137–55.

This study would have been impossible without tremendous help from a large variety of scholars and performers. I am particularly grateful to the following who have given me a wide range of information, responses, cautions and hints over the last six years or so: Wye J. Allenbrook, Suzanne Aspden, Katherine Bergeron, Anna Maria Busse-Berger, Dorottya Fabian, Fabrice Fitch, Lydia Goehr, Thomas Gray, Joseph Kerman, Richard Luckett, Anthony Newcomb, Max Paddison, Andrew Parrott, Joshua Rifkin, David Sherman, Mary Ann Smart, Reinhard Strohm, Richard Taruskin and Abbi Wood. I owe particular thanks to those who have read (or claim to have read) an entire draft of the book: Karol Berger, Georgina Born, my father, Wilfrid Butt, Laurence Dreyfus, Iain Fenlon, Christopher Hogwood, Daniel Leech-Wilkinson and Roger Parker. All errors are, I suppose, still mine, although it is comforting to have such a large and distinguished group of people with whom to share at least some of the blame.

My thanks also go to the two institutions that have employed me during the course of writing this book: to the University of California at Berkeley, which enabled me to begin the project with a sabbatical in the first half of 1995, and to the University of Cambridge, which enabled me to draw the project closer to completion with a sabbatical in the first half of 2000.

Last, but not least, my loving thanks go to my family: to Sally and sons Christopher and James; to Victoria, who was born after two chapters were drafted, in 1996; and to Angus, who arrived, somewhat unexpectedly, in 1999, at least in time for the composition of the last chapter and most of the first. I could not claim that this extensive and expressive group of people has sped up the project in any way whatsoever, but they have rendered the work infinitely more pleasant.

Abbreviations

BJA	*The British Journal of Aesthetics*
CM	*Current Musicology*
COJ	*Cambridge Opera Journal*
EM	*Early Music*
JAAC	*The Journal of Aesthetics and Art Criticism*
JAMS	*The Journal of the American Musicological Society*
JM	*The Journal of Musicology*
MQ	*The Musical Quarterly*

PART I

Historically informed performance in music criticism

I

Joining the historical performance debate

Some of the parameters of the debate over historical performance were set many years before the movement became a truly public phenomenon in the late 1960s. For instance, the commemoration of the year of Bach's death in 1950 occasioned diverse opinions on the way his music should be performed: the prominent composer and performer, Paul Hindemith, advocated the wholesale restoration of the instruments and performing practices of Bach's own age:

We can be sure that Bach was thoroughly content with the means of expression at hand in voices and instruments, and if we want to perform his music according to his intentions we ought to restore the conditions of performance of that time.[1]

Here we have the fundamental assumption that a composer fits effortlessly and contentedly into the culture of his own age, that what he got coincided with what he wanted, and that a restoration of contemporary performing conventions will thus coincide with the composer's intentions. Given that Hindemith himself was one of the major composers of the age, the suggestion that we might wish to follow the composer's intentions must have carried some considerable force in 1950. Both Hindemith's historicist attitude and his productions of early music were of tremendous influence on Nikolaus Harnoncourt who, perhaps more than anyone over the next twenty years, made the case for HIP.[2] He was recording with early instruments by the early 1960s and his countless essays from this pioneering period did much to popularise the virtues of associating earlier music with its original performance practice. More importantly, he was perhaps the first to stress that music and its performance before the nineteenth century involved a different

3

aesthetic attitude, one stressing the speech-like and rhetorical aspects of music. Each musical style and period before 1800 had a different ethos that brought with it different conceptions of performance, and it is thus wrong to think of changes in performance and instrument construction in terms of a necessary 'progress'.[3] Both in his rejection of the status quo and his early alliance with Hindemith, Harnoncourt's case is symptomatic of the association of HIP with a particular strand of modernism. Indeed Harnoncourt was one of the first to suggest that his historical reconstructions represented a 'modern' adventure and not simply a direct return to the past.[4] Behind much of his work as a performer and writer lies the sense that we have been in a prolonged state of cultural decline, one that HIP – by re-introducing us to conceptions of music more varied than our bland present – may rectify. In this pessimistic diagnosis of the present Harnoncourt comes remarkably close to Theodor W. Adorno, although his remedy is radically different.

Adorno in 1951 poured scorn on historical reconstruction: only the 'progressive' modern performance resources (indeed the modern arrangements by Schoenberg and Webern) could reveal the full import of Bach's music which stood head and shoulders above the pitiful concerns of its own age. Speaking at a time when the early music movement was still in its infancy, but when western Germany was undergoing an enormous process of rebuilding and restoration, he suggests that:

the neo-religious Bach is impoverished, reduced and stripped of the specific musical content which was the basis of his prestige. He suffers the very fate which his fervent protectors are least willing to admit: he is changed into a neutralized cultural monument, in which aesthetic success mingles obscurely with a truth that has lost its intrinsic substance. They have made him into a composer for organ festivals in well-preserved Baroque towns, into ideology.[5]

Adorno's specific comments about the levelling proclivities of 'historical' performance and the inadequacy of the older forms of performance sound very much like the types of criticism that became familiar over the next decades from musicologists such as Paul Henry Lang and musicians such as Pinchas Zukerman:[6]

Mechanically squeaking *continuo*-instruments and wretched school choirs contribute not to sacred sobriety but to malicious failure; and the thought that the shrill and rasping Baroque organs are capable of capturing the long waves of the lapidary, large fugues is pure superstition. Bach's music is separated from the general level of his age by an astronomical distance. Its eloquence returns only when it is liberated from the sphere of resentment and obscurantism, the triumph of the subjectless over subjectivism. They say Bach, mean Telemann and are secretly in agreement with the regression of musical consciousness which even without them remains a constant threat under the pressures of the culture industry. (Adorno, 'Bach Defended', p. 145)

Whatever we might think of Adorno's views today, he does raise some important questions that proponents of HIP frequently miss. He sees the fledgling movement to restore older instruments and performance practices as part of a wider cultural malaise in the wake of the depersonalising forces of industrialism and late capitalism. Instead of setting up a form of resistance to contemporary society, as was done by the increasing isolation, introspection and complexity of the Second Viennese School (Adorno's ever-pessimistic hope for the future of musical culture) the culture of restoration resorts to a facile objectivity that does not even notice the subjective challenge posed by great modern art. As mass culture becomes ever more superficial it substitutes the fetish for historical detail for a profundity of which it is not even any longer aware. Adorno is clearly representative of a form of musical modernism that sees the avant-garde as absolutely crucial in somehow revealing the truth of our desperate condition. Pessimistic though his tone may be, he evidently still believes in a form of progress, that music culture and composition must move forward, however bleak the prospects ahead. Perhaps this is more a sense of irreversibility than of progress as such.[7] But, whether this is progress or irreversibility there is clearly a fundamental antipathy between the modernism, as represented by the Second Viennese School and Adorno, and any culture of restoration, such as HIP. Hindemith and Adorno not only represent the two poles of opinion about HIP, they also show how the movement, in its post-war form, sits both within and without the culture of modernism.

As I hope to show in the following chapters, Adorno was surprisingly accurate in diagnosing a move away from a culture of progress and ever-renewing modernity towards one based more on restoration and recycling. Much that was profound or challenging may well have been lost in the process. But, given what I perceive to be crucial shifts in cultural consciousness, it is impossible for us to know what we have lost. Indeed to resort to Adorno's particular brand of modernism would itself be a sterile form of resurrectionism, since we have passed the historical moment from which he was talking and cannot authentically restore his ideals. The various forms of historical restoration, of which HIP is an obvious component, are, I believe, an 'authentic' expression of our contemporary cultural condition bringing new experiences and insights into our world. Most importantly, this lies largely in the realisation that the culture of inexorable technological progress is itself an historically conditioned phenomenon, that conserving what we already have or might already have lost is now at least as essential as forging new paths into the future unknown.

Adorno's later writing reveals what perhaps lay behind his strident antipathy in 1951. In his typographical sketch opening his *Introduction to the Sociology of Music*, those associated with HIP (at least as it stood in 1962) are christened 'resentment listeners'.[8] This category comes at the very bottom of the ranking of those constituting the culture of classical music, just above the 'jazz listener'. What is immediately striking is how Adorno relates the early music culture to totalitarian politics: the resentment listener normally sympathises with orders and collectives, together with the political consequences (p. 10); all expression and individuality is to be expunged, 'the gypsies are to croak now as they did before, in concentration camps' (p. 11). This culture yearns for the pre-individual state (witnessed by its penchant for Baroque music, which Adorno considers – apart from Bach – as a form of levelling mediocrity)[9] while it cannot escape its own post-individual state. Its process is 'formally comparable to the fascist manipulation that invested the compulsory collective of the atomized with the insignia of a precapitalist, nature-grown "people's community"' (p. 12).

Indeed, during the 1930s in Germany both the ecological movements and the popular youth movements in early music had been strongly infiltrated by the Nazis (see p. 210 below), so it is easy to understand Adorno's personal position. Yet Hindemith too had been a refugee from the same regime and he – together with several others in the same circumstances – did much to cultivate the early music culture of American campuses. Here there was no inkling of the political associations that had arisen in Germany and, more often than not, the American culture of HIP acquired liberal connotations. This would seem to suggest that a culture dedicated to restoring practices from a past age does not, by definition at least, seek to restore the political circumstances of that age. The notion of a 'lost innocence' can serve a number of political ideologies – sometimes fanatically – but we should refrain from prejudging all forms of restoration as inescapably reactionary.

So far then, we have the modernist–antimodernist identity of HIP, together with the reactionary–liberal dichotomy, both of which suggest that the culture of HIP is not so simply explained as it might first appear.

Hamilton, Kenneth L.
8/11/09

These two issues form major threads throughout the present book and receive a more thorough examination in the last two chapters.

THE HIP CULTURE OF THE 1980S – THE DIAGNOSES
OF LAURENCE DREYFUS AND ROBERT MORGAN

Laurence Dreyfus, building on some of the implications of Adorno's view, gives the most perceptive critique of HIP from the vantage point of the early 1980s, thus a full decade after it had become a major component of public musical culture. He also introduces several themes that become central to the debate as it accelerated over the next fifteen years. From the outset, he poses a question that is crucial to the present book (one that has perhaps received less attention than it ought in the meantime) namely, why the historically 'correct' performance of music should become such a particular issue in the late twentieth century.[10] Moreover, we learn that it is wrong to view it purely as a 'thing' since it is definable only as a social practice, the tacit assumptions and activities of a range of people.[11] And, as is taken up in the last chapter of this book, it is not just a matter of looking at the people producing the instruments, texts and performances but also at the consumers and audiences without whom the HIP movement could never have been a commercial concern in the first place.

The commonplace assumption that HIP resulted from 'progress' in musicology is simply inadequate, particularly since there has been an increasing rift between HIP and post-war musicology (Dreyfus, 'Early Music', p. 311). As Joseph Kerman observed around the same time, musicology has many things to do other than provide material for performers: history and criticism are the disciplines he mentions specifically in 1985,[12] but, by the end of the century, this list would have expanded almost beyond recognition to cover the whole gamut of cultural and critical studies. A recent and seemingly comprehensive study of the entire field of musicology (1999) contains no chapter on HIP as such and remarks that it is 'Modernist, and – as an intellectual concept, perhaps – exhausted . . . it proved impossible to find an author who could feel that there was something useful that could be said beyond a summary of conclusions of arguments current in the 1980s.'[13] Performance is more important as an element of musicology than ever, but now more as a feature of the ontology and receptive traditions of works, institutions or performing communities, or as a counterpart of analysis. Nevertheless, Kerman's assumption that most outsiders would normally associate musicology with the music they hear at concerts and particularly with the unearthing of older repertories, probably still holds true.

As Dreyfus argues, musicologists have taken particular relish in debunking the claims of HIP's often spotty and inadequate scholarship. But he also shows how this criticism often covertly defends the supposed monumental and unified institution of western music against the revolutionary force of HIP. He outlines the fundamental opposition that early music is supposed to make to the 'self-aggrandising individualism prevalent in Mainstream musical praxis' (p. 299), something that was to become far less the case in the later 1980s and 1990s, as HIP threw up more and more of its own self-aggrandising figures. Instead of reaching some sort of spiritual understanding with the composer, HIP in its orthodox mode of the early 1980s dealt mainly with empirical evidence, thus substituting objectivism for subjectivism, relativism for critical appreciation, precisely as Adorno had complained: 'Objectivity is not left over once the subject is subtracted' (Dreyfus, 'Early Music', p. 300). It is thus easy to brand the movement as profoundly puritanical, relishing its very denial of the subjective and emotional.

Yet even from Dreyfus's 1983 standpoint it was evident that the best performers (he names Gustav Leonhardt) used their history in startlingly imaginative ways. What was so beneficial about HIP was the fact that the best performers had to rethink their entire interpretative strategy, thus challenging the assumed 'natural' expressivity of the mainstream. In a deeply prophetic statement, Dreyfus notes that successful HIP does not (indeed, I might add, cannot) return us to the past 'but reconstructs the musical object in the here and now, enabling a new and hitherto silenced subject to speak' (p. 304). This realisation of the *present* significance of HIP had already been acknowledged by some of the more perceptive writers of the 1950s,[14] and also became a central point of Taruskin's critique around the same time as Dreyfus. It relates to one of Taruskin's more surprising claims, that HIP is a symptom of late twentieth-century modernism.

While it is already clear that there is a fundamental antipathy between Adorno's modernism – which requires the constant taunting of a progressive avant-garde – and early music, Dreyfus notes their reciprocal negation of a comfortable present. Just as modernism purposely engages in defamiliarisation, HIP renders strange favourite masterpieces inherited from the past and, in consequence, often experiences exactly the same sort of sharp criticism from the conservative mainstream. Almost unintentionally, HIP performers become branded as dangerous, counter-cultural figures. By overthrowing accepted models of musical taste, HIP threatens many of the supposed certainties of civilised society. Indeed critics both of the avant-garde and of HIP analyse the phenomena as though they were pathological disorders.

Yet early music performers are also counter-cultural in another, more conscious, way, which Dreyfus relates to the denial of envy. The practice of HIP (at least as Dreyfus saw it in 1983) builds purposely on the equality of its members, under no conductor, all sharing a number of performing functions, avoiding virtuosity, enjoying a cross-over between the professional and amateur world and thus experiencing a closer relationship with a like-minded audience and producing historically integrated – rather than sensational – programmes. He might well have added that many involved in the movement during the seminal decades of the 1960s and 70s were, in fact, counter-cultural in other ways, seeing in HIP a way of redeeming music from its elitist and hierarchical connotations. In an interesting – and perhaps underplayed – footnote, Dreyfus adds that much of the recent improvement in HIP standards resulted from an influx of conservatory-trained musicians, themselves eager to escape the rat-race of the mainstream.

It is worth outlining some of the interesting contradictions between the 'purist', non-hierarchical conception of HIP that Dreyfus so graphically formulates and the original historical practices with which it is assumed to correspond. First, it may well be that many forms of performance before the nineteenth century did not use a conductor in the modern sense. Yet most had a director (often the composer) who clearly had a status and will that dominated the other performers. Secondly, while performers were extremely versatile, they were often far more rigidly ranked than even a modern orchestra would require. Such ranking usually mirrored a broader social ranking and much of the music was written to confirm or exploit the hierarchical nature of society in general. Far from eschewing virtuosity, many forms of music making from the mid-sixteenth century onwards were extremely virtuosic, the technical agility required of singers in Baroque opera far exceeding that which became the norm by the twentieth century. And if velocity was not a feature of the performance practice there was often some element that sharply distinguished it from the amateur ethos outlined by Dreyfus: e.g. improvisation in Baroque and Classical keyboard performance, memorisation of an enormous corpus of liturgical music in the Middle Ages. Thus the stereotypical HIP milieu that Dreyfus describes tends to use an imagined utopian past as a way of criticising and 'improving' the present. The modern conventions of

safe, objectivist scholarship help sift out the diversity and messy realities
of history and present the past as a potent social practice with a political
relevance in reforming the present condition.

While Dreyfus attempts to explain how HIP happened by relating it to
a form of discontent with – even protest against – an assumed norm, he
does not fully address the issue of why it should have happened precisely
when it did, why it became such a tremendous commercial success in the
1970s and 80s. Robert P. Morgan considers this wider cultural issue in his
contribution to a valuable collection of essays, edited by Nicholas Kenyon
in 1988.[15] He links the sudden widespread concern for historical accuracy
with the contemporary situation in musical culture as a whole, characterised as it is 'by an extraordinary degree of insecurity, uncertainty, and
self-doubt – in a word, by anxiety' (Morgan, 'Tradition', p. 57). He outlines a fundamental change in our conception of musical culture, from
one based on unbroken linear tradition, which is not consciously aware
of the great difference between that which has survived from the past
and the present, to one in which the past has become an enormous 'field
of instantaneous possibilities'. One has complete access to a wide range
of historical data, thus obscuring 'the very distinction between past and
present' (pp. 59–60). Morgan goes on to observe a similar diversity in
compositional style and the increasing multi-culturalism in the music
scene. But this is possible 'precisely because, and only because, we have
no well-defined sense of the musical present' (p. 66). On the assumption
that the availability of all cultures is basically no culture at all, Morgan
suggests that our greed for diverse cultures grows so far that we are even
keen to assimilate the older versions of our own culture. The quest for
historical 'authenticity' thus reflects the very absence of a culture we can
still call our own. Adorno would surely have concurred with this, and
also – for different reasons – Nikolaus Harnoncourt, who suggests that
the historical approach to performance 'is a symptom of the loss of a
truly living contemporary music'.[16] HIP is thus to him a sort of last-ditch
rescue attempt of western musical culture. As Hermann Hesse put it in
the words of Joseph Knecht's friend Plinio, in *The Glass Bead Game*, 'our
resigned sterility proves the worthlessness of our whole culture and our
intellectual attitudes. We analyse the laws and techniques of all the styles
and periods of music . . . but produce no new music ourselves.'[17]

Morgan suggests that while tradition flourished we were quite happy
to adapt and arrange earlier music for our own purposes, but now everything must be restored since 'we have no clear idea of what "up to date"
means' (p. 68). Just as many contemporary composers borrow multiple

languages from others, the historicist performer recovers old musical languages as if they were fossils, and the resulting performance automatically lacks 'the immediate, unreflected, and "natural" delivery of a native speaker' (p. 70). A similar nostalgic spirit informs house restoration and furniture, and some even seek to restore the songs and shows of the 1930s to their 'original' performance style (pp. 75–8). In sum, music history, like history in general is over, and with no purposes of our own we can no longer interpret the past, only passively reconstruct it within the culture of the museum. This 'cultural identity crisis' Morgan sees as having roots as far back as the seventeenth century, part of a long process of the divided self and the increasing loss of individual identity (pp. 78–81).

Morgan's pessimistic diagnosis has much in common with Roger Scruton's, as I discuss below, and also shares with Taruskin a concern for the loss of tradition that HIP seemingly implies. The 'end of history' hypothesis is convincing and his suggestion that HIP belongs within a larger culture of nostalgia that restores other artefacts becomes the subject of chapter 6 below. But where I differ is in rejecting the sense of pessimism he seems to present. Indeed, his very tone suggests a nostalgia for a past order that is precisely of a piece with the culture of restoration itself. While the HIP scholar/performer typically wishes to return performance to a lost Eden, Morgan, in turn, laments the loss of an age in which stylistic difference was unnoticed owing to the strength of one's own tradition. Both these facets of the past are, of course, equally unrecoverable.

While Morgan is quite correct to suggest that the access to such a wide range of historical data effaces the distinction between past and present, this was surely also the case with 'tradition' as he describes it. Within tradition one used whatever was deemed canonical from the past entirely for presentist purposes and consigned everything else to oblivion. Both modes – restoration and tradition – thus evidence different ways of 'misusing' the past. Perhaps it would be truer to say that restoration movements such as HIP themselves represent the culmination of a long tradition, one stretching back to the Renaissance. It was that era which first became conscious of the past 'as a foreign country', one that was admired as a corrective to the present condition.[18] By the end of the twentieth century the collection of 'differences' had become so great that it was no longer possible to be certain of *any* similarity between past and present; we had better preserve everything it is still possible to know or collect, 'just in case'. Moreover, as Daniel Leech-Wilkinson argues, it was only in the twentieth century that there were enough people with the education, resources and money to make so much early music marketable, and recording technology has revolutionised the way music is used and the amount that is available.[19] Thus the interest in past music and practices, far from signifying a failure in the present condition, might actually reflect the luxurious possibilities opened up by modernity.

The view that HIP style will automatically lack the unmediated, unreflective delivery of a 'natural' speaker is, of course, the crucially contentious point. Dreyfus had already explored the notion that HIP could encourage imaginative performers to use history to discover new possibilities, new possible worlds of musical expression. And, by the late 1980s it was quite clear that HIP could engender its own traditions, albeit 'invented'. Given that (as Morgan stresses) constant change and adaptation is essential to tradition, and that the same is happening within the invented traditions of HIP, it is difficult to distinguish qualitatively between a tradition that is newly invented and one that appears to be continuous, without making claims for some mystical thread that validates the latter. It takes barely a single cycle of a generation to render any form of delivery seem unmediated, unreflective or even 'natural'.

Finally, there is the history of decline that Morgan outlines for the human subject, traumatically descending into the virtual loss of individual identity by the end of the twentieth century. This is surely back-to-front in suggesting that there used to be a strong sense of individual identity that began to disintegrate in the seventeenth century. It was, rather, in that century that Descartes first made it possible to conceive of human subjectivity in the modern sense, it was in the next that the concept of individual genius arose, and so forth. Thus the trauma that Morgan identifies in the present in fact represents the decline of a relatively recent and historically conditioned conception of humanity. Indeed, Arthur C. Danto views the 'end of art' (which is essentially coterminous with Morgan's end of history) in a much more positive light since it opens up new possibilities of cultural experience rather than necessarily evidencing a terrible decline.[20]

Morgan's final claim that HIP places older music in a museum (together with all the stuffy, nearly-dead connotations that may apply) is ironic, if we are to believe Lydia Goehr's later assertion that the entire bourgeois culture of western music as it arose at the turn of the nineteenth century is essentially a museum culture.[21] Moreover, Peter Kivy, in his defence of the 'mainstream' practice of music against HIP's emphasis on original context (see p. 36 below) suggests that the 'museum' of the concert hall is still the best place for the masterworks of the western

canon. If both Goehr and Kivy are right then, HIP does not represent
the internment of music in the museum but rather the transfer of music from one type of museum to another, perhaps to something akin to
the 'living museum' which tries to show old artefacts in action within a
convincing context (see chapter 6, p. 180 below).

Morgan's pessimism concerning HIP as the museum of a dead tradition turns to violent polemic with Roger Scruton, writing a decade later
in 1997. To him the efforts of *Musica Antiqua Cologne* or *Concentus Musicus*
have frequently come:

> to cocoon the past in a wad of phoney scholarship, to elevate musicology over
> music, and to confine Bach and his contemporaries to an acoustic time-warp.
> The tired feeling which so many 'authentic' performances induce can be com-
> pared to the atmosphere of a modern museum.[22]

He uses the analogy of the painting, 'gaped at by weary multitudes'
in a museum, as opposed to its proper place 'on the wall of a private
house, where it can bestow joy and dignity on the life surrounding it'.
This alludes to a political point, clearly evident elsewhere in his writing,
that mass culture reflects the sorry decline of a sense of aristocracy within
a developed bourgeois culture. Indeed, taste itself derives from 'the demands of privilege'. Following Nietzsche, democratic man is 'culture-
less', failing 'to strive towards the inequality which is the mark of the
truly human'; departing from Nietzsche, Scruton also relates culture to
a necessary religious form which leads to 'a conception of the sanctity of
places and times, persons and offices, customs and rites' (p. 505).

But surely HIP, particularly when it relates to specific royal customs
and spectacles, such as have been reconstructed by *Les Arts Florissants*
(such titles being 'twee extravagances' according to Scruton, *Aesthetics of
Music*, p. 448) can enliven the experiential context of past music. On the
other hand, many have criticised the concept of historical reconstruction,
and the belief in the value of 'ensembles' (at its most politically charged,
being the case of a painting, placed in the context of a country house, with
the correct furnishings, and occupied by some descendant of its original owner) as perpetrating a political system of inequality that would
seem so essential to Scruton. His direct reversal of this notion, namely
that a museum culture, as evidenced by HIP, is the enervating corollary of a levelling democracy, helps substantiate the point I drew from
Adorno's reflex action of disgust towards restoration culture: that the
opening up of historical context implied by the very venture of HIP (and
anything else connected with the culture of 'Heritage' and restoration)

does not automatically bring with it, or enforce, the original political connotations.

During the 1980s and nineties the field of 'performance practice criticism' became dominated by the powerful writing of Richard Taruskin, which culminated in the publication of his collected essays in *Text and Act* in 1995.[23] There have been several other fine writers on the subject – those, for instance, who appear along with Taruskin in a 1984 issue of *Early Music*, and in a volume by Oxford University Press in 1988[24] – but Taruskin's voice has been the loudest, the most influential and by far the most thought-provoking. His strengths as a scholar come not only from his own past experience as a significant performer of early music, but also from the sheer breadth of his scholarly expertise and critical range.

Taruskin's central argument (most comprehensively stated in his fourth essay) can be condensed into a diagnosis, a judgement and an axiom: his diagnosis is that very little historical performance is, or can be, truly historical – much has to be invented; that the actual styles of histor-ical performance we hear accord most strikingly with modern taste; and that the movement as a whole has all the symptoms of twentieth-century modernism, as epitomised by the objectivist, authoritarian Stravinsky in his neo-classical phase. Taruskin's concern with Stravinsky obscures the fact that very similar aesthetics of performance were promoted by Schoenberg and his students.[25] But this modification would only further support his judgement that historical performance practice, far from being intrinsically wrong, is, rather, a true and even 'authentic' represen-tation of modernist thinking (needless to say, he would prefer it to move in what he sees as the 'postmodernist', 'postauthoritarian' direction). And the axiom on which much of his work hinges is that the methods we use to base and judge scholarship are not those on which we base artistic per-formance. Each may inform the other, but one cannot be reduced to the other. Thus the inclusion of a couple of essays addressing the question of editing help to consolidate one of Taruskin's central points, encapsulated in the title: performance, of any kind, should be an *act* and not reduced to the status of a *text*. Performance is significant for its human compo-nent and not for its objective veracity. Taruskin's view perhaps helps us understand the increasing rift, also outlined by Dreyfus and Kerman, between mainstream musicology and the 'musicology' of those exclusively concerned with preparing their historicist performances. This distinction comes close to that posed by David Lowenthal, between 'History' and 'Heritage', the former concerned with understanding the past on its own terms, the latter more on ours. While I maintain that this distinction is fallacious, given that all forms of historical representation rely on fabrication and an inescapable presentist perspective, it does outline two essential poles in historical practice. Lowenthal's view that 'personal immediacy is a heritage hallmark' relates nicely to Taruskin's conception of the essential musical performance. By this token, HIP performers err when they consider their practice to be 'History' when it is really one of 'Heritage', that should consequently demand imaginative – rather than objective – recreation of the past.[26]

The relation between modernism and HIP was suggested in another way by Dreyfus, namely that the 'shock value' of HIP renditions of favourite classics drew much the same response as the more avowedly counter-cultural expressions of the avant-garde in the early years of the twentieth century. Taruskin relates HIP more to the chic modernism of Stravinsky, and not so much for its shock value but more for the actual style of its performance. Thus, if both Dreyfus and Taruskin are right, HIP is doubly unaware of its modernist credentials, its jarring effect for cultural conservatives on the one hand and its motoric aesthetic on the other. Taruskin's claim that many of the conventions of HIP performances were modern inventions had been brilliantly demonstrated empirically by Daniel Leech-Wilkinson's study of 1984 showing that various groups covering the entire historical range of HIP adopted similar mannerisms.[27] This observation might well relate to a wider phenomenon in late twentieth-century culture, with the increasing concern for 'minority heritage', the acceleration of ethnic, regional and cultural differences, the very public exchange and dissemination of these differences, all of which bring a new form of conformity, which, ironically, reflects the increasing standardisation of western culture.[28]

Taruskin's central arguments are supported by several other opinions: the 'seductive simplicities of determinism and utopianism have got to be resisted . . . and . . . the endlessly renegotiated social contract, dowdy patchwork though it be, is the only cause worth defending' (p. 192). This ties in with Taruskin's concern for the audience – an opinion that interestingly seems to grow in the later essays, as he becomes further removed from his own performing career – a move from a production oriented system to a 'proper' reassertion of consumer values (p. 47). This

development is also shadowed by Taruskin's growing distaste for the concept of *Werktreue*, something he sees as central to modernist performance
(whether 'historical' or 'mainstream') and one that 'inflicts a truly stifling
regimen by radically hardening and patrolling what had formerly been
a fluid, easily crossed boundary between the performing and composing
roles' (p. 10).

His reservations about the work-concept – the idea of individual, fully
formed and authoritarian pieces of music – ties in with his distrust of
the composer as an authoritarian figure. So much of historical performance, runs Taruskin's argument, is bogged down with questions of the
composer's intentions, and, what is worse, those of a most mundane
and provincial kind, when in fact we can never know intentions or even
'know we know them' if we happen to find them, and, furthermore,
composers are often wrong or change their minds (p. 97). In his view,
our need to gain the composer's approval 'bespeaks a failure of nerve,
not to say an infantile dependency' (p. 98). This argument is bolstered
with an impressive array of cases where composers change their minds,
did not expect their intentions to be followed, or were simply working
in an environment (especially opera) where adaptations and cuts were a
matter of daily routine.

So if authority comes neither from the work nor exclusively from the
composer, where are we to turn? To ourselves, would seem to be the short
answer from the Socratic Taruskin: 'Authenticity . . . is knowing what you
mean and whence comes that knowledge. And more than that, even, authenticity is knowing what you are, and acting in accordance with that
knowledge' (p. 67). In fleshing out this concept, Taruskin tends to draw
on two theories in modern thought: the history of *reception* as a major
carrier of meaning and *tradition* as an alternative to authority. According
to reception theory '[c]hange of context adds as much meaning as it may
take away' (p. 267); the meaning, for us, of *Don Giovanni* has been 'mediated by all that has been thought and said about it since opening night,
and is therefore incomparably richer than it was in 1787'. Reconstruction
of original meaning (and here Taruskin clearly includes reconstruction of
original performance practice) 'should add its valuable mite to the pile'
but cannot substitute for the pile itself. Taruskin's conception of tradition
also follows from this: tradition is 'cumulative, multiply authored, open,
accommodating, above all *messy*, and therefore human' (p. 192). For the
performer this means less fetishisation of documents and instrumental
hardware, more listening to one another, reaction and competition. HIP
is productive only when it spawns its own 'viable oral tradition' (p. 194).

Many, at this stage, might well be led to agree with the popular mythology that Taruskin is fundamentally opposed to the whole enterprise of historical performance. Furthermore, the temporal progression of the essays suggests that Taruskin has progressively distanced himself from it (only the earlier writings refer periodically to 'our movement'). But, as his introduction and postscripts to the essays often aver, he believes himself to be continually misrepresented as a crusty opponent to the movement when all he intends to show is its shortcomings. As Bernard Sherman reminds us, Taruskin has termed HIP 'the least moribund aspect of our classical music life' and recognised that it at least offers the opportunity to question 'knee-jerk habits' in performance.[29] Perhaps part of the problem is that his praise for the movement and his recommendations for its direction are argued far less strongly than his pointed criticisms, are often couched in ambivalent terms and are consequently less easy to summarise. Moreover, there are intimations that the movement has great critical and creative potential but, as a whole, has failed in some wider objective to revolutionise performance:

A movement that might, in the name of history, have shown the way back to a truly creative performance practice has only furthered the stifling of creativity in the name of normative controls. (p. 13)

Taruskin's relation to HIP parallels, in many ways, Nietzsche's attitude to history in the latter half of the nineteenth century. Nietzsche, like Taruskin, has often been accused of trying to dispense with history altogether when, in fact, his purpose was to destroy the belief that history led to a single, indisputable truth (i.e. 'History' in the objectivist sense as understood by Lowenthal). Instead, history should reveal as many perspectives on the past as there are individuals studying it; it should open up new possibilities rather than close down our perspectives. In short, it should promote life and individual development in the present, thus, in Taruskin's terms, leading to newer and better forms of musical performance (i.e. as 'Heritage' in Lowenthal's formulation).[30]

So what constitutes good historical performance for Taruskin? One thing that seems clear is that many performances need to be 'more historical', particularly if the historical evidence implies creative departures from the text, something he demands particularly for the performance of Mozart piano concertos (p. 167). He seeks a return to a conception of classical music that began to die out two centuries ago, something that would bring the music closer to the values of pop music than 'classical' (p. 170). Another useful comparison, which unfortunately he uses only in one chapter (essay 15), is that between 'crooked' and 'straight' performance. Straight performance is fine 'if what you want out of music is something to sit back and relax to' while the crooked performers are the 'real artists', such as *Musica Antiqua Cologne*, whose 'responses are conditioned not by generic demands that can be easily classified . . . but by highly specific, unclassifiable, personal and intensely subjective imaginings' (p. 317). In short, historically informed performance is all very well provided the 'literalism' (i.e. following of some documentary evidence) is 'inspired',[31] such as in the case of Roger Norrington's strict adherence to Beethoven's metronome markings. Taruskin also praises Christopher Page's Stravinskyesque approach to fifteenth-century courtly songs, which 'arose out of a fundamental rethinking of the repertory in its specific details, and on as close to its own aesthetic and historical terms as human nature and human epistemics allow, rather than from the acceptance of a standard of beauty or of audience appeal imported unreflectingly from past experience' (p. 351). Gustav Leonhardt produces joyful results in Bach performance through 'passionate and committed experiment with original instruments' (p. 148), while Nikolaus Harnoncourt refuses to succumb to the customary efforts to prettify and sanitise Bach's severe message in the sacred music (essay 14).[32]

Taruskin's view of 'good' history in performance seems to come quite close to Nietzsche's of 1874: history as a form of knowledge, 'known clearly and completely' has been neutralised and is in effect dead; but history that does not try to mimic science can be a service to life, something dynamic and opening up new possibilities.[33] Karol Berger suggests something similar by pairing art and history as forms of representation (i.e. of possible and past worlds) in contradistinction to philosophy and science (which have more to do with argument than with representation).[34] This wider sense of history, that Berger borrows from Aristotle, covers more than the academic discipline of history: 'Its scope includes any portrayal of the real world, present as well as past, journalistic as well as historical . . . History and art can be mixed, though usually one will predominate, as when a historian imaginatively reconstructs the thoughts of a historical protagonist that, strictly speaking, cannot be documented' (*A Theory of Art*, p. 61). Thus the point to which Taruskin may ultimately be most pointing is that performance should indeed be separated from history, insofar as the latter is a factual, scientific, discipline in Lowenthal's formulation, but that history in the wider sense – that which is akin to an art in suggesting a world that is not immediately present (i.e. Lowenthal's 'Heritage') – might be a useful way of regenerating performance. Historical evidence might be worth follow-ing to the degree that it causes us to refashion ourselves and produce a performance that is fully committed.

I find two of Taruskin's points specifically problematic: his desire to 'democratise' performance by catering to the needs and wishes of the audience, and his tendency to promote postmodernism as the answer to all modernism's ills. He introduces the issue of audience satisfaction within his argument that all classical performance is under the grip of the work-concept, all joining 'the ranks of museum curators, with disastrous results – disastrous that is, for the people who pay to hear them' (p. 13). Does this imply that there is some standard by which we may test whether or not the audience has had its money's worth, whether or not it has been cheated of some profounder experience?

Things become a little clearer with the next reference, for now Taruskin identifies himself as a member of the audience (this is the non-performer Taruskin of 1994): 'My first commitment is to the mortals – that is, the audience – and to their interests, since I am one of them' (p. 18). Using the force of the oppressed masses to justify one's own position is a common tactic among politicians. This impression is strengthened on p. 47 where he states that he is 'glad to see increasing impatience with an excessively production-oriented system of values in classical music and the proper reassertion of consumer values (yes, audience response) as a stylistic regulator', surely the language of a free marketeer. But most of the evidence he cites for this shift in priority concerns changes at the pro-duction level rather than a revolution on the consumers' side: pluralism in the concert scene, the breaking down of the walls between the 'high' and the 'low' in the field of classical composition. In other words, the shift is in the direction of that which Taruskin believes the audience should want rather than unequivocal evidence of the people's will at work.

What would count as evidence in any case? If consumer values are the issue, surely the remarkable prosperity of Taruskin's bête noir, Christopher Hogwood, must be strong evidence; somebody must have bought all those records. Of course, the audience may have been stun-ningly uninspired in its choice of purchase, perhaps cruelly hoodwinked by the hype of authenticity. But if this is the case, how can Taruskin insist that the audience call the tune? If he wishes to persist in so harsh a view of Hogwood, he must, along with 'virtually all important artistic movements since Romanticism . . . have shared in [the] contempt for the public as arbiter of taste' (pp. 72–3). This is substantiated by his comment regarding Roger Norrington on p. 234: 'I don't know whether his work

will prove as marketable as Hogwood's. Probably not: You have to pay
attention to it.' Here then there is a revulsion at the 'easy-listening' culture that seems to come with commodification, a revulsion similar to that
which Adorno experienced several decades before. Moreover, Dreyfus
had already suggested that there was considerable identification between
performers and audience in precisely that form of HIP which was most
objectivist and opposed to 'individualist' interpretation (Dreyfus, 'Early
Music Defended', p. 317).

Taruskin distances himself from the dictatorship of the market with
one of his 1994 postscripts: 'I have always considered it important for
musicologists to put their expertise at the service of "average consumers"
and alert them to the possibility that they are being hoodwinked, not only
by commercial interests but by complaisant academics, biased critics, and
pretentious performers' (p. 153). This is laudable enough, but it does
imply that the audience is incapable of making up its own mind and
needs the benevolent dictates of an inspired expert. But simply shifting
the performer's responsibility from 'upwards', to the work, composer or
whatever, to 'downwards', to the audience, does not solve any problems
of responsibility, since the identical issues (and perhaps more) simply
reappear in a new position. One is forced either to accept the judgement
of the audience in commercial terms, or to dictate what the audience
should enjoy (which is little different from dictating how, and in what
style, the performer should play, in the name of historical fidelity, the
composer spiritual intentions, or 'the artwork').

Taruskin might also be implying another sense of 'pleasing the audience', one with which I can wholeheartedly concur. This is the idea
of the performer taking on something of the audience's role, constantly
monitoring the performance from a listener's perspective, and reacting to
what she hears. While this is obviously a golden rule for all performance,
it might take on a special significance in 'historical' performance as a very
practical antidote to a surfeit of factual data. It is precisely this reflexive
attitude which is so often a sure sign of quality in visual and musical arts,
in which the earliest possible stages of reception are folded back into the
creative act (for a further exploration of this see chapter 3, below).

Taruskin must take credit for being one of the first musicologists to
introduce the term 'postmodernism' (in essay 13, of 1987); by the time
we get to the 1990s, the term is bandied around by virtually anyone who
wants to appear 'relevant' and up-to-date. We even get macabre disputes between scholars trying to be 'postmoderner than thou'.[35] The
fault of this approach is to see postmodernism as the answer to all the

evils of modernism, as the way for the future, even as a happy utopia in which all differences will live side-by-side in a pluralistic flux. Taruskin, in his first reference to the term (p. 16), tries to erase the utopian element since he directly associates utopia with 'authoritarian fulfilment'. Postmodernism, then, seems to have something to do with the subversion of authority (which was, incidentally, fundamental to modernism at the outset of the twentieth century). Next he implies that postmodernism in fact has much to do with 'premodernism', since it revokes the triple nexus (which solidified only around 1800) of 'serious-classical-work'.[36] This is already an odd situation, for however much a postmodernist approach to music (i.e. subversive of musical works) may share with the concepts of music before 1800, the cultural context in which music is conceived, produced and used is radically different. Indeed, this point was elegantly made by Adorno: the culture of early music pretends to substitute the pre-individual state for the real, post-individual state of its 'own collectivisation'.[37] The pre-modern era was essentially feudal and it was, ironically, bourgeois 'freedom' that led to the work concept in the first place. So unless Taruskin is prepared to talk about music and its performance in the abstract (absolute music?), divorced from its cultural environment (and I'm sure he's not), the pre/postmodernist association is considerably impoverished.

Later he approvingly quotes a definition of the postmodern stance proffered by two legal scholars, which entails 'rejection either of applause or of dejection, which are themselves . . . the products of specific cultural moments, in favor of a somewhat more detached acceptance of the inevitability of change and our inability to place such changes as occur within any master narrative' (p. 36). This seems to me a 'genuine' definition of postmodernism,[38] but one that hardly accords with Taruskin's approach elsewhere: rejection of judgement? a neutral stand, above culture and ideology? a detached acceptance? This sounds like classic, objectivist HIP as outlined by Dreyfus. Furthermore, many of Taruskin's most trenchant criticisms of historical performance seem to target an archetypal postmodern stance: 'The art works of the past, even as they are purportedly restored to their pristine sonic condition, are concomitantly devalued, decanonized, not quite taken seriously, reduced to sensuous play' (p. 138). Perhaps, then, postmodernism is precisely what is wrong with 'authentistic' performance. Taruskin's preference for strong, authoritative performances which creatively and virtuosically deviate from the letter of the score seem not of a piece with postmodernism insofar as the latter encapsulates decentredness and play (p. 176). It is, rather, the cult of the composer as the ultimate authority in music that he beats with the stick of postmodernism, not the concept of authority in general. In this way he does a great service in rendering performance *per se* much more crucial in contemporary culture. Rather than seeing it as the lapdog of the composer or of objective, factual evidence from the past, it is elevated as a mode of cultural production in its own right. Performance becomes the primary mode of musical being as indeed it so often was before the advent of the work concept.[39] Moreover, by considering the entire issue of the history of performance and the various roles it has played in the very concept of music it may be possible to regenerate western music. HIP can, and does, obviously play a part in this, but it has to be conceived in a sense that is both far broader and more critical than the old objectivist form decreed.

Perhaps Taruskin should have been more sceptical of postmodernism as a stance or ideal (although it is certainly acceptable – indeed indispensable – as a description of the condition we happen to be in; this will be explored below in chapter 5). In its earliest forms, of the late 1960s and 1970s, postmodernism has been taken to task for its irresponsible, amoral stance. Terry Eagleton, for instance, sees postmodernism as 'simply co-extensive with the commodification of all life in consumer capitalism . . . an aesthetic reflection of already aestheticised images',[40] and Christopher Norris quite rightly condemns Jean-François Lyotard's denial of any meaning or truth-value 'aside from the manifold language-games that make up an ongoing cultural conversation', since this allows Lyotard to affirm that there is no certain way of denouncing Faurisson for his assertion that the Nazi Holocaust never really happened – according to Lyotard, 'there is *no common* ground between Faurisson and those who reject his views'.[41] Jürgen Habermas, who sees modernity as an unfinished project, relates postmodernism to the neoconservatives, those who attempt to diffuse 'the explosive content of cultural modernity', a group that 'asserts the pure immanence of art, disputes that it has a utopian content, and points to its illusory character in order to limit the aesthetic experience to privacy.'[42]

Much of what Taruskin has to say, seems to me close to the spirit of Habermas's call for the completion of the Enlightenment:

What I am after, in a word, is liberation: only when we know something about the sources of our contemporary practices and beliefs, when we know something about the reasons why we do as we do and think as we think, and when we are aware of alternatives, can we in any sense claim to be free in our choice of action and creed, and responsible for it. (p. 19; see, too, the quotation from p. 67, above)

This, together with numerous criticisms of historical performance's reliance on documented authority and lack of self-resolve, could almost be a paraphrase of the opening of Immanuel Kant's famous essay of 1784 'What is Enlightenment'.[43] Even that most dubious section of Kant's essay – that advocating absolute monarchy over republicanism – strikes a chord with Taruskin's respect for the stronger-minded conductors and for the 'inspired literalism' of those performers who fanatically adhere to a particular historical principle: 'Argue as much as you will, and about what you will, only obey!', as Kant put it.

Thus to me, all that is excellent in Taruskin's approach – his avocation of passionate commitment, risk and vision coupled with self-awareness, a sense of choice in performance, and responsibility to both the audience and the richest and deepest possible meanings of pieces of music – could be read as a neo-Enlightenment stance. This posture is inescapably bound to a postmodern condition, to be sure, but it should not be confused with the playing of superficial surfaces of postmodernism as a conscious style, one that, at least in its earlier manifestations, placed the aesthetic in pride of place, above the ethical.

Finally, there is the question of what is 'authentic' to our particular age. Taruskin judges the entire HIP movement as being 'authentic', not for the criteria commonly proffered (i.e. historical accuracy, restoration of original), but for far more significant reasons:

Messrs. Brüggen, Norrington, and Bilson . . . have been rightly acclaimed . . . Conventional performers are properly in awe and in fear of them. Why? Because, as we are all secretly aware, what we call historical performance is the sound of now, not then. It derives its authenticity not from its historical verisimilitude, but from its being for better or worse a true mirror of late-twentieth century taste. Being the true voice of one's time is . . . roughly forty thousand times as vital and important as being the assumed voice of history. (p. 166)

So historical performance – almost always associated with modernism by Taruskin – is authentic as the true voice of the times; yet he continually suggests that the movement go in the postmodern direction. Now he must mean either that modernism is, in fact, no longer the voice of the times, or (probably closer) that postmodernism *should* be the voice of the times; this would seem to generate an authenticity more by edict than description. Moreover, if we were to take the postmodern condition more seriously, perhaps the very concept of a 'true voice of the times' should be de-emphasised. Surely it is the diversity of value systems and the surprising coincidence of multiple forms of authority that distinguishes our contemporary condition from virtually all earlier eras.

Perhaps the way out of these confusions is to show that the concepts of modernism and postmodernism cannot be so cleanly divided (their precise definitions would, in any case, demand a book many times longer than Taruskin's or this one). Indeed, it might be the case that the moment that an historical performance recording (however 'modernist' the performance) first became a best-seller, western 'classical' performance entered a postmodern condition, one with a splintering of tradition and authority. Postmodernism – with its slant on, rather than opposition to, modernism – may be here whether we like it or not, and historical performance has definitely played its part. A distinction that might come in useful is that which Arthur C. Danto makes between 'modern' and 'contemporary' art. The former term applies to that which is avowedly 'modernist' in the objectivist, geometric sense used by Taruskin, while 'contemporary' refers both to the broader picture of the present art world and to that type of art which is liberated from the tyranny of the modernist narrative of progress and innovation.[44] This might help to overcome the confusion between 'postmodern' as a specific style of ironic mixing of genres (e.g. the classic case of the Peter Sellars production with a 'period instrument' orchestra) and the wider contemporary culture that allows a considerable diversity of authority and practice, and that does not make automatic exclusions from an ongoing canon. Although I still believe it is useful to see this wider culture as a symptom of the 'postmodern condition', Danto's concept of an ongoing, non-progressive contemporaneity is an illuminating way of understanding the direction of artistic movements within this condition.

PETER KIVY AND THE DEBATE WITHIN ANALYTICAL PHILOSOPHY

1995 was an extraordinary year in the course of the 'early music debate', for not only did it see the publication of Richard Taruskin's long-awaited *Text and Act* but also of Peter Kivy's *Authenticities*.[45] It is striking how close some of the tastes and opinions of these two authors come: both lament the cramping of personal freedom and style in performance resulting from the application of historical musicology, and both focus on the tendency to reduce the art of performance to an element of the musical text, with all its connotations of accurate readings and blind fidelity to an assumed 'original'. On the other hand, their style and presentation could hardly be more diverse: Taruskin's approach is not particularly systematic but critically incisive and often rhetorically lethal. Kivy's takes the cool rational method of analytical philosophy, starting from the supposed certainty of dictionary definitions and arriving at its conclusions through the steady tread of rational reasoning and hypothetical tests. However, just like Taruskin, many of the results are in fact the result of strong opinion, (sometimes) prejudice, and a passionate belief in a certain cultural system.

Taruskin had spent at least a decade before 1995 trying to abolish the concept of 'authenticity' in relation to performance. Moreover, his efforts seem, remarkably, to have been almost universally successful (indeed, my frequent use of scare-quotes for this term is a direct result of the Taruskin heritage).[46] Even by the early 1990s most writers, performers and promoters were already substituting it with terms such as 'period' performance or – the most flexible, but perhaps the least specific – 'historically informed performance' (HIP).[47] Moreover, Nikolaus Harnoncourt, whose career in HIP is among the longest and most distinguished, has always distanced himself from the term 'authenticity', considering any claims of correctness and genuineness in historical performance to be simply fraudulent.[48] Thus one may wonder whether Kivy's engagement with 'Authenticities' was already outdated in 1995. But his first three authenticities – (1) authenticity as the composer's intentions for performance; (2) authenticity as the original sound of the music; (3) authenticity as the original practice of the performers – could all be renamed 'restorations' or 'ideal aims' without crucially altering their implications, and these do indeed correspond to three of the main topics of interest in the study of historical performance. It may well be that Kivy retains the word as a way of profiling his fourth and clearly preferred form of authenticity, 'The Other Authenticity', namely, the personal authenticity of the performer (in the sense of being original, unique, inspired etc.). This thus coincides directly with Dreyfus's imaginative 'advanced guard' in HIP and Taruskin's preferred manner of personally committed performance.

This does seem to be a legitimate use of the word, since it is dealing with genuine and irreplaceable entities (although the concept of sincerity and uniqueness in performance is perhaps rather more problematic than Kivy might imply). In a sense then, he has recovered the most *authentic* use of the word 'authentic' but, by the same token, the other three surely need to be seen as completely different categories. By pretending that the four authenticities are of equal conceptual status, Kivy creates false dichotomies between them: namely, that you cannot have authenticity of intention, sound or practice, together with 'The Other Authenticity' – that they are mutually exclusive.

Kivy notes the participation of philosophers in medical, business and environmental debates and their contribution to issues ranging from nuclear war to abortion. The philosopher thus arrives at the door of historical performance in the guise of the mandatory quality controller: 'a thorough philosophical critique seems to be in order, of the whole apparatus that has, to some extent haphazardly, been put together to support the practice of historical authenticity in musical performance' (xi). Philosophy will thus expose a field that has hitherto been characterised by piously inarticulate gibbering. But philosophical methods of this kind will only give a foolproof result if the parameters are absolutely stable: e.g. that the musical work is always and without exception one thing and performance another; that the composer and performer are consistent and mutually distinguishable entities. Kivy does indeed allow and demonstrate considerable flexibility in these definitions during the course of the book, but my overall impression is that philosophical analysis is there to give rhetorical support for the recently beleaguered Germanic conception of musical art, as passive aesthetic contemplation.[49] In this sense, then, his agenda is considerably different from Taruskin's, who would not want anything less than passive contemplation in the Germanic tradition.

Kivy's philosophical facility does have much to teach us, particularly when we might hold a view precisely because we believe it to be logically necessary. His examination of the issue of intention is particularly pertinent in this regard and is one of the most thorough to date (this will be discussed in detail in chapter 3, below). He also shows that the traditional 'restoration' argument for historical performance – that, just as the art restorer tries to return to us the physical object as it first came out of Rembrandt's studio, 'the goal of the historically authentic performance is to give us . . . the physical object as it issued from Bach's "studio"' (p. 191) – is flawed by the fact that the two arts are distinct in logical and ontological terms. Painting is, in Nelson Goodman's terminology, an autographic art, relying on the concept of a single, unique original, while performed music is allographic, infinitely repeatable. The work-performance relation of music is in no manner equivalent to the original–reproduction (or original–fake) relation in painting. Indeed, as Kivy shows us throughout the book, the tendency to reduce both the musical work and its performance to the status of a single object, whether analogous to an allographic text or an autographic painting, sounds the death-knell for the entire concept of performance: 'The "logic" of music as a performing art . . . is a logic in which the gap between "text" and performance is not merely a necessary evil but at the same time a *desired, intended* and logically *required* ontological fact' (p. 272). This is thus a more formal way of describing Taruskin's distinction between 'text' and 'act'.

Moreover, even if the concept of restoring paintings at least reasonably presupposes the possibility of an ideal original, 'the physical restoration of paintings is neither an obvious desideratum nor even as transparent a concept as it might at first appear' (p. 193). Using arguments taken from David Carrier, Kivy shows that there is an obvious problem in restoring a painting to its original appearance since this involves actually changing that which the artist has made, which itself has changed through the natural ageing process of time. Furthermore, even the perfect restoration of the original colours would not have the same effect on the modern viewer as it did originally on account of changes in perception and cultural context. One is faced with the almost contradictory aims of restoring either a physical object or the perceptual, intentional object whose very definition depends on a viewer with specific expectations.

This relates to one of Kivy's strongest observations about HIP. If we somehow achieve the same actual sound that was achieved in an historic performance ('sonic authenticity') this has to be distinguished from what the original audience actually heard, or rather, consciously experienced ('sensible authenticity'). Kivy was by no means the first to realise the distinction between an acoustical phenomenon and the musical phenomenon perceived by the listener, but his discussion is perhaps the most far-reaching.[50] It is at least theoretically possible that – with our changes in culture and listening practice – we might have to change the original sound to achieve the original effect (though how could this theoretical possibility consistently be realised in practice, one might ask?). This leads to one of Kivy's most interesting conclusions about HIP: despite its capacity to foster historical awareness and to rejuvenate 'even the most overworked warhorses in the concert repertory', all these attractions are profoundly 'inauthentic' in terms of what the original audience experienced (p. 232).

Related to this is the notion that the accumulated experience of western music culture means that earlier 'surprises' no longer have their intended effect. The Matthew Passion must have originally had an effect as overwhelming as the Berlioz Requiem (p. 53), while the opening of Beethoven's first symphony is now entirely unsurprising in the wake of later harmonic developments (pp. 54–5). Similarly, an HIP performance of the Matthew Passion sounds 'subdued' and 'chamber music-like' while

the original audience heard something new and striking (p. 197). Roger
Scruton uses exactly the same argument: we compare works with those
that came both before and after, 'To us the "Goldberg" Variations an-
ticipate the Diabelli Variations – that is how they sound, and one reason
why we wish to play them on the piano.'[51]

Both philosophers are surely right to suggest that we can make transhistorical comparisons and judgements. But to suggest that a later norm
automatically negates an earlier surprise is ultimately to suggest that
we cannot appreciate the historical difference between Bach, Beethoven
and Berlioz. Having heard the free atonality of the twentieth century we
would presumably have no appreciation of Bach's expressive use of dissonance. If this is to be used as an argument to modernise the instruments
it would surely apply equally strongly to the notated music: we'd have
to use twentieth-century harmonies to recapture the original opening of
Beethoven's first symphony, just as we'd have to use a large symphony
orchestra to recapture the aural effect of the Matthew Passion. What
seems to be more the case is that we very easily develop a relativity of
hearing: we really can hear the revolutionary in Beethoven, the pathos of
Bach. Just as humans can learn to express themselves in more than one
language they can pick up the essentials of any particular historical style
(or – to put it rather more accurately – the received view of the essentials)
remarkably quickly; we can actually hear unusual, surprising elements
within a style *in spite of* our knowledge of later music. It follows then, that
we could (and do) become accustomed to hearing Bach on the harpsichord, Beethoven on the fortepiano. This is not to suggest that we *must*
hear Bach on the harpsichord – perhaps the accordion would work just
as well with repeated hearings – but that the later norm of Beethoven's
piano does not automatically render earlier sounds obsolete for us. Indeed, it may well be a specific feature of our age that we are able to appreciate stylistic and linguistic differences better than ever before (see
chapter 2, p. 66 below).

Kivy introduces a related issue, namely that the original audiences always heard 'ahistorically', that the uniformity of modern 'mainstream'
performance is both ahistorical and transparent (i.e. unnoticed), and that
mainstream performance is thus in a sense more 'authentic' than HIP
(Kivy, *Authenticities*, pp. 70–4). This is debatable, not because mainstream
performance is to be condemned *a priori* as inauthentic but because each
stage of the argument lies on premises that are historically vague. Original
audiences might have had a much narrower historical awareness than
we do, but eighteenth-century audiences could distinguish between

music that was up-to-date or out of fashion, and, in the nineteenth century (in which the notion of disinterested, aesthetic listening first became
a possibility) the historicity of the music was almost more important than
it was to become in the twentieth. It does 'mainstream' performance no
service to suggest that it is, or was, uniform. On the other side of the coin,
it is by no means certain that HIP still sounds novel to those who have
experienced it constantly for several decades (this, of course, somewhat
weakens Kivy's – and indeed Dreyfus's – point about the rejuvenating
advantages of HIP). And, most importantly, how can we reclaim the vir-
ginity of the supposedly transparent, mainstream performance having
eaten the forbidden fruit of historical performance? Indeed, there is a
sense in which 'mainstream' performance of the hotspots of HIP (the
baroque repertory in particular) might now sound more historical (in
the sense of sounding as if from a period other than our own) than the
(by now) default idioms of HIP.

Kivy's critique of the 'composer knows best' ideology is particularly
acute: it may well be that performers often understand how to realise
a composition better than a composer. His model of the composer as
maker and the performer as marketer is a useful starting point that can
be modified to account for composers who were specifically virtuoso
performers or for those who expected considerable performer initia-
tive in the realisation of their notations. This relates to Kivy's point
that performing carries with it a certain element of the composer's art,
that 'performing is a species of composing' (p. 260). The only crucial
omission I perceive in this theory is the reciprocal view that composing must also be a certain species of performing. Indeed it is the very
development of HIP that jogs us into realising that past composers did
not make the same assumptions about performance as we do, that their
very different ideologies and styles of performance were not the transparent media for their 'higher' thoughts but often constituted their way
of composing and thinking musically in the first place (see chapter 3,
below).

Kivy suggests that if we are to commit ourselves to historical performance practice as an end in itself, 'then music as aesthetically appreciated
object must be construed as being something beyond mere sound, even
if sound is widely construed as intentional object of musical perception.
For practice . . . can thus be an end in itself only if it is an unheard but
otherwise perceived part of the total musical experience' (p. 89). This
strikes me as a very important consequence of the strong adherence
to HIP (i.e. as necessary, above and beyond the actual musical sound

achieved), one that challenges the notion of the essence of music lying in sound alone. Moreover, HIP has often made a virtue out of
sounds that are not specifically 'musical' but come as a consequence
of the instruments and techniques used. For instance, Martin Elste notes
the contribution of Nikolaus Harnoncourt in rendering the sound more
earth-bound and corporeal, as if speaking directly from the material of
the instruments; moreover, he has also made silence (through articulation
between the notes) an essential part of the musical experience.[52]

These attitudes are worth exploring for what they reveal about changing conceptions about how music should be created and presented
in our cultural practice. Perhaps the interest in the historical context
and the 'effort' of production acts as a counterweight to the increasing
disembodiment resulting from mechanical reproduction. Perhaps it reflects a growing interest in composition and performance as specifically
human and social activities, thus counteracting the idea of the performer
as merely the means to a formally independent, abstract end. Perhaps we
are even learning something from popular culture where the trappings
of presentation are virtually as significant as 'the music itself'.

Kivy's response is more to shore up the status quo: while music before
what he describes as 'the great divide' (i.e. the birth of the concert hall,
the 'sonic museum' in which music is heard without distraction or con-
tamination from other arts) is to a certain degree 'a mixed-media art'
(p. 94), the concert tradition cuts the visual and social aspect of the art
'to the bone, abstractly stylised . . . into one standard practice' (p. 101).
Thus, if I correctly understand what really lies behind this, HIP and its
threat to pure sound is counteracted by transferring all music, ancient
and modern, to the concert hall where the predictable etiquette and conventions of presentation somehow sublimate all the ritualistic and social
resonances of the past. A non-sounding (visual) element is retained as
essential to the best experience of the work, but in a strictly controlled
environment that does not let a diversity of historical production and
performance context run its evil course, ever thickening to dissolve the
work out of existence. In other words, here there is a tacit recognition
that HIP really does represent a counter-cultural threat, in the sense
formulated earlier by Dreyfus.

To Kivy, historical aspects of presentation can be justified only if they
make an 'aesthetic difference', i.e. if they somehow become internal to
the work. In this way, Kivy feels that he can halt the 'slippery slope' of
the 'wig problem' (i.e. once you let one historical factor in, where do you
draw the line?). Wigs don't make much of a difference in the performance

of the Brandenburg concertos but, on the other hand, blowing out candles rather than flicking off electric switches is more akin to the graceful rhythm and expressive character of Haydn's 'Farewell' Symphony finale; it could be justified as being 'part of the music'. There is certainly something attractive about this argument, although the line it draws is contingent on our interest in keeping the sonic museum – and all the listening practices that it implies – as the only licensed premises for the consumption of musical works.

There is one central problem in Kivy's study that undoubtedly colours virtually every argument: his apparently total ignorance of the actual practice of HIP during the 1980s and 1990s. He assumes virtually all the characteristics outlined by Dreyfus back in 1983 without noting Dreyfus's enthusiasm for the more inspired leaders of the movement. Kivy's objections often mirror Taruskin's without the latter's tendency to be at least as complimentary of the movement's virtues as he has been condemnatory of its vices.[53] We are reminded of the 'baleful effects of the authenticity movement in performance' (p. 21) as if these were common knowledge. In short, the HIP performer is one who won't deviate from the notation (pp. 32–3), and who 'mandates literal observance', of the *Urtext* (while the 'mainstream' performer may creatively depart from it). The HIP harpsichordist will play Bach's Chromatic Fantasy and Fugue 'straight' while the mainstream pianist will play it 'romantically' (p. 77). HIP inspires archaeology and sound-as-text rather than performance proper, and thus seeks 'closure' in performance (p. 272); it is a champion of the 'Kleinmeister' (echoes of Adorno, here); it is against any form of personal expression, and virtuosity is to be seen as a form of charlatanism. And in HIP the composer rules ('With the historically authentic performance you are dialing direct', p. 283 – a nice expression, were it true). While these assumptions do not affect the quality of Kivy's arguments, they are influential and indeed reappear – almost literally, if more ferociously – in the more recent work of Roger Scruton.[54]

Obviously it is impossible to refute all these statements in one go, and it should be acknowledged that many in the movement more-or-less hold these views. Taruskin, it should be remembered, linked objectivist performance to the high modernism of the Stravinsky and Boulez generations. Moreover, as Taruskin and others have observed, subservience to the composer has been fairly universal in most forms of performance in the late twentieth century, it is merely that HIP and the 'mainstream' have different emphases.[55] In any case, as Dreyfus had already suggested, there were plenty of performers within HIP who did not conform to the standard caricature of objectivist performance (e.g. the fantastical Medieval reconstructions of Thomas Binkley, the 'earthy' Bach of Nikolaus Harnoncourt or the inimitable subtlety of Gustav Leonhardt).[56] There are plenty of younger performers who amply (perhaps too amply for some) fulfil Kivy's criteria of 'personal authenticity', e.g. those who introduce improvisation into their performances of canonical masterpieces, such as Robert Levin and Andrew Manze. Had Kivy ever tried to accompany Marion Verbruggen, as I have, I think he would agree that *any* adherence either to the rhythm or pitches of the score would have made our job far easier. Indeed – quite contrary to the entire drift of Kivy's approach – there might even be a case for suggesting that there is now generally more freedom and latitude in interpretation within HIP than there has been in virtually all 'mainstream' performance within living memory.[57] Far from eschewing 'personal authenticity' HIP has attracted some of the strongest personalities in conducting: John Eliot Gardiner, William Christie, and, perhaps the most spectacular figure to span both HIP and the 'mainstream', Simon Rattle. As Joseph Kerman observed, performers in the first wave of HIP, most notably Dolmetsch himself, greatly emphasised the categories of feeling, impression and spirit, and that the association of HIP with objectivism was a symptom of the wider positivistic spirit of the 1950s.[58] But even in the period up to *c.* 1980, the numerous writings of the most public voice in HIP, Nikolaus Harnoncourt, continually stress the need for the performer to be foremost a musician and not a scientist, the need for us to prioritise the aspects leading to good interpretation, and that the instruments on their own do not create the correct interpretation.[59] Thus the notion that HIP *by definition* is neutral and objectivist is merely a short-sighted bias.

For Scruton spontaneity and the art of improvisation simply do not exist in HIP (*The Aesthetics of Music*, pp. 454–5); indeed they cannot exist, by definition, since HIP is the puritanical art of literal restoration and can be nothing more. For him (pp. 447–50) there is a direct line from nineteenth-century historicism into musicology as a discipline, and from musicology into HIP. The rot set in when Bach was first described and historically categorised as a 'Baroque' composer, rather than as the greatest composer of a still living tradition.[60] In stressing that performance should likewise be part of a tradition, Scruton comes surprisingly close to Taruskin, but Scruton turns to tradition for quite different purposes. Because of the unbroken polyphonic tradition we can hear in Victoria's music 'exactly *what it was like* to believe as Victoria believed,

seeing the world in terms of the Christian drama', the very lack of scholarly enquiry, and the immanence of the musical sensation allow us access
to states of mind that are otherwise no longer available to us (p. 449). It
is at points like this that Scruton's discussion seems to cease to be strictly
philosophical and becomes more a form of religious discourse.

I will address the issue of tradition more closely in the final chapter (see
pp. 201–3 below), but here it is necessary to note that there would appear
to be nothing HIP could do to redeem itself given these assumptions
about its unified aim, its identity as sounding musicology, and the 'tired
feeling' of the results. Just as Scruton abhors modernism's break with
the past and its avowed opposition to bourgeois culture, HIP has already
committed the original sin of separation and revolution: '[t]he authentic
performance is a kind of tacit reprimand of the audience' (p. 450). If it
were to reproduce exactly the same sounds as Klemperer or Munchinger
this would not do either since this would be stained with the blood of an
earlier break with tradition. Scruton follows Taruskin in believing that
'the authentic performance arises from a consciousness of the past which
is available only to those who feel themselves irremediably sundered from
it' (p. 450). Both are almost certainly right, as I will try and expound in
chapters 5 and 6 below. But Scruton's tacit assumption that there would
thus be a greater authenticity 'for those who feel themselves' inextricably
linked to the past (i.e. by living tradition) is surely as much make-believe
as any of the rasher historicist claims of HIP. To return to a tradition that
is unquestioning and unaware of history is as impossible as becoming one
of Nietzsche's cows, happily unaware of yesterday or today and somehow
stirring our envy for the immediacy of its experience.[61]

So much for assumptions about the essence of HIP – but what exactly
is the 'mainstream' with which Kivy so nostalgically compares it? First,
it does not blindly follow the performance instructions prescribed by the
composer, score or wider performance practice; instead it is a standardised practice that is relatively 'transparent', allowing a form of immanent, historically unconscious access to works of all periods. Kivy notes
'the tendency . . . of "mainstream" musical performance, with its uniformity of performance means and performance aesthetic, to encourage
ahistorical listening' (p. 77). But paradoxically – perhaps unusually so
for a thinker so systematic as Kivy – it is precisely this 'mainstream' that
fosters personally authentic performance:

we are praising it for bearing the special stamp of personality that marks it out
from all others as Horowitz's or Serkin's, Bernstein's or Toscanini's, Casals's or

Janigro's: we are marking it out as the unique product of a unique individual, something with an individual style of its own – 'an original'. (p. 123)

This leads to the suggestion that the interpretation of a great artist does not change every time she performs, that her performances of a particular work are 'tokens of the same type' (p. 127) – uniqueness of personality is thus presumably to be distinguished from a form of aesthetic schizophrenia. The work of a great performer has to be delimited much in the same way as the work of a composer, something that surely comes dangerously close to the sin of collapsing performance into text. In short, Kivy's ideal of performance seems to be an abstruse amalgam of a uniform wider practice, articulated by unique original performances that are uniform among themselves.

One point in this caricature of both HIP and the 'mainstream' needs further discussion. According to Kivy, the 'mainstream' violinist playing a Bach partita will add 'a good romantic dollop of vibrato' while the HIP performer will not: 'vibratoless sound has now become part of Bach's "text" ' (p. 270). Another 'rule' of HIP is that a dissonant appoggiatura is to be played as 'half the value of the adjoining note' (p. 271) leaving us to assume that the 'mainstream' practice is entirely variable in this respect. But, even if we assume that these practices are indeed standard rules of 'HIP', surely there are equally standardised practices in the 'mainstream', which, as Kivy acknowledges, is characterised by a uniformity of performance aesthetic? There is nothing intrinsically wrong in replacing one set of rules by another (except for the anarchist) and, in the actual state of affairs, the 'rules' of both HIP and the 'mainstream' are far more complex than this analysis would suggest. Enough recorded evidence survives to suggest that the 'mainstream' was quite variable before mass-marketing of recordings encouraged a certain degree of standardisation. Many aspects of 'romantic' practice – not least, continuous vibrato – do not become uniform until well into the twentieth century (indeed Dreyfus points that continuous vibrato is, by its very ubiquity, 'unmarked'),[62] and HIP has now been round long enough for a certain number of its interpretative features to be part of a constantly evolving tradition, in which most players learn as much (in fact, definitely more) from their peers than from their own scholarship.

If my thumbnail sketch of the way performing communities work is in any way correct, it suggests that many aspects of performance that Kivy implies are 'natural' (including his frequent suggestions that the ear is often the truest arbiter of interpretation) are largely a product of the historical situation. As Jim Samson notes, the concept of the performer as someone who develops a unique interpretation that is simultaneously subordinate to the work is a nineteenth-century development directly reflecting the increasingly fixed form of the notated text.[63] But the historical nature of performance conventions does not make them weaker or any less valid than if they really were 'natural' – first nature rather than second nature – and we all know how intensely any particular community will defend any values it considers intrinsic to its identity. Indeed, that which counts as 'musical' in performance subtly changes over the years and from one community to another:[64] many performers from the first thirty years of the twentieth century might sound to me casual, senselessly erratic and only accidentally expressive, while to their contemporaries they represented the pinnacle of musical interpretation. There would be nothing intrinsically correct about my observations, but I would defend the viability of the traditions of which I have become a part, my understanding and appreciation of dialects that have become second nature, just as much as I would expect of anyone else who belongs to a particular community. With the splintering of traditions that HIP has produced (in theory only two, but in practice many more) there is patently no way of recovering the lost innocence of 'mainstream' performance (other than by a fiat of conformity). The genie of historical thinking has been decanted into the world of performance – the recognition that things were not only once different, but that they were constantly changing; that musicians of the past had to make decisions based on a limited number of choices; that the origins of our own inherited practices were not inevitably foretold in the past and, in consequence, that our present could be different in an infinite number of ways.

The ultimate danger of HIP is thus not Kivy's fear of the restriction of freedom, but the spectre of unlimited freedom, the danger that everything we consider 'natural' can be undermined by historical thinking. One way of coping with this danger in HIP of recent decades is to take a pluralistic approach, so that one might alter equipment, style and expressive approach depending on the historical background of the music concerned. There's no way of proving whether these changes truly reflect the historical differences (in any case impossible, as Kivy would doubtlessly agree, without an equivalent historical change in the audience), but this is surely one of our ways of replacing an irrevocably lost authority of tradition with a variety of local conventions. Our musical culture stands a chance of being regenerated at the expense of rendering the concepts of the musical work and the canon less stable. Perhaps there *is* a loss of intensity, but we could never know, given that recorded performances from a century ago do not strike us all as immediately and incontrovertibly 'natural'.

I would not wish to condemn Kivy's strong view of musical art but there are one or two things that disturb me about it. The first is the dichotomy he makes between the history of progress and – as Dahlhaus would have put it – the history of decline (roughly equivalent to Kivy's dichotomy between 'mainstream' and 'HIP' performance).[65] It is undoubtedly true that the appreciation of Beethoven has grown since the many expressions of incomprehension in his own time. But to compare the situation of the Fifth Symphony with the fact that the progenitors of fire in prehistoric times, of the French Revolution, and of Newton's mechanics could not possibly have understood the full implications of their revolutions, makes the decidedly Platonist assumption that artworks are discoveries replete with true meanings that can only be unfolded through cultural evolution. I believe it is absolutely true that musical works *can* often be appreciated better with hindsight, but also that different ages have different parameters of musical quality (the 'best' works perhaps fulfilling the largest number of these historically contingent criteria), and, most importantly, that some elements of appreciation may be lost (both from the time of origin and from intermediate periods of reception, e.g. Dahlhaus's observation that Bach's 'pointe de la perfection' came around the time of Mendelssohn's Matthew Passion performance in 1829).

Despite Kivy's awareness of the origins of the concert tradition and the fact that many aspects of musical practice before 'the great divide' were not specifically aesthetic in character, he takes aesthetic listening as the ideal for modern practice (pp. 240–1). Certainly it is true that most pieces of music from most ages do contain elements that could be described as aesthetic, and there is nothing necessarily wrong with appreciating them as such. But what is disturbing is the way the concert hall becomes a sort of Procrustean bed for virtually all 'good' western music (the 'bad' pieces perhaps work better in their original performing context, according to Kivy). Given that the finales of Bach's two-part cantatas often match, Bach obviously had a sense of aesthetic whole (one that was perhaps at cross-purposes with the original liturgical context with a sermon in the middle). Thus Kivy suggests that we can follow up 'Bach's attempt at aesthetic damage control' (p. 248) by transferring them to the sonic museum, where the thematic connections will show allow them to be 'heard as autonomous, unified musical works'. This line of argument would be more convincing if, in fact, Bach's cantatas *were* a regular (and successful) element of concert hall life (ironically, it is generally only in the HIP concert world that this happens on a regular basis). Even less plausible is Kivy's argument for an Ockeghem Mass. By removing such a work from its original function in a 'multimedia' event, 'the richest aesthetic payoff . . .*from the music lover's point of view*, is to be had not in its original setting and choreography but in the sonic museum [which] . . . . optimizes just those "viewing" conditions that make this kind of musical complexity perceivable to the fullest extent' (p. 257). Such is Kivy's commitment to the concert hall as a *social* institution with its own quasi-religious ritual, that he perhaps misses a truer consequence of the formalist–aestheticist stance: that the contemplation of this music is often best served by the type of church acoustic that gives the whole a resonant bloom unavailable in most concert halls, sung by a group that specialises in this repertory (and thus veering towards the HIP perspective), and perhaps most perfectly heard through the format of a personal CD-player.

THE DEBATE AT THE END OF THE TWENTIETH CENTURY

One point that is signally absent in the HIP debate as it stood in the watershed year of 1995 is the question of technology and its influence on the public reception of music. This might relate to the fact that only around this time did the prophecies of the dominance of new technologies become plausible – if not inevitable – but it might also suggest that many scholars had undervalued the impact of technologies that had been in place for some time. This issue becomes central to a perceptive article by John Andrew Fisher and Jason Potter in 1997.[66] They observe the all-pervasive influence of electronic media across the arts and, particularly, the prevalence of unhistorical combinations of music and other sounds facilitated by synthesisers. Moreover, they consider this to be an extension of a practice of technological manipulation that has a two-hundred year history (p. 171). Thus the advent of mechanical reproduction (to use Benjamin's famous formulation) might actually parallel the progressive abstraction of art and formalism itself, since both mechanical reproduction and the rise of mass audiences 'decontextualize and recontextualize, distance, and alter artworks in all sorts of ways'.

The historical view of music is progressively effaced by new listening practices that tend to regard all musics as equal, juxtapose them ahistorically, use them as background, or play only parts of works (p. 172). Thus, in the face of whatever critics or experts might suggest about the 'correct' interpretation of works, the very behaviour of the audience has wrought a profound change in the way we conceive of works; social practice wins out over scholarly edict (p. 173). The central dilemma is thus clear: 'appreciative practice seems to construct a presentational concept of the artwork; critical practice seems to construct an historical concept of the artwork' (p. 175). Not only is there a dichotomy between the elite concept of art and that of the broader public, but there is also no obvious way how the insights of the former can be communicated to those who lie outside its immediate circle.

On the other hand, there are several different theoretical approaches to art, some of which come closer to the non-contextualist practice of the public. Closest are the 'presentational theorists' who focus on the artwork as 'monument' (to adopt Foucault's expression). It is these (normally formalist) theorists who make a conceptual distinction between the work as an historical document and as an 'artwork' to be appreciated ahistorically. Then there are the 'historical reductionists' who view the artwork entirely as a document and generally refuse to acknowledge aesthetic appreciation as an abstract experience. This is the position that comes furthest from the normal practice of artists, critics and audiences, according to Fisher and Potter (p. 178). Finally, the 'historical contextualist' theorists stand somewhere between the other two, suggesting that aesthetic response is itself (or should be) informed by historical and contextual knowledge.

While the historical concept of art may still persist, public practice is tilting towards the 'idea of the work as merely a free-floating pattern of enjoyable sights and sounds'. Indeed, the authors suggest (like some recent musicologists, see p. 7 above) that HIP itself may be waning, and that its actual attraction (for both musicians and audience) has lain in its sensory attractions rather than its historical claims. The authors conclude that the historical notion of art still functions as a regulative ideal (p. 180): the new audiences still retain an idea that there is a *'possibility* that historical contextual information will alter our experience'; they are – in principle – still open to historical information (p. 181). Yet the overall conclusion is that the 'more solipsistic relation between the spectator and the images or sounds experienced' as enabled by the new technology threatens ultimately to end the era of 'historically conceived artworks' (p. 182).

Is all ultimately lost for HIP, then? If it is no longer central to the cutting-edge of musicology, and audience practice is turning away from an historical appreciation of art, what possible value can it have? Fisher and Potter might be ultimately wrong for a number of reasons. First, there is a fundamental conflation that colours their account: that between the audience practices they correctly observe and the formalist, presentational view of art. Although, at one point, they acknowledge that historical views of art 'have begun to displace the pervasive formalism of the recent past in art criticism and philosophies of art' (p. 174) the general drift of their argument is to suggest that such formalism is of a piece with the new technology-influenced audience perception of art. For them, the formalism of Bell, Beardsley and Hanslick seems to run directly into examples of the effacement of historical provenance (p. 178).

While Fisher and Potter are perceptive to see an historical connection between mechanical reproduction and the growing possibility of abstraction, they go awry in suggesting that the historical conception of art is earlier and gradually disappearing. First, historicism in art appeared at precisely the same time as formalist abstraction (i.e. the early nineteenth century). Secondly, ahistorical formalism, of the three art theories mentioned by Fisher and Potter, is precisely that which has declined most precipitously in the latest technological age they describe. Indeed, it is the historical reductionists who are often the strongest voices in cultural criticism since their aim is not 'to describe the actual concepts of artworks' (p. 179), but, on the contrary, the political conditions of artistic production and, indeed, the conceptions of power that make concepts such as that of the artwork possible in the first place.

In short, the essential point they miss is that historical issues became important in the nineteenth century *as a consequence* of technological modernisation, *as a consequence* of the growing realisation that the past was profoundly different from the present. Moreover, in recent decades, the unprecedented progress in technology and – most importantly – its availability to an enormous segment of the population, has cut off our roots from the past in a very tangible way. Historicist movements like HIP are not part of an *ancien régime* that new audience practices are eroding, they are a direct consequence of a new historicist stance in public culture. This is the heritage industry, which I examine at length in chapter 6, something that is both a reaction to precipitous progress in technology but also something which is itself enabled by these same advances. Historicism, a fanatical concern with original contexts and the search for roots of phenomena that are still present, is thus the direct result of a haemorrhage of historicity, that sense of one's historical roots and embeddedness in an historical culture. This is the condition (most efficiently described as the 'postmodern') which I discuss at the end of chapter 5. Fisher and Potter account for the success of HIP recordings in terms of the sensual attraction: 'historical authenticity seems to take a back seat to what sells and what sounds exciting' (p. 180). They might be right about the sensual attraction, but surely it is the *claims* of historical authenticity that count (like the attraction of artefacts that might – or might not – be fakes). The 'authenticity' label sells to a public that is desperate for the 'original' in a culture of copies and virtual reality;[67] and a desperate person will often settle for outrageously low standards of verification. The fact that Hildegard von Bingen can be sung to electronic accompaniment or that the Hilliard Ensemble can perform Renaissance music underneath Jan Garbarek's saxophone improvisations (pp. 169, 172), does not necessarily – as Fisher and Potter seem to infer – suggest a rejection of historical thinking. It could equally well betoken the adding of 'the historical' to the patently modern. Exactly the same phenomenon is evidenced in the tendency of (post)modern directors (such as Mark Morris and Peter Sellars) to use a period-instrument orchestra with their daring and outrageous productions.[68] All these examples suggest the use of something purportedly 'old' as a way of grounding something that seems so new that we might otherwise feel severed from tradition, from the direct and continuous connection with the past. While this connection was taken for granted, historicist activities like HIP were merely the activities of a quaintly antiquarian minority. Fisher and Potter forgot to mention that their baby-boomers, using a variety of world musics, collaged and extracted for ambient sound on the ROM drive of their computers, were probably searching the internet for *National Trust* paint for the recycled fixtures of their neo-Georgian town-houses.

The span of time from Dreyfus's analysis of the culture of early music (1983) to Scruton's condemnation in 1997 might seem extraordinarily short; certainly it was short enough for Kivy and Scruton to discount virtually anything that had happened in practice in the meantime. Yet it has been precisely during that time that HIP has come of age. Dreyfus's perception of a 'dominant social code' and a smaller 'Advance Guard' of the more interesting figures would now have to be expanded into countless further categories that almost defy a single description.

Michelle Dulak, for instance, while acknowledging Taruskin's claim that HIP had hitherto shown every sign of twentieth-century high modernism, observes a softening of the verbal rhetoric and a more luxuriant performing style, starting in the late 1980s:

The 'vinegar' that record reviewers once found in 'period' violin tone has turned to honey in the hands of the latest generation of players... this new sound-quality is not just a retreat toward 'mainstream' ideals, but a distinct new timbre, gentler than the 'modern' string sound, more plaintive and more resonant, more suggestive of the physical gestures of performance.[69]

She notes one reviewer's slight embarrassment about enjoying Anner Bylsma's second recording of the cello suites (1992), which displays a degree of expressive 'romanticism' that would be all but banned from 'mainstream' performances.[70] Another reviewer attributes Bylsma's style more to a 'sense of strain' that tends to detract from the spirit of the dances.[71] This observation might reflect just how unfamiliar certain forms of expression (whether or not labelled 'romantic') have become. Bylsma's choice of instrument is also significant: an 'original' instrument, to be sure, but as a Stradivari from the Smithsonian Institution it is not in its original state – no restorer would dare 'put back' an instrument of such value.

Dulak thus suggests that there has been a turn away from Taruskin's pejorative 'authentistic performance' moving 'toward the use of a newly expanded catalogue of expressive resources, developed in the shadow of the modernist mainstream – a set of resources whose applications will surely not long be confined to "period" instruments'.[72] She notes that this is surely a discomfort with the 'modern' and may represent the beginnings of a postmodern performance practice (while acknowledging the ambiguity and ever-expansive category of the 'postmodern').

I have suggested that HIP has generated several of its own traditions and that much of the diversity we now hear results from performers reacting to one another; indeed, even the mainstream itself is reacting to developments within HIP.[73] This seems to substantiate one of the more optimistic moments in Taruskin's writings, when he discerns within HIP the growth of 'a hardy social practice ... that obeys its own dictates, has its own momentum, is becoming more and more eclectic, contaminated, suggestible'.[74]

Moreover, in the light of the very proper criticism of literalism and objectivist performance, many performers may well be developing a more critical attitude towards historical evidence, even deciding to use historical information selectively. As before, many will employ the experimental connotations of 'historical performance' as a licence to produce something new. Dulak, in a later article (1995) goes so far as to suggest that HIP performers 'are expected merely to sound in some way different and are given such wide latitude that they can be different in nearly any way that pleases them'.[75] Perhaps that which twenty years before was so often believed to be a puritanical movement, thwarting our desires for individual expression, was really the covert entry of anarchy into the western performing tradition. Indeed, Dreyfus goes so far as to suggest that the most significant work produced under the umbrella of HIP is that which actually flouts 'musicological authority', thus seeming to substantiate Taruskin's call for the divorce of scholarship and performance.[76] Perhaps this all reflects HIP's embrace of otherness. Indeed, Kay Shelemay, in her ethnomusicological approach to the early music movement, suggests that 'this "otherness" is inevitably and sometimes dramatically inflected by a late twentieth century sensibility with difference articulated by many as a central value of the movement at large'.[77]

The most comprehensive attempt to account for the situation at the end of the 1990s is undoubtedly Bernard D. Sherman's volume of conversations with performers. While there is the obvious problem that what performers say may not necessarily correspond to how they play or sing, the conversations show how the performers themselves have engaged with the early music debate and how they place themselves within the various traditions that have arisen. Sherman summarises the diversifying nature of HIP (including various 'cross-over' ventures with forms of popular music, such as the Hilliard project mentioned above) and also makes the obvious point that with more familiarity with early instruments, players are able to do more with them (*Inside Early Music*, pp. 5–7). As William Christie states later in the book, 'specialisation' is a far better word for the movement than 'authenticity'. All this substantiates Taruskin's point that adopting old instruments will not on its own result in a particular, 'correct' style (see p. 14 above); both the player's competence and taste must have a considerable influence on the result.

What is immediately evident from the interviews is that, for many of these scholar–performers, pure factual scholarship is simply no longer adequate and the puritanical attitude of twenty years before can be entirely absent: 'You can't sing a footnote', states Susan Hellauer (p. 50). Kerman's perfectly common-sense assumption in 1985 that interpretation is an individual matter while '[h]istorical performing practice . . . is by its very nature normative' is clearly in need of modification.[78] Instead, these figures often believe – some passionately – in forms of 'authenticity' other than normative practice and that their work on earlier repertories actually effects a change in one's state of mind. Like many 'pre-HIP' performers, they often sense a form of spiritual or emotional connection with past performers, but one that is (re)discovered rather than directly inherited.

Some of those interviewed treat their field somewhat like ethnomusicologists trying to understand a foreign culture, a phenomenon greatly substantiated by Shelemay's recent study ('Toward an Ethnomusicology pp. 18–21), which suggests that the connection between early music and world music is a broad cultural trend that has not sufficiently been acknowledged. While the ethnomusicological approach generally involves transferring the traditional horizontal axis of the ethnomusicologist (i.e. across various world cultures) to the vertical one of European cultural history, there are occasions when the performers seek an historic authenticity in parallel cultures of the present. Marcel Pérès, noticing that Old Roman chant contained some pieces in Greek sought out a Greek singer to try out the chant (p. 33). The fact that the singer had absolutely no experience in this field was apparently an advantage: somehow an inherent 'Greekness' would reveal truths about the music. Alan Curtis similarly favours Italian singers for Monteverdi. Foreigners like himself can only get close to the essential sound (and, presumably, understanding) of the language, however hard they try (pp. 138–9). It would be interesting to know whether any native Italians would share Curtis's concept of (or perception of) authenticity with regard to their own music, or whether his is the fervour of the 'convert'.

Christopher Page has made a case that English choral singers, trained in the Oxbridge tradition, cultivate a level of purity and precision, but also a sense of routine, all of which may well reflect something of the original performance practice of Medieval and Renaissance singers.[79] Despite the obvious danger of cultural chauvinism, Page is careful to stress that this 'authentic' link comes from the repeated practices involved rather than something inherently 'English'; in this respect he is more relativistic than either Pérès or Curtis.

Yet essential to much of Page's writing and music-making is a sense of 'transhistorical humanness', evidenced by the seemingly obvious fact that we do understand and respond to music of the past while the utterances of any other species remain entirely foreign (p. 76).[80] In contradistinction to much post-structuralist critical theory, Page believes in the continuity of substantial aspects of human nature and that the enterprise of HIP should have an ethical concern with rediscovering such continuities.

Moreover, the scholar should reject the puritanical sieve of positivism as the sole basis for performance and use one's intuition (p. 79). Presumably this is the flexing of that thread of human nature connecting us to the past – it is the intuition that finds the continuities in the fragments from the past and brings them to life. However, as Shai Burstyn remarks, the fact that past listeners had aesthetic preferences like we do does not guarantee their similarity.[81] But, given that we could never know – even with the greatest amount of historical knowledge imaginable – whether our aesthetic reaction were ever the same as that of the original listeners and performers, perhaps we should follow Page in using historical knowledge to build upon intuitions we already have rather than dismissing the latter entirely. Peter Jeffery employs ethnomusicology as a way of filling the obvious gaps in our historical knowledge of Gregorian Chant, since '[o]ral transmission is not a peculiar feature of some music at certain times, but rather a universal characteristic of almost all music at almost all times.'[82] This trust in universal human practices is fundamentally antihistorical – but it is clearly a major component in much of the thinking behind HIP and, obviously, of musicology that tends in the direction of ethnomusicology.

Page's belief in 'transhistorical humanness' is paralleled by Joshua Rifkin's view that HIP can often reveal a mode of performance that has temporarily fallen from human consciousness. He suggests that there are elements that are more or less universal (e.g. structural cohesion, detail, declamatory speaking, beautiful sounds), but that doing justice to one will often underplay another. Thus 'every era will slice it differently' and HIP basically reinvents wheels that have temporarily rolled out of sight (p. 389). Page and Rifkin thus come remarkably close to Scruton's notion of our achieving states of mind that were experienced in the past: i.e. '*what it was like* to believe as Victoria believed' (see p. 32 above). Yet for Scruton this could be achieved only through '[t]he unbroken tradition of polyphonic writing' and the continuous, changing tradition of performance. Belonging to a tradition somehow connects us to feelings that are nowhere else available in our culture. For Page these feelings are latent, but, conversely, obscured by recent tradition. Historical research, exhaustive experimentation and practice in performance and transhistorical intuition re-establish the link. Page's ideology perhaps comes close to Arthur C. Danto's conception of transhistorical essence in art, always and everywhere the same but disclosed through history. Danto's essence is distinguished from that of a modernist (such as Clement Greenberg, in Danto's case), in that it is no longer to be identified with a particular style that would imply 'that art of any other style is false'.[83] Even more significantly, Danto distances himself from essentialists such as T. S. Eliot who make a distinction between the aesthetic and the historical. Such a move confuses artistic and natural beauty and thus obscures the fact that both artistic perception and artistic beauty are historical through and through (Danto, p. 165).

Barbara Thornton's approach to Hildegard's music suggests that she tends towards the radical end of the Early Music Movement: rationalism has been exhausted so our era looks back towards the so-called primitive, whether African music or early music in the western tradition (Sherman, *Inside Early Music*, p. 56). Her interest in Hildegard, and the enormous enthusiasm with which the 'first' female composer is greeted also evidences a renewed interest in women and music in general. This provides an alternative story of music history, one that is presumed to reveal shades of humanity that have hitherto been unavailable. Anthony Rooley takes immersion in Renaissance as a means of capturing Ficino's Orphic frenzy; he believes his art to go beyond mere play to the actual 'being of life' (p. 152). As with the cults of the primitive and women's mystical music, Rooley's approach to HIP represents the New Age wing of the movement.

Within this increasing diversity within the 'new' HIP there are still performers who use some of the 'old' rhetoric – fundamentalists, as it were, who utter precisely the sorts of statements that Taruskin and others have rendered so unfashionable. Gustav Leonhardt affirms categorically that 'an instrument of the composer's period and country is certainly the best' and that 'it's been proved for people with a refined ear' (p. 203). Moreover, he subordinates himself to the composer to a degree that few others approach: 'I have nothing to say, I am only a player ... [not] a real musician, which is a composer' (pp. 203–4). Robert Levin applies the antiquarian's 'thin end of the wedge' argument: he plays continuo in Mozart piano concertos because the composer called for it; if that doesn't matter, perhaps the fortepiano doesn't matter either, if the instrument doesn't matter, neither does Mozart's articulation, and so on (p. 327). True historical performance for him is thus a delicate ecology in which seemingly unimportant differences contribute to the whole, to 'the cake that Mozart baked'.

The arguments of Leonhardt and Levin are precisely those that virtually all critics of HIP, both within and without the movement, believed

led to dull, literalistic performances. Yet, most of us would agree, these
two performers represent the very acme of the movement in their virtuosity, imagination and expression. Christopher Page describes his ideal
performance of Medieval music as relatively inexpressive (at least in the
modern sense) and devoid of rhythmic caprice (p. 82). Nevertheless, the
intensity of the result has been widely praised, even by Taruskin (see
p. 18 above), who could hardly share Page's ideals as they are expressed
verbally. Conversely, I have described the case of one performer, whose
liner notes promise a vital, rhetorical style that no one has previously
accomplished, but whose performances struck me as entirely ordinary
and uninflected.[84] In other words, it is impossible to predict how any
particular ideology of HIP will influence the quality of the resulting
performance; we should refrain from condemning performers before
actually hearing the results of their encounter with history. As Kerman
suggested '[r]eading books by the great artists is not the best way to gain
understanding of their artistic secrets';[85] this seems to hold as true of HIP
figures as it ever did of the mainstream. But, given the supposed scholarly credentials of HIP, the dislocation between artistic achievement and
verbal utterance is extremely interesting as part of a cultural – rather
than purely 'musical' – inquiry.

Where does all this lead? First, it is clear that the best performers are
excellent because of their insights and talents as performers, not necessarily because they are good historians in the professional sense. To this
extent, Taruskin's distinction of Text and Act seems to make sense. Yet it
is equally clear that these performers would not have achieved what they
had without some form of encounter with history and, above all, an intense belief in what they could learn from history. History, in a wider sense
than historical scholarship, can thus teach us how things were different,
how they could have been different; it helps us create imaginary worlds,
just like those of fiction, that chime with our own while revealing crucial
differences. History need no longer be merely the pessimistic one of decline followed by patchy restoration, or the optimistic one of Whiggish
progress to a redeemed present. Morgan's sad patchwork of undifferen-
tiated historical allusions can actually become lived realities if we, in the
present, can believe in something more than linear progress, and can
rediscover resonances in past human achievements. The professional
historian must be sceptical about apparent continuities or uncanny fa-
miliarities with the past. But in live, spontaneous performance, not only
can these experiences actually happen, they must.

Sherman outlines three basic types of HIP artists in the epilogue of his book: first, there are the traditionalists who firmly believe that we must perform as much as possible according to the times of the composers concerned. Secondly, there are those who reject the ideal of historical authenticity; having learned what they can about the history of performance they often decide to go in a different direction. Thirdly there are those who use 'history radically, to undermine a more basic assumption, one that the first two groups share with the mainstream' (Sherman, *Inside Early Music*, p. 393). This might include those performers who capitalise on the improvisational practices of an age in order to undermine the concept of *Werktreue*, a fidelity to the work that often ossifies a score that was merely intended as a starting point for performance. There are those who use history to rebel against the seamless perfection of modern, clean performance; the composer of any age may, after all, have anticipated a certain amount of imperfection as central to how the music was written.

These categories come surprisingly close to Nietzsche's three types of history which, it should be remembered, contained positive as well as negative qualities and all of which he considered necessary in their own particular ways. Sherman's traditionalists in HIP clearly parallel Nietzsche's category of the *antiquarian*. In this, one preserves as much as possible from the past, particularly of one's own culture and heritage. It pays equal respect to those who were less favoured in that past as to those who stood above their contemporaries; in its fibrous historical groundedness it parallels the contentment of the 'tree in its roots' (Nietzsche, 'On the Uses', p. 74). In the use of the term by Fredric Jameson, this type of history thus cultivates one's 'historicity', that sense of belonging within a densely textured cultural fabric, most of which is otherwise inaccessible (see chapter 5, pp. 158–63 below). But the details, small and large, significant and insignificant, give us a glimpse of that past, cultivating a sense of depth in our origins. As Nietzsche warns, this mode can easily suffer from a levelling of value, 'an extremely restricted field of vision' in which everything that is seen is 'much too close up and isolated'. The result can often be a 'blind rage for collecting' and an obsession with 'bibliographical minutiae' that represents the mummification of cultural life rather than its revivification (p. 75). Here Nietzsche uncannily prophesises views of culture in the late twentieth century, particularly those of Jean Baudrillard, who suggests that the collecting mania and thirst for historical detail 'comes from a headlong flight forward from the hemorrhage of objective causality'.[86]

Sherman's second category, which is perhaps the least typical within the context of HIP, comes closest to the 'mainstream' practice insofar as this also tends to reject the letter of historical practice. Nietzsche's *monumental* history is that of the great human achievements of the past, a chain that 'unites mankind across the millennia like a range of human mountain peaks' (p. 68). Exactly as Scruton suggests, greatness shows the 'solidarity and continuity' of all ages and underplays the *differences*, as though 'history' in all its details and diversity is really the story of mediocrity (p. 69). According to Nietzsche, this type of history deals in 'approximations and generalities, in making what is dissimilar look similar', exhibiting the *effect* at the expanse of the *cause* (p. 70). This inspiring, heroic sort of history runs the risk of becoming 'quite incapable of distinguishing between a monumentalised past and a mythical fiction' and whole segments of the past are forgotten and devalued. The political danger lies in its deceit by analogy: 'with seductive similarities it inspires the courageous to foolhardiness and the inspired to fanaticism' (p. 71). Just like the antiquarian mode, there is also the danger that monumental history will undervalue the achievements of the present: 'the dead bury the living' (p. 72).

Sherman's final category, of the HIP figure who uses history to confound an assumed convention, parallels Nietzsche's *critical* mode of history. For Nietzsche, the emphasis is on the immediate past and in exposing the historical contingency of present assumptions; '[i]t is an attempt to give oneself, as it were *a posteriori*, a past in which one would like to originate in opposition to that in which one did originate' (p. 76). In its strongest sense, critical history renders one suspicious of everything in history (thus it is almost the opposite mode to the antiquarian). But it clearly sums up the service that HIP does in opposing the normative modes of musical behaviour, showing how things were, and still could be, different.

Nietzsche's list of dangers within the critical mode involve our assuming that we can be free of the aberrations of our inherited nature and ignore the fact of our own origins; to believe ourselves to be entirely free is a characteristic of 'dangerous and endangered men and ages'. But the lesson learned is salutary: just as we learn to realise that our 'first nature was once a second nature' we should understand that 'every victorious second nature will become a first', and so on (p. 77).

While part of Nietzsche's plan is to show the *uses* of history and its necessity for the human condition, the bulk of his essay attempts to show that there was too much history for its own sake at the time he was writing, namely the last third of the nineteenth century. This had rendered the present dowdy, uncreative, satiated with more information than it could assimilate, jaded and relativistic, and cynical about the individual's ability to make any difference in the world. This was, of course, precisely the era of the 'first wave' of early music and HIP: the time of the Caecilian movement, the Solesmes project, the Schola Cantorum in Paris and the first musings of Arnold Dolmetsch. Of course, such a historicist turn was relatively slight compared with the tremendous commodification of early music and HIP at the equivalent point in the twentieth century. There is no doubt that the Nietzsche of 1874 would have been doubly appalled by the later phenomenon. Rather like Adorno of 1951, he noted that the 'historically educated' person is a neutered being, becoming eternally subjectless and merely objective: 'the hollowed-out cultivated man at once looks beyond the work and asks about the history of the author' (Nietzsche, 'Uses and Disadvantages of History', p. 87). Much of his concern related to the nationalistic desire to promote a Wagnerian German culture, one that needed something of an unhistorical horizon in order to flourish freely. Yet Nietzsche was soon using history again, believing historical criticism to be the most potent weapon to debunk many of the central dogmas of Christianity. History was thus a powerful weapon in the process of 'disenchantment', a process that to many is absolutely central to the cultural work of modernism (see chapter 5, p. 131 below). With the collapse of the communist world in the last decades of the twentieth century, many would suggest that this process of disenchantment has run its course. Virtually all the 'grand narratives' of historical progress and destiny are seemingly undermined by an 'excess of history', limitless information and, potentially, an infinite plurality of competing systems of belief (see pp. 145–58, below).

The situation at the outset of the twenty-first century is quite different from that for which Nietzsche was writing. Perhaps the domination of history and surfeit of information are such that it is no longer possible to escape these modes, as Nietzsche thought he could in 1874. In a postmodern climate – if that is the name of what we are experiencing – the notion of 'monumental' history can no longer have claims to sovereignty over the others, although rumours of its death might be greatly exaggerated. The antiquarian mode may well be more important than before, since its gift of historicity is indeed a comfort in a world that has outwardly changed beyond recognition within the space of a couple of generations. And in a world that is inherently pluralist, the critical mode of history is surely one of the most potent means we have to question our inherited habits and seek viable alternative 'second natures'. Just as Nietzsche warned, history can render us inactive or fatalistically relativistic. Yet, just as he hoped, it can still serve life, albeit a life of a very different nature from what he could possibly have envisioned. The remainder of this book is an attempt to explore the potentials for new life within the culture of music, and the service that HIP might do in promoting it.

PART 2

Historically informed performance and the implications for work, composer and notation

Historical performance and 'truth to the work': history and the subversion of Platonism

> I have often heard it stated by scholars and others interested in performance on early instruments that they would rather hear a great artist on the wrong instrument than a mediocre player on the right one. I am no longer willing to accept that statement. Perhaps it is wrong to put the instrument before the artist, but I have begun to feel that it must be done . . . There is simply no way that the greatest, most sensitive artist can ever come close to a true Mozartean sense with [modern instruments].
>
> Malcolm Bilson, 1980[1]

Many involved with performance on historical instruments may now find Bilson's remarks extreme; the rhetoric of historicist performance has become progressively milder since the early 1980s. Yet something of Bilson's sense is probably still harboured by any of us who choose the old instruments over modern ones; why, after all, make this choice if one does not believe that there is some positive advantage? Bilson's famous remark may thus still represent a *reductio*, however much *ad absurdum*, of the historicist enterprise. Moreover, the same type of thinking is evident in reconstructionist approaches to other arts, such as the Globe Theatre project. Andrew Gurr implies that Shakespeare's plays as we have hitherto known them are somehow incomplete without the precise reconstruction of the 'original instrument', the theatre for which the dramatist wrote his plays:

We lose or distort much of what is valuable in his plays so long as we remain ignorant of the precise shape of that playhouse, and of how Shakespeare expected his plays to be performed there . . . A play in performance is a dynamic event, the product of a huge complex of details, from the penetrating quality of an actor's voice to the hardness of the bench a spectator may be sitting on or the state of the weather. We need to know these details, the precise shape of the stage and the auditorium, the quality of the light, the effects on sound and vision of an open-air arena and a crowded auditorium, the interplay between actors performing on a platform in an open yard and the packed mass of thousands of spectators, many of them standing, all in broad daylight. None of these effects, each of which influences the others, can be gauged without a full-scale reconstruction. Shakespeare's works were composed in full knowledge of the intricate and dynamic interplay through which his plays were to be performed at the original Globe. We owe it to ourselves to attempt some reconstruction of the more tangible features of that interplay.[2]

The attention to the 'ensemble' of details contributing to the phenomenological impact of what we often regard as a written text is certainly stimulating, but two crucial questions immediately arise. First, there is the obvious issue of whether we can ever be sure that we have actually reconstructed all the original details. Secondly, and more crucially, both Gurr and Bilson seem to assume a consistency of listenership, that an ideal human subject will somehow respond identically to the same sensual stimuli regardless of age, period or social background.[3] Thus there is a profound sense in which this 'strong' concept of restoration is *anti*-historical, assuming as it does that there are essences in artistic production and reception that are entirely unaffected by the passing of time or place. This attitude could be termed 'modified autonomy' – the retention of the concept of the timeless artwork, but embellished with as many details as possible from the circumstances of its production. And these details are relevant to the degree that they proceed from the work outwards and not so much from the outside world – inwards – to the work.

This chapter first examines the nature and implications of this essentialist approach, since I suggest that HIP has gained much of its prestige through its appeal to a pre-existing concept of *Werktreue* ('truth to the work'). Yet, as I hope to show, the very concern with history destabilises the notion of consistent essences. HIP, quite against the intentions of its more 'hard-line' advocates, has – like a Trojan Horse – actually served to loosen the hold of the work concept and to change profoundly the culture of music and performance.

So what conception of music, musical works and composers underlies Bilson's statement? And what part does performance play in this equation? First, it is clear that the performer has duties and responsibilities to composer and work. This is, in itself, an unremarkable stance, common to many accepted performing ethics concerned with the concept of *Werktreue*. What is more contentious is the view that the instrument is privileged above the performer; it is to have a status equal to that customarily accorded to the musical text. To the degree that a performer feels duty-bound to use a score that conforms to an authentic version of the work (whatever the difficulties this may entail), he should also use the 'authentic' instrument that the composer had in mind. The tenor of Bilson's argument (and indeed of many writings on historical performance) presumably stretches to the next level of regulation, in which performance style and interpretation are also to be governed by the historically correct norms. Indeed, he suggests in a later interview that Mozart's slurs and other performance markings are sometimes more crucial than the notes, if the performer wishes to follow Mozart's intentions (note, though, the milder imperative implied by the reference to the contemporary performer's wishes). In all, Bilson develops an interesting viewpoint that extends the customary respect for the literal accuracy of the score with an equally strong belief in aspects of the broader context that, he believes, bring out the essence of what the composer sought to express.[4] This sort of shift of emphasis, which retains the moral fervour of a pre-existing system of beliefs, is typical of HIP in general.

Much of this presupposes that the works concerned have an identity – a correct form of being – that the performer is morally bound to realise in sound; it is not enough to provide a recognisable performance or even one that is in some respect interesting. There is a sense that the listener (and presumably also the performer – both kinaesthetically and as a critical listener of his own performance) is deprived of some experiential truth if exposed to the 'wrong' sort of performance. Perhaps this truth has something to do with a composer's mind and personality, with a particular historical style or with the essence of a single work. But most writers on HIP adopt an ethical tone in this regard without offering any explanation of the basis of the imperative.

This ethical tone undoubtedly borrows something from the traditional Germanic conception of 'the work' as that which we are duty-bound to interpret. Ludwig Finscher articulates a typical post-Adorno view of HIP in 1967 when he suggests that there is a dichotomy between the *work* as something we wish to interpret and the 'work' as the objectivication of an historical moment. He proposes that an interpretation on modern instruments might sometimes allow us to get closer to a 'true' interpretation of the work than the original ones and that the surest guide to that interpretation is through analysis and contemplation of the 'work itself' in its notated form.[5] The 'hard-line' HIP view seems to conflate Finscher's two notions of work by concretising the historical moment *as* the essential work. Philosophical justification for this position comes, not from within the Germanic tradition but from the Anglo-American brand of 'analytical philosophy'. Might this express in logical terms that which the HIP hard-liner intuits?

A performing musician's concept of music should not necessarily be as coherent as that which a philosopher might demand. Aesthetic theory comes, more often than not, after the event and will usually trail a more broadly based ideology concerning the status of music.[6] It is quite striking that there is very little interaction between the writings of philosophers concerned with HIP in music and those by musicians and musicologists. But recent philosophical writers do perceive a need to account for historical performance and those who favour it do seem to be in broad agreement with Bilson's statement.

Werktreue in historical performance finds its most fully developed theoretical home in one of the most traditional formulations of the musical work, Platonism. Platonism has long been a feature of music theory, particularly when theory has veered towards the abstract, mathematical and formal, or even towards the unheard and ideal. In many ways 'pure' Platonism would seem to privilege musical works in the abstract over their realisation in sound (as in Keats's 'Ode on a Grecian urn', where 'Heard melodies are sweet but those unheard are sweeter'). Thus the unattainable ideal in music is analogous to a belief in divine aesthetic and moral order.[7] In short, Platonism, with its uncreated, eternal repertory of musical masterworks, affords music a metaphysical status similar to religion, a point not lost to aestheticians of the nineteenth century onwards.

At first glance, things do not look promising for historicist performance in a Platonist world. Platonism stresses that the best music transcends its time and context, that no performance can match the ideal and that history is merely a local phenomenon. Jerrold Levinson suggests that pure Platonism is particularly well served by Schenker's theory of musical analysis which tends to take the universal essence of each piece as a starting point and sees good performance in terms of its secondary role as the successful realisation of the musical structure.[8] On the other hand, composers from the nineteenth century onwards seem to have been all the more concerned with the specifics of performance practice, the choice of instruments and performance directives. Here the related concept of original genius might also be significant, with composers trying to make each work as individuated and exhaustively defined as possible. But this trend might also reflect much more mundane matters: e.g. the developments in copyright law and the opportunities afforded by the very mechanical reproduction of music (see chapter 4, below).

Peter Kivy gives the most thorough account of the obvious sort of musical Platonism that privileges the pure sound structure over the performance means. Works are universals while performances are merely particulars or instances. If instrumentation (and presumably performing style) are ever essential to the realisation of the work, they are only temporarily so, during the few years after composition; after this instruments and performers might well have 'improved'.[9] On the other hand, one of the 'purest' Platonists, Nicholas Wolterstorff, surprisingly maintains that the original instrumental directives are essential to the composition (at least in the last 200 years) as are any interpretative directives expressed by the composer.[10] However, it is only with the considerable modifications of Platonism offered by Stephen Davies and Jerrold Levinson that HIP receives its most thorough justification.

Davies notes that an interest in the performer's role is a concomitant of an interest in the composer's achievement *per se*.[11] For him, the sounds heard and intended by the composer should be as crucial to the identity of the work as the notes themselves:

A highly authentic performance is likely to be one in which instruments contemporary to the period of composition . . . are used in its performance, in which the score is interpreted in the light of stylistic practices and performance conventions of the time when the work was composed, in which ensembles of the same size and disposition as accord with the composer's specification are employed, and so forth.[12]

Davies associates 'authenticity' specifically with the sounds specified by the composer in their most ideal form, and believes any factors that are not directly associated with the sounding of the music (e.g. social circumstances of the composer and performance) to be irrelevant. Most binding of all are the composer's determinative intentions, although, as Wolterstorff also stresses, the non-determinative intentions might be subject to variation. Whenever the composer's intentions are not determined, or improvisation is essential to the music, the authorial element will play less of a role in determining authenticity; now general issues of contemporary style will come more to the fore. There is a certain circularity to Davies's scheme, since 'only those intentions which conventionally are accepted as determinative are relevant to judgements of authenticity' (Davies, 'Authenticity in Musical Performance',

p. 42). Thus authenticity is defined in accordance with determinative intentions and vice versa. I shall address the general problem of intentionality, and specifically the supposed hierarchy of determinative and non-determinative intentions in the next chapter.

Here it suffices to note that Davies gives a value to authenticity in performance that can be assessed independently of valuations of the musical work itself; indeed:

> A performance is better for a higher degree of authenticity (other things being equal) *whatever* the merits of the composition itself. A performance praiseworthy for its authenticity may make evident that the composer wrote a work with little musical interest or merit. It is the creative skill required of the performer in faithfully interpreting the composer's score which is valued in praising the authenticity of performances of that score. (Davies, 'Authenticity in Musical Performance', p. 47)

Although he admits the performer's originality and creativity in generating the necessary authenticity, this theory seems to be largely a matter of bibliographic housekeeping, similar to the fundamentals of producing a good edition.[13] The correct sound involved in 'authenticity' seems to relate directly to the *identity* of the work; the more correctly the notes are realised in accord with the specifications of the score and the sounds implied, the more it seemingly exists in performance. In this way Davies comes close to Nelson Goodman's notorious nominalist conception of music, in which works are defined as a class of performances that reproduce exactly the notes of the score.[14] Although this leads to certain absurdities, such as that a performance lasting ten years can count as an instance of the work, while a performance with a single wrong note does not, it does have a certain use as a *regulative* concept for the performer (i.e. the performer usually *intends* to get all the notes right).[15] Davies, in effect, adds those elements he supposes to confer 'authenticity' in performance to Goodman's call for correct notes. In all, his theory is to some degree successful in describing the intentions of many concerned with HIP, although it is still difficult to see where the moral imperative lies. Nor does it explain why works are both readily identified and enjoyed when performed 'inauthentically'.

Levinson concurs with much that Davies has to say, but formulates his attitude to historicist performance within a much more extensive general theory of the ontology of musical works. First, he modifies the pure Platonist approach by drawing in the creativity of the composer as part of the essence of music. One consequence of this definition which seems initially to conflict with common intuition, is that two composers coincidentally producing exactly the same notated piece of music actually provide two distinct works:

> The reason for this is that certain attributes of musical works are dependent on more than the sound structures contained. In particular, the aesthetic and artistic attributes of a piece of music are partly a function of, and must be gauged with reference to, the total musico-historical context in which the composer is situated while composing his piece. Since the musico-historical contexts of composing individuals are invariably different, then even if their works are identical in sound structure, they will differ widely in aesthetic and artistic attributes. (Levinson, *Music, Art, and Metaphysics*, pp. 68–9)

This line of reasoning obviously shares something with Jorge Luis Borges' satyrical 'Pierre Menard, Author of the Quixote', where the fictional author seeks to produce an exact verbal analogue of Don Quixote, but due to the entirely different circumstances of production and historical context, claims at the same time to produce a work entirely distinct from Cervantes'. Levinson's semiotic turn is also instructive: the same verbal sound – even sometimes with the same spelling – can signify entirely different concepts according to the language or to the context within any particular language. Thus the same musical sound structure can bear an entirely different significance according to its historical and creative contexts. But this comes dangerously close to accepting musical works as arbitrary signifiers that have meaning only in relation to their position in history and having none of the intrinsic identity that Platonism would surely demand.

If we provisionally accept Levinson's appeal to history as essential to musical works, two factors have come into play: the creativity of the composer (his background, assumptions and experience etc.), and the time at which he wrote (in terms of the position of a piece both in the course of his career and in the basic musical languages of his era). In Levinson's words, the musical work becomes 'a sort of universal brought down to earth' (p. 216). In the light of these two factors, it is not difficult (although not obligatory) to claim also that the Platonist sound-structure is also directly connected with the original performing medium. According to Levinson, it is simply not enough to claim, as Davies does, that the sound determined and expected by the composer should be reproduced. The way the sound is produced is crucial since it affects the attitude and experience of the performer and, with a little background knowledge, that of the listener too:

Part of the expressive character of a piece of music *as heard* derives from our sense of how it is *being made* in performance, and our correlation of that with its sonic aspect – its sound – narrowly speaking . . . Not only the qualitative nature of the sounds but also their specified means of production enter into the equation that yields the resultant aesthetic complexion of a piece of music in the tradition with which we are concerned. (p. 395)

In this respect Levinson distances himself from Kivy, who regards all sound-producing elements as secondary to the basic sound structure, and also from Randall Dipert, who ranks compositional intention from the lowest level, of sound production, through the actual sound intended, to the highest level of expressive intent.[16] According to Dipert's view, if the correct sound were to be produced more efficiently by some other means, the lowest level would no longer be significant; furthermore, if the composer's expressive intentions can be better produced for a later historical audience with other means or sounds, both lower levels should be dropped. Dipert's concern for the ulterior intention (although even this is not to have automatic priority over other conditions) does have the advantage of allowing a more vital, critical factor into the argument (in contradistinction to the objective concern for identity conditions that pervade the Platonists' arguments). However, there is an obvious problem in assuming that a composer's expressive or 'spiritual' intention will necessarily survive its historical context (for more on the ranking of intentions, see chapter 3, below).

Levinson draws some support from Kendall Walton, who stresses the importance of the listener's beliefs concerning how the music is being produced, and how this affects the expressive content derived from the piece.[17] Clearly, by this account, it might be possible to deceive the listener with synthesised sound and miming performers but this, for Levinson, is not performance in good faith. This argument is certainly compelling: a certain speed on one instrument is not so impressive on another, virtuosity plays a part in Handel's oboe concertos which is lost on a modern oboe that can play the part more easily. Moreover, this line of reasoning could be extended to show how crucial it is to preserve this instrumental factor in those cases where such virtuosity is about the only aesthetic advantage of the piece concerned. A performance which negates this or any other performance skill (as is the case with certain études) necessarily removes virtually everything that is valuable about the piece. However, Levinson obviously goes too far when he essentially dismisses entire traditions of performance, interpretation and insight. He comes close to Bilson when he suggests that, even if a modern clarinettist can produce exactly the original sound Mozart would have expected in his Thirty-ninth Symphony,

such a performance would not be expressively equivalent to *any* performance achievable on those older, and different, instruments. What expressiveness it would have is hard to say, bastardy being no simpler to deal with in the aesthetic realm than in the social one. (p. 407)

Obviously, Levinson, like Davies, allows that performance elements not determined by the composer are open to a wide degree of variation. While the work as notated is normally a singular entity, there are an infinite number of possible performances. He also allows certain deviations from 'correctness' if these take account of elements of modern practice in a conscientious and insightful fashion. But here the cool detachment of his modified Platonism must, by necessity, break down into personal preference: for instance he can allow for Glenn Gould's interpretations of Bach, but not for the gratuitous ones of Wendy Carlos which appeal only to the '*dull, lazy, unpractised* listener' (p. 384). He also allows some departures from historically authentic performance if these bring across qualities that the unpractised (but presumably not dull or lazy) listener would otherwise miss.

On the whole though, much of Levinson's attitude to both musical works and their performance is characterised by his quotation of 'Leibniz's law': if two things differ in any respects then they are simply not identical (p. 222). This thus takes into account those aspects which are not immediately (or perhaps ever) perceptible. Actually Levinson's Platonism has much in common with Leibniz's famous dictum that the predicate is necessarily contained within any particular subject; it is part of the definition of Julius Caesar that he should be slain by Brutus, just as it is part of the definition of Mozart's clarinet concerto that it uses a particular instrument (although, ironically, the choice of instrument for this concerto is a particularly contentious case). Of course, to be truly Leibnizian, rather than Platonist, Levinson would have to view the entire history of performance and reception as essential to the work (as perhaps he should), but his insistence that apparent accidentals of the creative context are of a piece with the most durable and recognisable aspects of the composition (the 'recognitional core' to use Levinson's expression) is a typically Leibnizian viewpoint.

Levinson's theory of 'authentic' performance is, I think, particularly important in that it actually defines what lies behind many assumptions made by 'hard-line' advocates of historicist performance (most overtly exemplified by Bilson's comments, above). Composers, repertories and specific musical works have an essence that is both universal and historically conditioned, and the use of the correct historical instrument will facilitate a performance that is definitive for the music concerned. Interpretative and creative aspects of performance can be allowed only after the correct 'performing definition' has been attained.

However, it is still difficult to see how this can or should be binding as a conception of music; much can be taken only as a matter of faith and force of opinion. Questions concerning the status of instrumental specifications 'ask too much of a practice that is indeterminate and complex', to quote Lydia Goehr. As she also notes, whether we believe or not in the essentiality of instrumentation depends on our conception of what a work actually is.[18] Furthermore, while it is clear that knowledge about the creative context of the piece is going to affect the conceptions of both performers and listeners alike, it is perfectly possible to have a profound appreciation of the music without this background.[19]

Goehr calls into question the entire tradition in which philosophers such as Levinson play a major role, suggesting that the very structure of arguments in analytic philosophy, concerned as they are with the conditions of identity, are incompatible with the objects they purport to define:

the lurking danger remains that the theories will probably become forever divorced from the phenomena and practices they purportedly seek to explain, as well as from any non-philosophical interest we have in those phenomena. The problem with the search for identity conditions resides just at this point, then, in the incompatibility between the theoretical demands of identity conditions and the phenomena to be accounted for. (Goehr, *The Imaginary Museum*, p. 86)

Not only does theoretical abstraction have little point if it is entirely divorced from musical practice, or if it is not clear as to what aspect of musical practice it refers, but the musical practice itself cannot be understood without an awareness of the complexities of history. Ontological arbitration alone cannot answer definitively questions relating to works, transcriptions, versions and performance (p. 60).

In Goehr's account, no analytic theory adequately accounts for the historical boundary of the music that it concerns; here she is perhaps rather unfair to Levinson who repeatedly stresses that his theory is to be applied only to music since 1750. Nevertheless, he does not show how the work-concept is itself dependent on an historical viewpoint. According to Goehr it is an 'open concept', allowing for the subtraction or addition of defining characteristics provided that its continuity is assured and that it is consistently recognisable over its period of operation. Open concepts are thus ' "signposts" facilitating language use' (p. 93). The work concept is also a 'regulative' concept, one that defines certain normative and interrelating practices that are implied when we talk of musical works (pp. 102–3).

Goehr seeks to show how the many strands constituting the work concept came together around 1800, so that it is to be basically associated with Romantic aesthetics of music. While many of these strands are present before that date (thus certain pieces and composers show a superficial affinity with pieces and composers from the period in which the work concept was operative), in the strictest sense works do not exist before 1800, only pieces of music. In some ways, Goehr's study is less satisfactory in dealing with the status of music before 1800 than in defining the work concept and its operation after this date. She tends to homogenise the considerable history of western music up to the end of the eighteenth century and give short shrift to earlier swings towards and away from a work concept. Indeed, the move towards the profiled composer and the perfection of individual works (as was happening in the fourteenth and fifteenth centuries, if not before) is precisely that character which Reinhard Strohm considers essential for the European tradition.[20] It would thus be false to suggest that the western tendency to abstract art from its context and function, treating it as if it were a world in itself, is just a nineteenth-century invention.[21] What is unique to this later conception – Goehr's 'work concept' – are the specific social, aesthetic and analytic practices attached to music, ones that resonate with earlier 'work concepts' but which do not necessarily constitute a more refined, perfected version of a consistent concept. As Goehr later writes, the fact that the origins of the work concept can often individually be traced back to earlier periods does not mean that the fully fledged concept emerged then; indeed, they become origins only in retrospect after the concept becomes operative.[22] One essential distinction may lie in Karol Berger's suggestion that a clearer division of labour between composer and performer developed in post-Beethovenian music.[23] Goehr's study is extremely successful in showing how modern analytic theories of music are all beholden to the work concept, in the guise in which it arose at the end of the eighteenth century, and thus tend to apply only to values and repertories of the nineteenth century and a little beyond. In all, Goehr's study would suggest that the very notion of defining HIP in terms of the intrinsic essence of musical works is doomed to failure on theoretical grounds, however much, and however usefully, it might define certain beliefs today concerning the relation between pieces of music and its original performing context.

Levinson's 'modified Platonism' is also problematic epistemologically: given that there is no certainty as to whether we have ever created the actual sound of original performances, we having nothing other than historical conjecture as a means of determining what the correct sound should be. The concept of Platonic forms of perfection is at least plausible in cases where we have several authentic examples to compare and experience, such as cars and lumps of cheese, but in the case of HIP we have only one conjecture to pit against another. Furthermore, were we to hit upon exactly the 'right' historical performance of a piece of music we would never be able to know it as such; it would not conveniently leap out at us leaving all the other attempts in the dust. In short, the 'modified' Platonist historical performance is by necessity both impossible to achieve and impossible to recognise and therefore it is difficult to know what practical purpose it could possibly serve. So where does this leave the actual practice of HIP, to the extent that it rests on certain theoretical assumptions that do not hold up under scrutiny?

Before suggesting ways in which HIP might actually be beneficial to our practice, particularly in regard to how we define and use musical works, one specific objection to HIP needs to be addressed. Intuitively it might seem that instruments have an obvious and immediate effect on both the sound of the music and the performer's attitude. However, Richard Taruskin, in attending particularly to the implications for tempo in 'traditional' and 'historical' performances of Beethoven's Ninth Symphony, observes that the old instruments, by themselves, do not create faster tempi, and indeed that Furtwängler's supposed slower approach often produces tempi faster than Norrington's with period instruments. In exasperation, he implores:

So please, let there be no more uninformed, deterministic talk about period instruments and their magical power to make a performance all by themselves. Such talk is evasive and simplistic at best, destructive of all judgement and values at worst.[24]

Even more devastating for the case for 'instrumental essentialism' are the changes in HIP sonorities which many have observed during the 1990s (see p. 41 above). While this does not exactly represent a return to the sound of 'mainstream' performance, it at least shows that the sound produced on early instruments is partly a matter of choice. Another issue to take into account here is the fact that by the 1990s there were more capable players on the 'period' instruments, players who had had more time to master the techniques required to make the instruments sound well (a process that would inevitably take a long time in the case of a reinvented tradition).

At the very least then, if instruments are to have any crucial normative value, as Bilson suggests, they can only have this if coupled with the 'right' kind of player and performance. Yet if players seem to have discovered the art of alchemy and can (within reason) make any instrument sound as they choose, the value of instruments seems to fall well below that of players. Does this then take us back to the square one of Kivy's strict Platonism, for which the sound structure, or Levinson's 'core', is the only important factor of the work, while everything else is a matter of contingent, historical interpretation?

The answer to all these issues is perhaps to take the argument outside the question of definitions and beyond moral absolutes that require us to opt for the 'instruments' on the one side, the 'players' on the other, or to ground the ontology of musical works in performance on the one hand or timeless Platonic forms on the other. For a start, instruments *do* make *some* difference, whether for a player more used to another type or for one who has a number of instrumental choices to hand. But this usually has little to do with actual historical accuracy, since it is clearly impossible to duplicate the kinaesthetic experiences and aesthetic attitudes of the original players for any particular repertory. What is significant is the fact that the instruments do alert the player to historical difference. Different versions of a particular instrument or family will force the player to rethink his techniques and interpretative capability, and thus the repertory will have to be seen in a new light.

In this respect, Adorno had it back to front when he suggested that historical performance undermined the essential distance with which we must relate to the past.[25] Rather than leading us to impersonate the practices of a past age as if they were our own, HIP more often leads us to appreciate a difference that we would not otherwise have noticed. To take a leaf out of Levinson's book, even if the historicist performer eventually produces exactly the same sound and style that he would have achieved with 'modern' instruments, the fact that he has had to go through technical hoops to achieve this will mean there is a difference in his experience of what he produces, something which may make him consider the issues involved in more detail.

Indeed many historicist performers have realised that novelty – rather than a return to original and 'better' practice – is one of the main things they have to offer.[26] In certain cases of music that was specifically progressive for its time, the use of hitherto unfamiliar instruments and performance practices might reproduce something of the sense of shock and surprise that the first performances engendered. Ironically then, the supposed introduction of an old practice will create a new experience in keeping with the composer's ulterior intentions, even though the original audience would have experienced the novelty in quite a different manner. Randall Dipert usefully makes a similar point when he observes how shocking the new clarinet must have sounded in certain works by Gluck.[27] However, he does not make the inference that the reintroduction of an *old* clarinet today might have a similar effect.

Evidently, the time will come – indeed it has come for certain instruments, such as the harpsichord – when 'old' instruments will no longer sound 'new'. However, the net result is a much greater variety of performing styles and sounds. Our ability to appreciate a plurality of styles is perhaps one of the greatest advantages of our present condition,[28] something which seems to negate those views which claim we are unable to appreciate earlier stylistic nuances. Young, for instance, evoking Wittgenstein's famous example of a picture that appears as a duck to some, as a rabbit to others, insists that the historical progress of western music is such that we can no longer appreciate that thirds in Mediaeval music are dissonant, or the significance of dissonance in tonal repertories, because we are used to atonal music.[29] This runs totally in the face of our ability to make stylistic distinctions, to hear the shock of dissonance in one style as the norm in another; there is evidently something equivalent here to our ability to understand more than one verbal language (see p. 28 above).

Young extends his argument to include musical connotation and symbolism: we don't hear trumpet flourishes as trumpets of the Sun King, we don't hear passages for oboe or flute as being rustic,

Of course, we can and do learn that period listeners heard certain sounds as rustic or regal. But it is one thing to know that others heard them thus and quite another to hear them so ourselves.

However, while we must allow that we can never duplicate the experiences of earlier listeners, Young misses an important point concerning the way listeners react to style and symbolism. All these conventions needed to be learned by the first listeners just as they are by those of the present – period listeners were not born with conceptions of the Sun King or the rustic muse. In both the original and modern instances, the symbolism is learned in the same way as any language or convention. While we could never relate to this in the same way as the original artists, we at least have a privilege of a plurality that was unavailable to them.

So far then, the value of instruments and performing styles would seem to lie in specifically contemporary needs rather than in considerations of eternal musical truth or essence. Does this imply that there is no means of proving whether or not an historical performance is better than a mainstream one? Here again, the conflict should not be one of absolutes. To affirm that historical performances are, by nature, better runs in the face of contemporary practice and evaluation within the world of performance. On the other hand, to affirm that the choice of instruments (and performing styles) is of no importance is to come near to returning to the 'pure' Platonist view of works as fixed eternal entities, unaffected by the contingencies of performance.

One particularly insidious consequence of the latter type of thinking is that entire repertories of music can be devalued. Most music of the French Baroque, for instance, entirely fails when performed in the standard 'mainstream' fashion. We cannot know whether any historically based performances today approach the originals, we can only observe the more-or-less uncontroversial fact that those that attempt to do so are immeasurably more successful in rendering the music valuable than those that do not. It may indeed be the case here that the performance practice is linked particularly strongly to the identity and quality of the music. But what may be even more crucial is the fact that the performers concerned have given exhaustive attention to the repertory at hand. Their greater absorption of both style and performance practices may give their performance an intensity and level of commitment that prevailing 'mainstream' traditions could simply not achieve. Stan Godlovitch suggests that HIP should aim for a 'thick' reading of 'authenticity', one that makes no brash claims or rouses no pretentious expectations. The culture simply cultivates more practical knowledge of the past, arousing curiosity and giving the opportunity to develop new skills.[30] In all, this seems to parallel Nietzsche's contention that history is useful insofar as it serves the purposes of life.

It might seem reasonable, then, to admit that there can really be no hard-and-fast rule regarding the relation between instrument, player and music; every piece and every repertory should perhaps be considered on a case-by-case basis. Sometimes the music and performance exist in a symbiotic relationship, in that the music simply doesn't make sense without something approaching the original performance medium (perhaps because it was the *performance*, rather than the abstract 'sound structure', that crucially identified the music in the first place). At other times the relationship might be far less important.

While one has a perfect right to 'prefer' what one takes to be the original sound, and one has a right to argue that this can present the music in a better light, this does not mean that the music is thus eternally defined by its original sound, given that the definition of musical works themselves is also a matter of contingent, human practice. Adorno suggests that there is little point in reconstructing the instrumental sound of the Baroque since the concept of the 'clearly authentic composition' was not yet established.[31] By this he means that composers used whatever was to hand, in a world of anarchic, pluralistic instrument building; Bach was more content to specify no instrumentation in his late contrapuntal works as if to show the inadequacy of the instrumentarium of the day. Moreover, the very principle of the thorough-bass and the freedom it implied shows that nothing was fixed in sound. Yet it is clear that Adorno is speaking of instrumentation in the nineteenth-century sense – as something structurally necessary: the instruments of the Baroque were indeed not so central to the identity of the music as the valve-horn or clarinet family became in the nineteenth and twentieth centuries. Thus, insofar as HIP performers might share this same attitude – transferring nineteenth-century concepts of instrumental specificity to earlier repertories – Adorno's critique is absolutely correct. But what he refused to countenance was the notion of the definition of music as lying as much in its performance as in its abstract 'workhood'. In other words, the variability suggested by thorough-bass practice is not so much evidence of a weak approximation to the fully rationalised, determined work, rather it reflects an alternative mode of musical being. HIP, as a concept, thus enables us to break away from the modernist imperative to condemn Baroque music either to abstract workhood (i.e. the 'best' music) or to the dumping-ground of inferior music, barely worth entombing in the archives. The instrumentation and performance is crucial – not in revealing something structurally essential about the music – but in suggesting to us how the surviving music emerged from a variable practice of performance which, in turn, conditioned the way the music was notated in the first place. We should perhaps follow Shai Burstyn in conceiving of works with a 'softer' ontological nature than is traditionally implied by the work concept.[32] Not only does HIP suggest that some earlier music is better understood in terms of *event* than abstract *work* (a point that Goehr strongly stresses) but it helps us focus on the role performance plays in defining all works. Even pieces which are strongly associated with the ahistorical, work-based view of music history are profoundly influenced by their performance history and, if José A. Bowen is correct, the 'study of the performance tradition of a musical work *is* the study of the musical work'.[33]

A knowledge of the historical context and the parameters of the original performance is sometimes the best means we have of realising a specific character or style in music that seems 'unfinished' or that does not seem to stand 'structurally' on its own. HIP thus actually produces (however contentiously) a stylistic identity that later works would have by virtue of their more individuated sound structures. This again suggests that we should not rely on an *a priori* separation of work and performance. The fact that a style of performance can completely transform the affect or another aspect of a work cannot simply be dismissed as misinterpretation of a stable original, especially if performance (whether assumed to be variable or fixed from one occasion to another) played an important role in the way the music came to be written in the first place.

The more recent arrival of HIP in interpreting music from the era of 'the work concept' (i.e. after 1800, to borrow Goehr's definition) has gone some way towards bringing the human elements of production back into play, often 'domesticating' works with mundane facts about their first performances. Following Taruskin, we might concede that this is hardly an ideal direction for performance *per se* to take. The notion that the amateur nature of the first performances of Beethoven symphonies should always be recaptured in contemporary performance is hardly going to result in performances that reveal new depths of human experience. Nevertheless, it does force us to take a stand on the relevancy of the work concept, its historical development and application, a stand that we might not otherwise have taken. Beethoven was indeed writing pieces that were soon to be seen as 'works' (and perhaps he even intended them as such) although they were still performed by players who viewed them as 'yet more pieces'. By witnessing an apparently 'amateur' performance of a Beethoven symphony we can learn how Platonism and other essentialist attitudes to pieces of music are not only historically contingent but also absolutely vital for the productive reception of certain repertories. Thus, if we are to take the implications of HIP seriously, it should help us recover elements of the 'work concept' for repertories for which it might be appropriate. As Leo Treitler has suggested 'the "work" concept has a history that is at least a thread in one of the central plot-lines of western music history; it cannot sensibly be taken as a premise for that history'.[34] The time is surely near when something of the aesthetic tradition of the nineteenth century is itself ripe for a form of restoration.

Another way of addressing the issue of how essential original instruments and performing practices are to the identity or 'meaning' of music is to see it as a parallel to the role of etymology in linguistics. The connection with etymology seems particularly appropriate in the light of frequently heard comments such as 'But, how did this music originally [i.e. correctly] sound?', analogous to the question 'But, what did this word originally [i.e. correctly] mean?' The primacy of etymology was dealt fatal blows by Darwinism in the nineteenth century and, specifically, by Ferdinand de Saussure's seminal *Course in General Linguistics* 1906–11. This was the fountain-head for the structuralists' preference for the synchronic over the diachronic. Saussure was the first to affirm that synchronic language study (i.e. study of how a language works across the board at any one time, rather than in its historical development) was essential if one wished to understand the practice and knowledge of a specific speaker and community, for whom the history of the language is normally irrelevant.[35] As Derek Attridge affirms, the view that etymology reveals 'authentic meanings' rests on a contradiction that historicist performers should well note:

Although it flirts with history, it's a deeply anti-historical attitude, replacing the social and historical determination of meaning (operating upon the arbitrary sign) by a transcendent 'true' meaning. Just as some literary theorists cling to the notion of authentic meaning for a text, not because this notion is consistent with itself or with the facts of literary history, but because they assume that to give it up is to invite unbridled relativism (and perhaps even revolution), so there's a common assumption that every word must have its authentic meaning, or else meaning could not exist at all. (Attridge, 'Language as History', p. 188)

Obviously the direct association of musical works with words is problematic given that musical 'meaning' is hardly reducible to verbal meaning.[36] Furthermore, the meanings of musical works cannot be arbitrary in the same sense as individual words, since they are intentionally created by historical subjects who, in effect, create both new works and their first meanings in one act. Nevertheless, Attridge's observation of the 'ahistoricism' in the search for authentic meaning could also be applied to the Platonist interpretation of historicist performance, in which a supposed historical situation is rendered eternally binding. 'Historically informed performance' under this definition is actually a profound misnomer. To be most thoroughly historicist (in the sense of being true to the original meaning and circumstances) one would have to acknowledge that no historical situation is exactly repeatable.

Yet many theorists, not least Saussure himself, do turn to etymology on occasions; indeed it is a temptation that few seem to avoid. It is most successfully employed when it is no longer viewed as something scientific and logical, when it has more to do with rhetoric and the po-etic or creative aspect of writing. Correctness is not the issue as such, more whether we can make an imaginative, persuasive and creative use of the past to change the present. Moreover, there is no reason why we should have to make a choice between the synchronic and the di-achronic; the latter – and the beliefs we may hold about it – can, and do, become an aspect of the former. History can be a very real part of our present concerns without necessarily replacing them.[37] One of the rea-sons why the issue of the historical circumstances of performance became an issue in the first place may have been the stagnation of the received traditions.

It is thus in the ability to change the present in a convincing and imaginative way that HIP may have its greatest strength. Those who (correctly) affirm that we can come to like 'the original way' of performing a piece of music, even if it's difficult initially, must come to terms with the fact we are capable of 'coming to like' many things if we believe in them for long enough. In other words, it doesn't seem to matter if our etymology is 'authentic', simply false or 'folk etymology'. It is in our wholehearted dialogue with the past – to the extent that it survives in the present – and our ability to make it into a convincing story (i.e. performance) that we make the most productive use of history.

This sense of 'feedback' between past and present is a useful way of avoiding the old diachronic/synchronic dichotomy. It may also explain what has been successful in the enterprise of HIP as well as pointing towards the manner in which it could develop. This model shares some-thing with the semiology of music which Jean-Jacques Nattiez developed from Jean Molino in which the meaning and significance of a musical work is located in the flux between the creative background of the work (the 'poietic' process), the surviving trace and the history of its reception (the 'esthesic' process). Many of Nattiez's complex developments of this model show how our perception of the poietic process is interfolded into our reception of a work in performance. In the case of Wagner's *Ring*:

To interpret the work's meaning we must return to Feuerbach and Schopen-hauer . . . Wagner, occupying an esthesic position in relation to them, read them in a certain fashion; we, in turn, understand the two texts according to our own personal bias, and furthermore we can suggest an interpretation of both informed by *Wagner's* understanding of their works. Finally, the spectator judges Chèreau's and Boulez's work relative to his or her knowledge of Wagner and the *Ring, and relative to the idea that he or she has formed of both* . . . What, in effect, is a *judgment* about the fidelity of this or that performance? It is the juxtaposition of one *interpretation* (the spectator–listener's interpretation of the musical performance and mise-en-scène) with another *interpretation* (that same spectator–listener's suppositions about the true Wagner, or the essence of the *Ring*).[38]

The crucial significance of the level of reception in defining musical works and performances is suggested by this semiotic approach: we learn that it is basically impossible for us to conceive of music in the abstract, untouched by human awareness.

Goehr concludes her remarks concerning historical performance on a remarkably positive note:

More than any other movement currently existing within the European tra-dition of classical music, the early music movement is perfectly positioned to present itself not only as a 'different way of thinking about music', but also as an alternative to a performance practice governed by the work-concept. By posi-tioning itself as a viable and dynamic alternative, even as a challenge to another practice, it is able to serve as a constant and living reminder to all musicians that the *Werktreue* ideal can be delimited in scope . . . It keeps our eyes open to the possibility of producing music in new ways under the regulation of new ideals. It keeps our eyes open to the inherently critical and revisable nature of our regulative concepts. Most importantly, it helps us overcome that deep-rooted desire to hold the most dangerous of beliefs, that we have at any time got our practices absolutely right.[39]

As Goehr herself notes, many practitioners of historicist performance are too closely wedded to the concept of *Werktreue*, something which still begs a satisfactory defence and, incidentally, can engender a practice that is both repressive and musically unimaginative. However, it is unlikely that the idea of HIP would have got off the ground without the notion of the essentiality of musical works in the first place. Ironically, it has also been significant in its own turn by enabling us to challenge this hegemony, acting as a litmus test for our own concepts of music, history and the relation of composition to performance.

This pattern of appropriating history for non-historical ends, which are themselves thereby destabilised, is captured with remarkable perceptiveness in Hermann Hesse's modernist allegory of 1943, *The Glass Bead Game*. Here, in the future state of Catalania, early music and performance on ancient instruments become a crucial component of general education, purging tradition of excessively personal Romantic traces and helping to engender a stable, uncreative and ascetic society.[40] Joseph Knecht, the protagonist who rises to be Grandmaster of the esoteric Glass Bead Game, finds that it is precisely his awareness of history (presumably informed by his early training in historical instruments and performance) that causes him to see the contingency of the Order and ultimately to take the heretically individualist step of resigning. Only by returning to the wider world would he be able to work more effectively towards preventing the decline of an order complacently regarded as inviolable by its members. Only from a standpoint outside the culture would he gain the necessary insight into how it must change and develop in order to adapt itself to the relentlessness of history. Might this not then suggest some of the ways in which HIP could relate to the wider culture of western music? Can it not act in the manner of Nietzsche's critical history, ultimately preserving the culture by calling some of its most cherished concepts into question?

Historical performance and 'truth to the composer': rehabilitating intention

> Performance malpractice . . . is not permissible, nor in the remotest
> degree forgivable . . . when tolerated or fostered by radio and tele-
> vision corporations, record companies, and concert-giving bod-
> ies . . . If there is to be rhyme or reason in musical performances, it
> is essential that they should reflect, as nearly as possible, the inten-
> tions of the composer. What these intentions were, and the correct
> way to interpret them, are as much the province of the professional
> musicologist as microphone placement and tape-editing are the
> concern of the professional sound engineer. When proper advice
> and interpretation are ignored, chaos results.
>
> Denis Stevens, 1972[1]

For many performers throughout the twentieth century it has been self-
evident that one's foremost priority in the theory and practice of performance should be to follow the composer's intentions. Those who espouse
the concept of HIP often believe that this can be achieved by finding out
as precisely as possible what the composer desired and expected of his
performers, an attitude that has been ubiquitous since the 1950s. Denis
Stevens (above) articulates the common conception that it is the musicologist's task to discern 'the facts' and then pass these on to the obedient
performer. In the same passage he asserts that this is the only responsible
policy for the media promoting performance, who have a duty to provide
the public with 'entertainment or instruction of the finest possible quality,
born of the best possible brains'. Discerning the composer's intentions
is thus evidence of an active and finely honed intellect. Anything else is,
we might infer, brainless (appealing merely to the heart, perhaps?) and
will encourage a slackening in the public's experience of music.

On the other hand, those who adhere to 'mainstream' values in performance often believe that the composer's intentions lie rather in the
metaphysical and emotional implications of the musical work, following
a sense of the composer's eternal spirituality rather than the letter of his

contingent age. This conception has a much longer pedigree than the positivist position (of which Stevens's is a virtual caricature). It has its roots in the very concept of subjectivity which arose in the seventeenth century and came to be virtually synonymous with Romanticism in the nineteenth century.[2] Thus, just as I have argued that HIP gained much of its early prestige by capitalising on an existing concept of *Werktreue*, Laurence Dreyfus notes that the appeal to objective historical intentions likewise relied on the pre-existing respect for composers' intentions: 'The great paradigm shift toward historical performance arrived therefore not as the imposition of a new structural metaphor for musical performance but rather as a remarkably clever annexation of traditional territory, albeit with a new appeal to authority.'[3]

Both traditions of this belief in the 'intentional imperative' are challenged by Richard Taruskin. To him, reliance on intentions rests on a fallacy:

We cannot know intentions, for many reasons – or rather, we cannot know we know them. Composers do not always express them. If they do express them, they may do so disingenuously. Or they may be honestly mistaken, owing to the passage of time or a not necessarily consciously experienced change of taste.[4]

Here he cites some striking examples, particularly the extraordinary variability of Stravinsky's own recordings of the *Rite of Spring*, so ironic for a composer who devalued performer choice and variability. Moreover, to Taruskin, a reliance on composers' intentions weakens the performer's own artistic resolve, bespeaking 'a failure of nerve, not to say an infantile dependency' (*Text and Act*, p. 98).

Peter Kivy questions Taruskin's overly sceptical attitude towards intention by suggesting he is simply 'placing on "know" the burden of *certainty*',[5] which would thus invalidate virtually any historical or empirical inquiry. Indeed, we work on 'justified true belief' every day of our lives. Anecdotal evidence suggesting that some composers had either few specific ideas or contradictory ones about the performance of their works does not prove that composers never had strong intentions regarding performance. Kivy urges that we critically appraise each individual case rather than being radically sceptical about intention across the board.

He suggests that the term 'intention' might cover quite a wide range of wishes and instructions that come from a composer, flirting with the idea of restricting intention proper to that which has the force of a command (p. 12). Many of the composer's expressed wishes may not be intentions in the sense of *commands* but suggestions open to the performer's judgement (p. 31); indeed, following all forms of instruction as if they were commands may go against the spirit of the composer's higher-level intentions.

Kivy uses Randall R. Dipert's critique of compositional intention as the basis of his argument. Dipert distinguishes three levels of intention: low-level intentions include such factors as the type of instruments, fingering etc; middle-level intentions are those concerned with the intended sound (temperament, timbre, attack, pitch, and vibrato); high-level intentions – those which he privileges, though not unconditionally – relate to the effects that the composer intends to produce in the listener. Some of these latter may be specific *purposes* that a composer had in writing: to entertain, inspire or to move an audience. To these, all lower intentions are subservient. Dipert further affirms that low-level intentions are not the automatic and sole progenitor of the middle-level since, for example, a synthesiser could technically produce the correct sound and attack, thus fulfilling the composer's middle-level intentions, but not the low-level ones. Much of Dipert's conclusion provides a useful rule of thumb for the discussion of intentionality: we have no more *moral* obligation to Mozart than we have to Napoleon, we don't necessarily want to recreate a historical environment, nor can we become historical listeners; and finally, only '*generally speaking* we are likely to perform a piece of greater aesthetic merit if we follow the composer's intentions than if we do not'.[6]

Following Dipert, Kivy concludes that although we can never really be certain about the order of a composer's wishes and intentions, the 'mapping of high-order, aesthetic wishes and intentions is part of . . . an *interpretation* of the music' (Kivy, *Authenticities*, p. 45). What is particularly useful here is the admonition that following intentions cannot be a matter of blind obedience but involves interpretation and an understanding of the context in which they were expressed. Another important distinction is that a composer's performing intentions are not to be confused with the meanings of his text, with what he had 'to say' (pp. 153–4), a confusion which might often account for the moral fervour that Kivy perceives in the HIP movement.

Where Kivy's argument goes awry, in my opinion, is when he draws the hypothetical case of William the harness maker who, by the possibilities afforded by the eighteenth century, could not possibly have wished to become an aviator; 'But it does make sense to ask whether, were he alive today, William would want to be an aviator; and if the answer is affirmative, then that *is* what he really wants, whereas harness making is not' (pp. 34–5). One hardly need read on to guess where this is leading:

to the possibility that Bach would have wanted modern performance forces had he known about them and had they been available:

Bach's actual wishes and intentions . . . like anyone else's actual wishes and intentions concerning anything whatever, are determined not merely by what they implicitly or explicitly convey, relative to the circumstances in which they actually find themselves, but by what they would explicitly or implicitly convey concerning their wishes and intentions in other possible circumstances. (p. 36)

The logical clarity of this argument belies some crucial assumptions: namely, that Bach, were he alive today, would still be a composer (and not − like William − an aviator), that, if he were still a composer, he would still be concerned with the works he wrote over 250 years ago, and that, were he to be impressed by the possibilities afforded by modern instruments, he would still be writing or performing the same kind of music. Kivy's argument thus relies on an almost religious belief in the consistency of human personality and genius over the centuries, that works have a transhistorical ontology, and, most importantly, that the composer would believe this in whatever time-zone he happens to appear. It is difficult enough to assume the consistency of a composer's personality during his lifetime; indeed, when Schumann came to revise his early piano music, there is a real pathological sense in which he was a 'different' person.[7] I would certainly not condemn the practice of playing Bach on modern instruments, but only suggest that it is unwise to consider hypotheses regarding a composer's transhistorical intentions as any part of an argument in its favour.

Roger Scruton makes the same assumption as Kivy in terms of 'an ongoing dialogue between composer and performer, a dialogue across generations'. This metaphor makes sense *insofar as the composer can be inferred from the surviving music* (an 'implied composer' as it were), but in referring to the composer's actual persona it can only imply a timeless subjectivity. Scruton also perceptively adds our own relation to transhistorical Bach's intentions − i.e. what would he have liked *us* to use for his fugues: 'a reproduction harpsichord, or . . . the Steinway grand to which we are accustomed, and which is, for us, the medium through which Beethoven, Chopin, and Bartók also make their way to our ears?'[8]

The assumption that most people will have wishes for future generations makes sense up to the point at which Scruton states 'we are accustomed' to the piano. What he means is that *he* is accustomed to the piano, and that he has nothing to say to those of us who might now be more accustomed to the harpsichord. To force us back to the 'norm' of the piano will no longer guarantee authenticity for us harpsichordists, any more than our forcing him to listen to the harpsichord will do for him. To wish HIP out of existence falls into the same trap as those pioneers of the movement who believed they could use historical reconstruction to escape the preconceptions of the present.

We can certainly learn from the implications of Kivy's conclusion (Kivy, p. 45): that we should understand intentions relative to the conditions pertaining today, to avoid the absurdity of executing Napoleon's design for unifying Europe by restaging the battle of Waterloo in original costumes (although this would be an eccentric choice of battles for this particular purpose, to say the least!). But is there not something equally absurd – or disturbing – about considering Napoleon's grand design as remotely relevant to the present condition of Europe? There is something crucially distinct between executing today a political plan from 1815 and playing a symphony from that year. This argument therefore doesn't really invalidate the assumption that the period instruments were part of a composer's intention for performance. Moreover, only tortuously can we avoid the fact that historic instruments are a significant part of our performing culture today, that they are part of a practice far more acceptable and effective than Napoleon's higher intentions, weaponry or costumes.

In all, we can greatly benefit from the critical attitude towards intention that is proposed by Taruskin and Kivy. But the whole concept of HIP brings up the issue of intentionality in a way that it has never been formulated before. It encourages us to rethink our customary sense of the relationship between composer, work and performer. Most importantly, it is an awareness of intention that helps us discover the human presence in composition, it can work as an antidote to the attitude of seeing musical works purely in formal terms.[9] As Aaron Copland put it: 'Examining a music manuscript, inevitably I sense the man behind the notes. The fascination of a composer's notation is the fascination of human personality.'[10]

Indeed, much of the antipathy towards authorial intention in recent years comes from a specifically formalist ideology of art. Even Taruskin – hardly a formalist in other respects – draws much of his argument from the field of American 'New Criticism': 'The intentional fallacy', as famously articulated and criticised in the 1940s by Monroe Beardsley and W. K. Wimsatt.[11] Many of their points are more or less accepted in literary criticism today: an intentional design, as the cause of a poem, has nothing to do with the standards by which the poem is subsequently to be judged. Just as Taruskin distinguishes between musical performance and scholarship, they insist that the art of poetry is of a different order to that of criticism. On the other hand, certain aspects of Wimsatt and Beardsley's approach run counter to Taruskin's: theirs is uncompromisingly objectivist and positivistic; only the poem itself provides the means to its interpretation, meanings and quality. As Beardsley states in his introduction to aesthetics, we should not ask, 'What is this supposed to be?' but, rather, 'What have we got here?'[12] Anything external to the poem is to be considered private and 'idiosyncratic' – in other words, irrelevant to the autonomous aesthetic object. This point is shown at its most extreme when the authors compare the artwork with other objects:

Judging a poem is like judging a pudding or a machine. One demands that it work. It is only because an artifact works that we infer the intention of an artificer . . . Poetry succeeds because all or most of what is said or implied is relevant; what is irrelevant has been excluded, like lumps from pudding and 'bugs' from machinery. In this respect poetry differs from practical messages, which are successful if and only if we correctly infer the intention.[13]

Moreover, the authors imply that the objectifying impulse is the natural mode of human thought and perception: 'For all the objects of our manifold experience, for every unity, there is an action of the mind which cuts off roots, melts away context – or indeed we should never have objects or ideas or anything to talk about' ('The Intentional Fallacy', p. 8). In all, this intensely objectivist approach relies entirely on the integrity and totality of individual artworks. The attitude can be traced back to nineteenth-century writer–critics such as Browning, Arnold and Wilde,[14] but finds its first theoretical formulation in the literary theory of Eliot and Pound.[15] A similar formalist–objectivist attitude has been taken towards music sporadically during the last two hundred years (first clearly articulated by Hanslick), and finding its most vociferous articulation in the writings of Stravinsky (at exactly the same time as Eliot and Pound were promoting the autonomy of literary works). It is precisely this attitude which Taruskin very properly observes as a failing in HIP (which he terms both 'authenticist' and 'modernist'), in which objective facts sometimes count for more than interpretative imagination.

In a later article, defending his assault on the intentionality, Wimsatt stresses that the background language system (the *langue*) is more important than the personalised exemplar by the author (the *parole*).[16] Certainly this might be the only way in which authorial intention might be the criterion of validity in the interpretation of meaning (i.e. what something is likely to mean given a particular background of practice). But if it is used as the sole basis of validity in performance interpretation it might well ironically play into the field of those historical performers who reduce a composer to the norms of his historical environment, those characterised by Adorno's famous complaint about the 'Telemannisation' of Bach (see chapter 1, p. 5 above). Thus things seem to have come full circle: the new critics' quest for 'objectivity' in interpretation and the concern for the wider system rather than the idiosyncrasy of the author are – if applied to performance interpretation – strikingly reminiscent of some of the very worst vices of HIP in which musical works can be diluted by an over-emphasis on contextual matters. As a whole then, it is unlikely that the 'intentional fallacy' argument can be accepted in the strongest sense (namely, that authorial intentions are irrelevant) for our purposes, although we might follow Taruskin in using its central premise that an artist's interpretation of a work after its completion is not privileged. We should be on our guard against limiting musical interpretation merely to what we think a composer allows us to do. Karol Berger suggests that an interest in intentions is a matter of courtesy, more a moral matter than one of certain knowledge. We should find out what we can about the artist and his environment and then take our interpretation beyond these.[17] Intention and historical context are thus the starting points of study and not our ultimate goal.

Wimsatt's resort to the traditional structuralist distinction between *langue* and *parole* points towards another strain of anti-intentionalist thought in the fields of structuralism and, particularly, post-structuralism. Perhaps the greatest difference between post-structuralism and 'New Criticism' is in its flight from metaphysics, its refusal to grant unity or integrity to any artefact. Both Roland Barthes and Michel Foucault view the very concept of an author as historically conditioned, something bound up with an ideological concern with true meaning, unity and value in texts.[18] To paraphrase Roland Barthes, the author is merely the past of his own book; a text is not a line of words releasing a single 'theological' meaning but the place where a variety of non-original meanings blend and clash. Everything a writer wants to express is only a ready-formed dictionary, its words explainable only through other words. If there is any unified meaning to be discerned, this lies in the destination of a text, not at its point of origin. As Barthes famously put it: 'the birth of the reader must be at the cost of the death of the author'.[19]

Something of this attitude is also evident in those philosophers who deny that human agents have the capacity for 'intrinsic' or 'original' intention. They suggest rather that human intentionality is *derived* from other circumstances, just as the intentionality of a machine is derived from the human purpose to which it is put. As Daniel Dennett proposes, meaning and significance are only to be found in the contingent adaptation of an artefact to particular circumstances; the fact that the panda's thumb was originally a wrist-bone does not detract from the excellency of its present role as a thumb. In short, an entire component of the Darwinian revolution is often ignored in contemporary thought:

After all these years we are still just coming to terms with this unsettling implication of Darwin's destruction of the Argument from Design: there is no ultimate User's Manual in which the *real* functions, and *real* meanings, or biological artifacts are officially represented. There is no more bedrock for what we might call original functionality than there is for its cognitivistic scion, original intentionality. You can't have realism about meanings without realism about functions.[20]

Thus for Dennett, as for Barthes, meaning and significance are to be located, albeit contingently, in the activity, function and use of the reader or interpreter. Of course, some would claim that musical performance has always privileged the reader, if the latter is defined as the performer; performers are popularly idolised above composers for their insights and unique personality.[21] Furthermore, there are many instances in earlier music history when far more performer freedom was expected than has been allowed in 'mainstream' twentieth-century performance, instances where the performer was also the composer or played a large part in completing the process of composition (see Chapter 4, pp. 106–14 below). Here then, the transfer of the reader-orientated approach to musical performance seems to support certain attitudes in the history of performance. The composer's intentions are imaginatively ignored particularly if there is no strong sense of composer or intention to ignore in the first place.

There is a further field in which intentionality has been questioned as the sole basis of interpretation: the editing of verbal and musical texts. Editorial theorists have noted that in certain source situations the author's intention is hard to define: sometimes there might not be a single original author (e.g. Homer), at other times a writer might produce more than one valid version (e.g. Shakespeare, *King Lear*). As Philip Brett has stated:

The problem with authorial intention for the editor as historical critic, once one grants the certain degree of ethical imperative it entails, is that it is too narrow a concept to adopt as a base of operations. Almost every work has implications beyond what its composer can consciously have intended; and often other people determine much of what transforms a composer's text or idea into what we conceive of as a work.[22]

Jerome McGann has also stressed that authorial intention cannot always be the sole arbiter in textual problems; indeed in some cases it may be overridden by other factors. However, he has also considerably refined our conception of where the author's intention might lie, showing that it is not a simple matter of a single act or process of intention. He perceives two codes at work in a text, the linguistic code – the basic verbal text which is the stuff of editing – and the bibliographic code – the other aspects of presentation such as the printing and layout of the page. In the normal course of events, the author will have most control over the linguistic code while the publisher will have the final say in the bibliographic code. However, there are obvious cases where the author has attempted to control both, particularly when the text involves illustrations (e.g. some of the publications of Blake and Pound).[23]

Much of this can be transferred to the music sphere, both with regard to making editions and to performance. The notion of a linguistic and a bibliographic code could be related to two different intentional levels, similar but not equivalent to what I will later describe as the 'active' and 'passive' levels of intention. With regard to the bibliographic code, we might ask how much control a composer had in the preparation and distribution of manuscripts. What do bibliographic matters (e.g. the layout of a score, the use of punctuation for the text) tell us about his performing intentions and expectations? We might also consider which composers took the most care and assumed the most control in the production of their scores and the conditions of their performance. None of these factors, to which an editor should be held accountable, provides a normative index of good performance. They do, however, give us some notion of the degree to which the presentation of the music on paper may relate to the various levels of the composer's intention.

Despite the challenges to the concept of authorial intention this concept has been by no means dead since it was first attacked in the 1940s. The whole debate has received enormous attention during the 1990s, some fifty years after it began.[24] This has generally concerned the question of meaning in literary texts and thus does not directly impinge on the issue of musical performance. But it may well evidence a general dissatisfaction with formalism and a search for alternative ways of understanding the arts. Quentin Skinner, like Kivy, attacks the position of total scepticism (in his case, Derrida's) with the blunt observation that even dogs can tell the difference 'between an accidental and deliberate kick',[25] while Jerrold Levinson extends the issue of intentions to the way an audience constructs plausible intentions on the part of an author.[26] These 'counterfactual' intentions allow us to construct the intentionalist stance of the author through consideration of the tradition surrounding him, his oeuvre as a whole, and his general public image. This has the advantage of allowing multiple interpretability, since there are an infinite number of ways of configuring the available contextual evidence and it also allows us to overrule what is known of the author's *actual* intentions, should these be known. Clearly, there is the question of whether counterfactual intentions are really intentions at all (especially when they are, literally, anti-intentional), but Levinson's position may evidence a profound shift in scholarly attitude. First, the audience's, interpreter's or critic's role in constituting intention is paramount (thus absorbing something of the post-structuralist critique of intentionality). Secondly, it suggests that the notion of the author as an active, human figure (rather than as merely the facilitator of perfected form), who works within a particular social and cultural environment, has become a more significant element in the way we conceive of art.

Even in the field of reader-oriented criticism, where one might assume that there was the greatest resistance to authorial intention, there are nevertheless some scholars who have relied on the concept. These include those theories that rely on a communication model for literary texts, such as Roman Jakobson's concept of author and reader as being related as the sender and receiver of a message.[27] Wayne Booth, concerned with the rhetorical aspects of textuality, gives attention to the ethical implications of the message, discerning an 'implied author' in the text who must be constructed in the act of reading by the 'implied reader':

Regardless of my real beliefs and practices, I must subordinate my mind and heart to the book if I am to enjoy it to the full. The author . . . makes his reader as he makes his second self, and the most successful reading is one in which the created selves, author and reader, can find complete agreement.[28]

Whatever the plausibility of these approaches in literary studies, the notion of sending a message or of the direct agreement between author and reader is not only too restrictive for music but also virtually impossible to prove in the absence of a codifiable linguistic equivalent for music. Nevertheless, I shall return later to the question of whether Booth's model of an 'implied reader' could be applied to music in the guise of an 'implied performer' who can be discerned in the notation of music.

Even those writers who most loudly proclaim their independence from the author's intention, have recourse to it on occasion. Beardsley and Wimsatt suggest, rather awkwardly, that an author's notes on the interpretation of his work (such as Eliot's notes on *The Waste Land*) can be used by the critic if they are viewed as actually being part of the work.[29] Wimsatt also acknowledges that intentions may come into play if there is something missing, some imperfection in the work; here knowledge of intentions might act like a crutch for the lame or an extra stone for the sagging arch.[30] Even Richard Taruskin will refer to some aspect of a composer's intention if it suits and substantiates one of his own points: in his review of Harnoncourt's recordings of Bach's cantatas, he notes that the performers frequently capitalise on the sheer difficulty of the music, often creating an ugly effect. This ugliness actually brings out a particular message in the music that could well have been intended by the composer, a sense of the drabness and imperfection of the earthly condition which is actualised by the struggles of the singers.[31] In all, he is complimentary of performances which involve creative departures from the notated text and is prepared to support this with historical evidence (e.g. for Mozart) that shows this was part of a composer's wider intention. Furthermore he laments the absence of a personal voice in much recent composition and performance, noting that most pre-modern composers had no difficulty in believing that they were the principal speaker in their compositions. Thus, in this sense Taruskin turns his back on Beardsley and Wimsatt and, particularly, the objective and impersonal approach to performance, and he positively encourages an intentional stance, provided this does not mean blind fidelity to a composer.[32] In other words, our own critical stance is essential in the valuation of intentions and thus conditions how we might employ them for our own interpretations.

One of the most productive points to emerge out of the critique of intentionality is the sense of flexibility between an author's intentions and a reader's interpretative insights. As Theodore Redpath affirms: 'The prize term "*the* meaning" seems to float between the two parties, like a balloon floating above two parties of children, each of which wishes to reach and appropriate it.' While affording priority to historical meanings (just as we would take the historical meanings of individual words as a starting-point for interpretation), Redpath perceptively suggests that: 'there is no universal rule that we ought to attach the same importance in all cases to what the poet meant by his poem, in determining the meaning of the poem: but that the degree of importance we should attach to it in any particular case is a matter for *aesthetic decision*'.[33]

Such an approach is particularly useful in the field of HIP. Far from reducing the artistic to the scholarly – perhaps the major conceptual flaw of many approaches to the field – this suggests that the scholarly enterprise of seeking an 'original' historical meaning should veer towards the artistic.

Precisely this dynamic attitude towards intention informs the work of two contributions to the philosophy of art, Michael Baxandall's *Patterns of Intention* and Richard Wollheim's *Painting as an Art*. Their inferential approach to intention is of a completely different kind from that which is normally discussed in the literary debates and which is applied to HIP. But not only may it be of great significance in making us reconsider the concept of historical performance, it might also show how HIP could be valuable in revising our conception of notated musical works. For Baxandall 'inferential criticism' relates not to

an actual, particular psychological state or even a historical set of mental events inside the heads of [the artists] . . . One assumes purposefulness – or intent or, as it were, 'intentiveness' – in the historical actor but even more in the historical objects themselves. Intentionality in this sense is taken to be characteristic of both. Intention is the forward-leaning look of things.[34]

This view of intention is evidently a construct of the contemporary critic/interpreter, something to be strictly distinguished from the more traditional static view of intention which

would deny a great deal of what makes pictures worth bothering about, whether for us or for their makers. It would deny the encounter with the medium and reduce the work to a sort of conceptual or ideal art imperfectly realized. There is not just *an* intention but a numberless sequence of developing moments of intention.

The account of intention is not a narrative of what went on in the painter's mind but an analytical construct about his ends and means, as we infer them from the relation of the object to identifiable circumstances. It stands in an ostensive relation to the picture itself. (*Patterns of Intention*, pp. 63, 109)

Thus, in the field of music, we should be concerned not with specific biographical events, but should imagine pieces as the result of an infinite sequence of decisions. This helps us to temper the view of musical works as static, timeless objects and allows us to see them as something much closer to the process of performance itself. What Baxandall most profitably gives us is the sense that we must reject the concept of a 'formal cause' in art and that the causal process is both dynamic and malleable:[35]

in a picture . . . it is not quite a matter of the painter first working out a finished design and then picking up the brushes in an executive role and just carry-ing it out. The phases interpenetrate, and one would surely wish at least to accommodate this sense of process. (*Patterns of Intention*, p. 39)

His insistence that the critical viewer take an active role in interpret-ing the picture is arguably even more important as a maxim for musical performance (however 'historical' one's intentions). This point is further developed by Wollheim for whom the viewer's perspective emerges as a crucial element for both original artist and subsequent interpreters. He assumes a universal human capacity of 'seeing-in', prior to that of picto-rial representation. In other words, we all have the tendency to discern representations within seemingly abstract patterns in nature before at-tempting such representations ourselves (Wollheim also goes on to claim a similar status for 'expression' in represented images). It is precisely this capacity of 'seeing-in' that the artist mobilises as he paints. His intention to represent rests on the same psychological abilities as the viewer has in 'seeing-in'.[36] Wollheim goes on to discern how the spectator's ability can be improved through the cultivation of particular kinds of knowledge:

a spectator needs a lot of information about how the painting he confronts came to be made. He needs a substantial cognitive stock.

But, once we allow information in, is there any principled way in which we can decide that some information is legitimate, and some illegitimate? . . . there seems to be only one limitation that should be placed upon what information can be drafted into the spectator's cognitive stock. It relates, not to the source from which the information derives, nor to its content, but to the use to which it is put. The information must be such that by drawing upon it a spectator is enabled to experience some part of the content of the picture which otherwise he would have been likely to overlook. (*Painting as an Art*, pp. 89–91)

This approach does contain an echo of the formalism lying behind the New Critics' dismissal of intention in the first place: much of the 'correct' interpretation can be fostered by looking at 'the work itself'. But there is the important admission that knowledge of the surrounding context is potentially infinite and relevant insofar as it allows us to find something new within the picture. Baxandall's entertaining discussion of the intentionality surrounding the architect of the Forth Bridge shows that much depends on our own frame of reference. Is our concern general history, the history of bridges, or economics? Are we interested in the general or specific conditions under which the designer worked, or in the things that, by necessity, must 'have been in the reflecting minds of the actors'? (*Patterns of Intention*, pp. 27–8).

How appropriate is the inferential approach to intentionality for music, particularly as a basis for the practice of performance? Traditional approaches to intentionality in composition and performance, such as Kivy's, tend to see the musical work as a concept or ideal provisionally realised in performance. The inferential approach rather sees the art object as resulting from an infinite sequence of intentions, a causal process that was both dynamic and malleable. Certainly, there is a great deal of sense in the notion that the composer functions not only as a composer but also as a performer and listener during the course of composition, reacting to what he plays and hears and altering and developing the composition accordingly. As Roger Sessions once usefully proposed, the practices of composition, performance and listening belong essentially to the same process, and anyone participating in any one of these activities tacitly (sometimes even actively) participates in all three.[37] Furthermore, Wollheim's view that information external to the painting is vital if it allows us to appreciate something we would not otherwise have noticed, justifies the search for historical facts relating to the performance of a piece of music. Rather than merely setting a standard of correctness these may allow us a musical experience of which we might not otherwise have conceived.

How, then, can we reformulate intentionality in music along the lines of inferential criticism so that it can be more productive for performance interpretation? Dipert's three-part categorisation of the low, medium and high levels of intention still provides a good starting point. A composer normally intends a specific means and medium of performance that result in an intended sound that, in turn, engenders the intended effect for the listener. However, in practice there are several problems both with Dipert's division of intentions and with his evaluation of their hierarchy. First, the primary *purpose* of the piece might not be one that was determined by the composer in the first place, particularly in the case of those repertories prepared for a specific extra-musical function. Such purposes might be entirely irrelevant to a modern audience's concerns, or, if the music is still used for its original purpose (e.g. church music) the theological and liturgical presuppositions might often be entirely different. Moreover, it is both impossible and undesirable to recreate the preconceptions of an historical audience (as Dipert himself affirms). In certain cases then, the high-level intentions (e.g. to serve God, through the liturgy) might not be specifically of the composer's own making and might not be those we most desire in contemporary performance.

It is also unclear as to how Dipert's high-level intentions fit into the realm of performance: much of the effect that a composer intends to produce in the listener (insofar as this is ascertainable), lies in the elements of the music that are not a choice in performance interpretation (e.g. harmony, melody, text-setting). In fact, it is often more in the 'lower' levels that the performer's choice and imagination can be exercised. Finally, and most importantly, consideration of the 'lower' levels quite often reveals possible 'higher' intentions that might not otherwise have been evident.

Thus Dipert is too dismissive of the low-level intentions, limiting the function of playing techniques to the ulterior purpose of the middle-level intentions, the specific sound required.[38] This approach tends to presuppose that musical works are discrete and static entities that merely require a particular sound to be realised. But the player may react to the medium or technique employed, something that can result in inter-pretative differences that are not quantifiable merely in terms of sound quality.[39] This might, in turn, facilitate a style of interpretation that was previously obscured, something perhaps to do with stylistic pacing, ar-ticulation and phrasing and, above all, the overall expression.

Furthermore, to come closer to the inferential approach of Baxandall and Wollheim, the instrument, playing technique or the abilities and style of the assumed performer may have played a major part in the way the music was written in the first place. Different 'low-level' inten-tions could thus have resulted in an entirely different piece of music. Here then, it may be more profitable to conceive of the three levels of intention in reverse order: rather than having a specific end in mind and then employing the requisite tools and personnel, the composer's ends are at least partly the result of what he discovers during the process of composition, his interaction with the medium. Thus Dipert's demonstra-tion that Bach hypothetically would have preferred the modern piano to the clavichord since it better fulfils an assumed middle-level intention for greater dynamic expression does not necessarily follow. After all, the greater fulfilment of one middle-level intention – dynamic expression – might inhibit another intention of the same ranking: tone, articulation, voicing etc. The modern piano may have caused him to write in an entirely different way (this is not to condemn performance today on the 'wrong' instrument, but merely to point to how the medium influenced the way the piece was written in the first place). Dipert's assertion that Beethoven is a proven master of form but not necessarily a good judge of pianos relies on a specific formalist ideology of music and is thus of no more intrinsic value than the assertion that Beethoven's remarkable dialogue with the developing styles of piano building of his day accounts for his daring and experimental approach to notated composition.

Sometimes an instrumental limitation actually contributes to the composer's creative act, such as in the case of Bach's unaccompanied works for violin and violoncello. Mendelssohn and Schumann saw fit to provide piano accompaniments for some of these works in order to make Bach's supposed intentions clearer to the listener. Some historians in recent years have even proposed developing bows (in the name of historical accuracy!) which allow for the performance of double-stops as indicated in the notation. Yet it was surely the very limitation of the medium of solo violin (even more so in the case of the solo violoncello) that provided Bach with much of his compositional incentive. The music is pregnant with textural implications: the reader/performer/listener constructs musical lines and gestures that are not necessarily notated. By being forced to write fewer notes Bach was able to imply many more.

It is also unclear as to why Dipert's assertion that 'the less conscious, informed, or deliberate the composer's indication, the less strong is our prima facie obligation to follow it' ('The Composer's Intentions', p. 212) necessarily holds. So much of the quality of a good composer must reside in his unconscious assimilation of techniques and in his intuition. Indeed, he might often alter his most conscious intentions for performance (e.g. Stravinsky's tempi in the *Rite of Spring*), while his unconscious assumption of a particular kind of instrument or playing technique may be integral to the way the music was written in the first place. This same misunderstanding pervades the considerations of intentionality by Stephen Davies and Jerrold Levinson, for whom the composer's 'determinative intentions' are the ones that count for 'authentic performance', as opposed to concurrent or unexpressed wishes and the social milieu of composer and work.[40] Their approach assumes that musical works have a timeless, essential core (something which is, at best, an historical conception), that this core brings with it certain imperatives in performance, and – what seems patently incorrect – that these imperatives are identical to, or at least directly parallel with, the composer's conscious decisions.

In short, I propose to drop the concept of a fixed hierarchy of performance intentions and instead divide intention into two non-ranked areas: 'active intention' – a composer's specific decisions concerning such matters as instrumentation, tempo, dynamic, ornamentation, articulation etc. (all of which may, or may not be, consciously notated); and 'passive intention' – those factors over which he had little control, but which he consciously or unconsciously assumed. On the whole, the active intentions will be more conscious and the passive ones less so, but this association is by no means fixed. E. D. Hirsch suggests that the distinction between an author's conscious and unconscious intentions is not to be confused with the distinction between what an author does and does not mean. Following Husserl, the unconscious factors form the wider horizon that helps us to reconstruct the author's mental and experiential world.[41] The composer's 'horizon of expectations' might relate to how he expected the music to be played and perceived, but might also, in turn, have caused him to write in a particular way. As Maurice Merleau-Ponty proposed, our interrelations with our environment ingrain 'carnal formulae' on our bodies and each new experience becomes sedimented into our 'intentional arc', thus influencing our future actions.[42] Consideration of intention, even at the lowest 'passive' levels, makes us aware of the artist's actual individual embodiment and helps us experience this afresh in the surviving works.

In some cases active and passive intentions might run into one another, such as when Handel chose a particular singer to perform a particular role (conscious, active intention) and then that singer's abilities, technique and style caused him to write in a particular way (passive intention, both conscious and unconscious). This issue is aptly demonstrated by particular arias from *Messiah* where multiple versions of 'But who may abide' and 'Thou art gone up on high' reflect a changing cast of singers and some radical changes to the music. Here the changing passive intentions prove a significant aesthetic point, that the influence of performance considerations was more important to Handel than the creation of a timeless, unified masterwork. Passive intentions of this kind are often conscious, extremely so in the case of Benjamin Britten:

During the act of composition one is continually referring back to the conditions of performance . . . the acoustics and the forces available, the techniques of the instruments and the voices – such questions occupy one's attention continuously, and certainly affect the stuff of the music, and in my experience are not only a restriction, but a challenge, an inspiration . . . I prefer to study the conditions of performance and shape my music to them.[43]

But such passive intentions may equally well be unconscious. As Mattheson remarked, in the most comprehensive survey of compositional invention in the early eighteenth century, 'Ten good composers are often not capable of creating a single good singer; but a single good singer, especially a beautiful and talented female, is easily capable of inspiring ten good composers; so that the latter sometimes do not know whence the magnificent ideas come to them.'[44] If Mattheson is right, the composer's unconscious passive intentions should be precisely those we should privilege if we are concerned with the intentionality latent within music of this kind.

In another sense, passive intentions could refer to active intentions that were impossible to realise. These may relate to the composer's desire for the best possible performance (even if this was not immediately available to him) or a particular style of performance practice that did not pertain to his local environment. In cases such as these, the composer's intentions, so far as they can be inferred, should surely override the actual historical conditions. Such intentions need to be seen in the context of both the actual set of choices open to the composer but also to possible sets of choices.[45]

In this sense, intentionality, far from being synonymous with the notion of historical fidelity, actually works against it. One would have to be an antiquarian of the most dogged type to wish mediocre performing circumstances as a norm for most of the music we choose to perform. Nevertheless, some have argued that since most earlier repertories were designed for performance within a regularly occurring multi-media event we perhaps need to recover at least the possibility of art music functioning as a form of routine or as background music, which is, after all, one of the main uses of popular music today.[46]

It is against the field of 'active intentions' that much of Taruskin's scepticism is aimed. He proves, at the very least, that composers' attitudes to interpretation in performance vary as much as any performer's might over the course of a career. Thus we might be able to find a more satisfactory tempo for a Beethoven symphony, a more elegant ornament for a Couperin dance, a more ingenious bowing for a Bach violin solo, than the composers specified. Furthermore, the fact that an intention may be active, does not necessarily imply that the composer was fully conscious of it or considered it indelibly fixed. In the case of marks of articulation, phrasing, dynamics and ornamentation the composer may have had diverse reasons for including them: perhaps barely considered, almost unconscious notations or a rather carefully worked scheme; directions for the inexperienced or reminders – perhaps limitations – for the experienced; exceptions to or reinforcements of an assumed rule.

Furthermore, it seems that composers' sense of their own 'active intentions' developed relatively late in history, reaching a peak in the

mid-twentieth century (for the issue of 'progress' in the notation of performance issues, see chapter 4). But it is not always the case that earlier
composers are silent on their opinions about performance, indeed they
sometimes insist on obedience to their intentions.

The anecdote is probably spurious, but at least it portrays a late-
Renaissance view of how Josquin the composer related to his performers:

You ass, why do you add ornamentation? If it had pleased me, I would have
inserted it myself! If you wish to amend properly composed songs, make your
own, but leave mine unamended.[47]

Whatever its veracity, this remark should not be taken literally as an
injunction to respect Josquin's notation with the awe of a fundamentalist.
We know that he himself was a singer and teacher of consummate artistry,
that he probably trained his best singers to ornament with the hindsight
of the strictest instruction in composition and that his notation represents
as much his own activity in performance as in composition.

Moving forward a century or so, Frescobaldi, in the preface to his
Capricci of 1624, affirms that:

I have wished to advise that in those things, that would not seem ruled, by the use
of counterpoint, one must first seek the affetto of that passage & the purpose of
the Author for the delight of the ear & the manner that it is sought in playing.[48]

A more direct equivalent to Wollheim's injunction to discern intention through protracted contemplation of art would be difficult to find
in the sphere of music. Roger North provides a remarkably subtle notion of compositional intention, when he describes the art of 'voluntary',
in which the roles of composer and performer are rolled into one: the
principal purpose of 'voluntary' is to conjure up many moods; even if
the composer/organist is not entirely successful in this, the fact that he
has an intention 'will signifie more than if nothing att all was intended
or thought on'.[49] In other words, the fact that there is intention is more
important than the idiosyncratic details of that intention; the notion
of 'intentionality' alerts us to the human and dynamic elements of the
notated piece, its 'forward-leaning' quality. Moreover, this takes us beyond the positivistic, objectivist view of intention towards a sense of the
subjectivity inherent in music, regardless of its age and style.

For Wollheim, certain pictures exemplified by Manet, Friedrich
and Hals contain one particular element that is essential for their
interpretation: an internal viewer, placed within the picture, who has
access to the same field as the external viewer and who thus influences

the perspective of the entire picture and the attitude of its characters. The notion of the 'implied performer' in the notational text of certain pieces of music (equivalent to Booth's 'implied reader' in the literary text), seems to me particularly productive. The anecdote about Josquin complaining of singers ornamenting his music which is already elaborated suggests that the notation might actually reflect an historical performance on its own terms. Much of my own work has centred on the interplay between notated composition and improvised elaboration on the part of performers during the German Baroque, and has suggested that authority in performance does not go merely from composer to performer but can quite often go the other way.[50] In other words, as the theorist Bernhard perceptively noted in one of his treatises on composition, composers had learned a lot from the elaboration of performers; there was clearly a fluid interplay of influence between the two.

The case of J. S. Bach is particularly significant: in his once-criticised tendency to restrict the performer's freedom to ornament he has actually preserved his own particular type of performance in the very symbols of the notation. On the other hand, the various figures of ornamentation are compositionally integrated (e.g. by consistency of figure and imitation) in a manner that could not have been achieved by the improvising performer. So we may envision Bach the composer adopting the attitude of a performer and then dialectically integrating the two roles within the notation. In this sense, any performance of his music that reproduces most of the right notes is an historical performance, one which follows the very active performing intentions of the composer.

The same sort of approach could be made to composers whose music is frequently preserved in a plethora of manuscript versions. David Fuller has advocated an open but critical attitude to the several different texts preserving the music of the French harpsichordist, Chambonnières, a state of affairs he conveniently sums up with the neologism 'heterotextuality'.[51] Here the player must take over much of the responsibility usually demanded only of the editor, sifting through the various versions, becoming familiar with the composer's style and, above all, *not* taking the printed notes as established, immutable facts. Exactly the same reasoning could be applied to the more celebrated case of Corelli's violin sonatas, where various printed versions claim to represent the composer's original performance style; the most obvious error to make here would be to take those publishers at their word who claimed to represent the only 'authentic' version.[52] In cases such as these each version could be regarded as the notation of one particular performance by the composer, something which would be completely obscured by approaching the score as an immutable *Urtext* (see chapter 4, p. 110 below).

Not every composer produces this sort of performer-in-the-notation. It is certainly most evident in the case of composers who were themselves superlative performers: Josquin, Couperin, Handel, Bach, Mozart, Schumann, Chopin and Liszt come immediately to mind. Their notation thus works as both a record of past performances and a mnemonic for the future.[53] As Jim Samson notes, even the detailed substance of much early nineteenth-century piano music may relate to improvisation.[54] Recognition of a performing persona in the notation greatly informs our own interpretative role as 'external spectators' or music critics, but the same persona may also enliven our musical experiences as performers and listeners.

It could be argued that much of what I discuss under the heading of 'intention' should be subsumed under some other title since it addresses elements found in pieces and repertories as they survive today and it is not specifically concerned with biographical details and the precise thoughts and decisions of any particular composer. Wimsatt and Beardsley would doubtless claim that anything of value revealed by my approach is a feature immanent in the work itself and not associated with the creative context. However, I believe it is important to appreciate the latent *intentionality* in music as an art to be performed, something that can be distinguished from the more local concept of 'the composer's intentions'.[55] Just as our interest in art *per se* rests on our understanding that it is *intentionally* created as art (otherwise it would be of the same status as an object in nature), our interest in pieces of music should be directed towards the human subjectivity involved in their creation and, particularly, in the intentionality towards (and occasioned by) performance. The value of a composer's specific intentions for performance cannot be legislated across the board; each issue needs to be constantly evaluated on a case-by-case basis. As Redpath and Baxandall's approaches to literature and art suggested, the choice and evaluation of intentional factors should itself be an aesthetic one. This approach to intention also influences our conception of the so-called 'higher' spiritual intentions of a composer, the 'message' that he supposedly communicates through the fallible media at his disposal. For these are surely mediated within the pattern of intentions and interact with all the details of the work's actual embodiment.[56]

The inferential approach is obviously irrelevant if we take a strictly formalist view of music, independent and adequate in its own mode of existence, but it surely becomes crucial if we wish to understand music as the product of human action and decisions to be taken within a relatively constrained range of choices.[57] As Fredric Jameson has remarked: 'restoring the clumsiness of some initial thought process means returning to the act of thinking as praxis and stripping away the reifications that sediment around that act when it has become an object'.[58] Studying both the historical context and the methods of performance widens the field from which aesthetic choice and evaluation can be made.

As Hesse shows us in *The Glass Bead Game*, history should not be used as a way of denying the struggle that brought countless artefacts and practices into being. It should not be a mode of preservation that returns us to countless original details if it merely treats these details as objective fact. Even if the best works 'no longer show any signs of the anguish and effort that preceded them' such works do, in fact, embody aspects of a time and conflict of which – without historical study – we would otherwise know nothing.[59]

Moreover, historical knowledge should not simply be fixed and exhaustible, it will change and develop as our own priorities change. Our reception of any particular piece, composer or repertory will develop as we learn more about its creative context and this, in turn, will inform our evaluation of what is significant within the context. Paul Crowther suggests, following Merleau-Ponty's theory of art, that the artwork expresses the relationship between the artist and a wider shared world and is thus important for 'its implications for other lives'. Our own changing historicity will enable us to draw inexhaustible meanings and experiences out of the work: 'As the patterns and meaning of personal and collective existence take on new meaning, so will our understanding of particular works of art and their creators.'[60] In short, the ultimate value of studying intention for the purposes of HIP might rest not so much in telling us how a piece should or should not sound but rather in how performance, as the medium of sounding music, conditions our idea of how music relates to the world in which it first sounded and that in which it continues to sound. It can be a counterbalance to the traditional way of viewing music history as merely the history of musical works.

4

Negotiating between work, composer and performer:
rewriting the story of notational progress

Evolution of notation indicates a tendency to make creation or
production constantly more complex and important . . . to make its
performance or reproduction constantly more mechanical.

John Cage, *Notations* (1969)

Scores are more than just tablatures for specific actions or else some
sort of picture of the required sound: they are also artefacts with
powerful auras of their own, as the history of notational innovation
clearly shows us.

Brian Ferneyhough (1990)[1]

Many observers of the early music movement may overestimate the degree to which 'historically informed' musicians actually foster a distinctive approach to the interpretation of their parts, normally cleansed of
every romantic accretion. Indeed, many purists might be shocked on
their first visit to the rehearsal of their local Baroque or Classical band.
The conductor will often give a long list of dynamics to be inserted into
the parts, and will provide indications of tempo changes and ornaments.
Moreover, the players – in the course of rehearsal – will make their
own markings to remind themselves of various issues such as bowings,
difficult fingerings, and those places where they must reluctantly resist
the co-operative urge of the early music ethos and actually watch the
conductor.[2] Our purist will be further disappointed to compare the level
of marking in the performers' parts with those of a 'mainstream' symphony orchestra. For the most part, the symbols used and the detail of
the marking will be similar. Obviously, the relationship of the performance markings with the notes may be different and to some degree
more 'historically informed' – shorter slurs, closer spaced dynamic nuances, more ornaments – but there would generally be little sense of the
performers intuitively drawing on a large reservoir of historical stylistic
awareness with which they spontaneously interpret the original notation.

There might be two explanations for this tendency to mark as many interpretative details as possible in the notation. First, much might reflect the circumstances of the present age: players and singers could rightly claim that they are being required to perform a far wider range of styles than any 'original' performer and that modern life is simply too frenetic to facilitate a ready stylistic ambidexterity. Furthermore, many might claim that western society has moved from a reliance on the power of memory and mental calculation to dependency on written records and detailed notations. Another side to this might be the influence of recording and broadcasting technology, which requires a greater degree of precision in the details of performance and a consistency from one performance or recorded 'take' to the next. As Robert Philip observes, 'The changes in recording and the recording studio have in turn fed back into the concert-hall. If pre-war recordings are remarkably like live performances, many late twentieth-century live performances are remarkably like recordings.'[3] Interestingly, Adorno makes a similar, if more damning, observation in 1938, precisely during the period that Philip now credits with particularly live-sounding recordings. Adorno believed performance style to suffer from the influence of the culture industry and recording technology, to be too concerned with the rationalisation of superficialities at the expense of the structural truth of the music:

The new fetish is the flawlessly functioning, metallically brilliant apparatus as such, in which all the cog wheels mesh so perfectly that not the slightest hole remains for the meaning of the whole. Perfect, immaculate performance in the latest style presents the work at the price of its definitive reification. It presents it as already complete from the very first note. The performance sounds like its own phonograph record.[4]

A second explanation of the tendency to notate interpretative details concerns the concept of autonomous musical works and the notion of the composer as the supreme controller of each work. This undoubtedly accounts in part for the dramatic increase in performance markings added by composers and editors during the nineteenth century, when the concept of the unique and autonomous musical work took hold. Not only the basic pitches and rhythms, but also many details of performance interpretation became part of the distinctive character of each work insofar as this was recorded in, or stipulated by, the score. Moreover, such details were often retroactively applied to earlier repertories in the various performing editions of the time. José Bowen, in a study of three of the most significant composer–conductors of the nineteenth century

(Mendelssohn, Berlioz and Wagner), sees the origins of the adherence to a composer's spiritual and notational intentions as lying precisely at the high point of musical Romanticism, when composers developed their respect for the intentions of their predecessors partly as a way of justifying a growing sense of their own individuality.[5]

The traditional periodisation of music history tends to support this view of the fully formed work solidifying in the nineteenth century, and of the composer taking ever more control over the notation of performance directives in the music. The medieval period was the time when first pitch and later rhythm were notated; in the Renaissance complex tempo relationships were established; in the Baroque, details of expression, tempo, dynamics, ornamentation and articulation were added to the notation; in the Classical period diminuendos and crescendos came to be notated and all expressive directions were notated in greater detail and in greater precision; and, with Beethoven, tempo itself could be established with the aid of metronome marks. The same 'story' can be continued to encompass the specification of many other musical and extra-musical factors in performance by Wagner, to Stravinsky's belief that the performer need do nothing more than read the notated instructions, to the serialisation of dynamic and attack by Messiaen, Babbitt and Boulez, and, finally, to tape music and its successors, in which both performer and notation are subsumed by the medium of data storage.

There are plenty of historical anecdotes to support the notion of the composer exercising increasing control over both notation and performance even before the early nineteenth century and the era of unique musical works. The mileposts might include Josquin who allegedly complained of singers adding ornamentation to that which he had already notated (see p. 92 above); there is Couperin who designs his notation of harpsichord pieces to be as prescriptive as possible; and, at the outset of Adorno's bourgeois period, there is Beethoven, who chided Czerny for not playing the music exactly as written.[6]

This story is also bolstered by cultural–materialist interpretations of music history. As early as 1911, Max Weber related developments in music to the increasing rationalisation of western society and man's increasing domination of nature. He gives particular attention to the development of tempered keyboard tuning and the developing technology of instruments. The progress of notational systems inevitably finds a place in this all-embracing system of rationalisation.[7] He sees notation as essential to the existence of a complex modern (western) work, and, indeed, to the very notion of a composer. Although he does not provide a detailed

history of the development of notation his concept of progressive rationalisation – in which the means towards specific ends become increasingly
efficient and precisely calculated – would clearly support the story of
notational progress.

Adorno develops this approach in a way that runs forcefully against
the ideals of historical performance. Musical works change throughout
their history and, most pertinently, the degree of freedom allowed to the
interpreter has progressively diminished during the bourgeois period.
While works of music achieve autonomy with the rise of the bourgeoisie
at the end of the eighteenth century, the music becomes more rationalised and any performer freedom that remains becomes arbitrary and
no longer part of the creative process and realisation of the work. If certain parameters of interpretation in earlier notations were purposely left
to chance, this no longer works in the modern age, when the construc-
tive unity of earlier music has been recognised and thus becomes the
goal of all performance: 'Subjected to more careful observation, older
and, above all "classical" German music – if it is to be realised as its
construction presents itself to the eye of today – demands the same strict
reproduction as does new music, resisting every improvisational freedom
of the interpreter.'[8]

As odious as Adorno's standpoint – making the high modernism of his
age a historical necessity – might seem today, it remains a perceptive
diagnosis of the notational rationalisation of music during the last two
centuries. HIP performers may have taken a step in the direction of performer freedom and a return to what Adorno saw as the intermingling of
the boundaries of production, reproduction and improvisation before the
end of the eighteenth century, but, I suggest, many are still dominated
by the urge to notate; even 'freedoms', even non-rational elements of
expression often have to be added to their performance parts.

Interestingly, performers do not seem universally to have added many
markings to their parts until well into the twentieth century – in other
words, the period of expanding recording technology and regular re-
hearsals. However much Bach added performance directives in his performing parts, the performers themselves seemed to have added little
more.[9] A century later, instrumentalists in Donizetti operas seem to
have added only cartoon-like annotations and left even obvious mistakes uncorrected.[10] As Robert Philip has observed, Oscar Cremer (1924)
advises violinists not to insert fingering into their parts so as not to inhibit the choices for other players; in the same period concert-goers in
Manchester were startled by the uniformity of bow-direction in the

visiting Berlin Philharmonic.[11] This was, incidentally, something that Corelli and Lully had aimed for over two centuries before; but clearly it had not become universal practice. All these examples might seem surprising from a twenty-first-century perspective, particularly given the detail of performance marking in nineteenth- and twentieth-century notation. Perhaps the composer's markings were seen as part of the inviolable work as preserved in notation, and the performer's own interpretation was something contingent, not necessarily to be notated or rationalised. The prescribed markings, at least from the nineteenth century onwards, may have been included to give the illusion of the completeness and uniqueness of each musical work, their success as performance directives depending on the practical experience of the composer.

Moreover, however much a composer may ostensibly wield supreme authorial control over the production of a musical text, there are going to be many external factors – and indeed other wills – in action. By the late nineteenth century, the golden age of the musical 'work', the creation of a definitive score, and, by analogy, the creation of an authorial figure, was a collaborative venture. James Hepokoski's study of the creation of Verdi's last opera *Falstaff* (1892–4) provides a particularly pertinent example of a composer who lived from an age of singer-dominance to one in which the composer exerted supreme control over matters of musical text and performance decisions. It comes at a crucial juncture in the development of the unique musical work:

> The *Falstaff* orchestral score was the product of a thoroughly industrialized editorship under the guidance of Giulio Ricordi at the height of his powers, and its printing history intersects – for the first time among Verdi's works – with such complications as the new American copyright law. From the beginning, the *Falstaff* project celebrated the modern principle of the marriage of art to the economic and legal powers of big business; from the beginning, it was conceived both as something to be received and treated as a 'masterpiece' and as something to be marketed aggressively within the norms expected by the modern institution of art music . . . To try to reduce this to a concern with Verdi's intentions alone – with the implication that these intentions may be investigated apart from the collaborative and commercial process with which they were inescapably intertwined – is grossly to misunderstand the multi-layered reality of this opera. *Falstaff* was very much a 'socially produced' work. [12]

What is most significant about the performance indications in the authorised published score is the fact that two members of the La Scala orchestra, Gerolamo De Angelis and Giuseppe Magrini, were commissioned to edit the performance markings in the orchestral parts. Verdi clearly knew of and sanctioned their participation, although he presumably held the right to modify their work and made suggestions of his own during rehearsal.[13] Clearly the comprehensiveness, rationalisation and plausibility of the performance markings were of prime importance in the definition of the authorised printed score.

The story of notational rationalisation should clearly not be accepted uncritically. First, it may lead to the belief that music history has always had the goal of precise performance specification, which was only imperfectly attained in the earlier periods (this is something which Adorno was perceptive enough to avoid). This belief may be precisely the reason some 'historically informed' performers today might give for covering the performance part liberally with interpretative indications (whether playing from a modern Urtext or a facsimile of an original source). But it is all too easy to assume that the 'goal' – only imperfectly attained in each successive development in notation – was always the same, that composers from Machaut to Josquin to Monteverdi to Corelli to Bach and to Mozart all desired (and performed with) the same variety of phrasings, attacks, crescendos and diminuendos. Moreover, many earlier repertories might be distorted and undervalued if current rules of musical interpretation are applied, in the belief that they constitute a universal system of human expression.

On the other hand, if many 'modern' parameters of interpretation are to be considered as simply absent from earlier repertories and if a piece is performed with a degree of neutrality concomitant with its sparse notation, there is now a danger that the music may come to be seen as more expressively deficient than it may actually have been originally. It requires a great deal of insight and imagination to envision parameters of musical interpretation and expression that are not directly equivalent to those that can be notated in nineteenth-century symbols, and we can be sure only of their difference and not their historical certainty. Nevertheless, it is within this concept that some of the most imaginative and incisive contemporary performances of early music may take place.

Given the striking evidence from recordings of the early twentieth century, it is, furthermore, quite clear that however didactic and precise a composer's – or, perhaps we should now say, a *score's* – notation there are still many unnotated aspects of performance style (e.g. rubato and portamento) and numerous cases where the composer's directives are modified or ignored. However much Stravinsky tried to control the flexibility of conductors that was fashionable until the 1930s, his own recordings up to that time show that he himself did not always maintain a strict tempo;

by 1960, when strict tempi were more the norm, he likewise became far more controlled.[14] Only in the last decades of the twentieth century did it seem that most performers and some composers saw a direct and literal correlation between the notation (marked up with directives, whether from the composer, conductor or performer) and the performance itself, a time, moreover, when it began to seem possible to hear what many performers had marked in their parts.

In all, the story of notation tends to support the concept of inexorable progress towards the perfected musical work, and, like all grand narratives, it often serves a purpose that is by no means innocent and universally valid. There is the obvious sense in which it renders music ever more distant from the practical production and reception of music in performance. As Alan Thomas put it in response to a questionnaire from John Cage, 'Notation fails in proportion to the singlemindedness with which it fails to enhance the social act of music.'[15] Furthermore, the idea of a goal of a fully rationalised musical work also implies the notion of an end to the story. In many ways, this end might already have come and gone given that tape music must have represented something close to the point of ultimate saturation – the point at which both performer and notation can be dispensed with.

The end of the story may thus be placed somewhere in the late 1950s, vividly symbolised by the demolition on 30 January 1959 of the Philips Pavilion at the Brussels World's Fair. Edgard Varèse's *Poème électronique* (1958), a masterpiece of *musique concrète*, had been designed to be played in the pavilion, ostensibly designed by Le Corbusier but largely realised by Iannis Xenakis. Sounding from around 325 speakers it was designed to be performed together with a two-minute interlude by Xenakis himself, continuously to successive groups of visitors. That Varèse saw his tape music as representing the ideal medium for a composer's supreme control over his music is suggested by his statement that 'Anyone will be able to press a button to release the music exactly as the composer wrote it – exactly like opening a book.'[16] However, Varèse was perhaps not so free of the intermediary of performance as his comment suggests; the piece was, after all, written with the simultaneously emerging building also in mind, and – more importantly – the sound engineers working directly on the site installed the sound equipment directly in accordance with the composer's instructions (Treib, *Space Calculated in Seconds*, p. 197).

Thus with the demolition of the Pavilion there is a sense in which this most specific of musical works is rendered incomplete. As Marc Treib suggests:

In [some] ways . . . the music no longer exists. Conceived and executed for a specific space, and perhaps more importantly, utilizing a specific sound system related to that space, no recorded performance today can equal the sounds experienced within the pavilion . . . no recording can conjure the space as well as the sound . . . Like the building, the full experience of the music can be described as demolished. (p. 211)

Not only is this 'full experience' demolished, but it cannot, in fact be recreated: certain aspects would be very difficult to reproduce – the acoustically absorbent asbestos sprayed on the interior of the building, the sound-technology of the late 1950s – and other aspects of the project were unrecorded (namely the exact number and placing of the loudspeakers, p. 49). In short, once the original performing venue is removed the piece can be heard only as a husk of that which was intended by its creators.

This piece also seems symptomatic of the breaking point in the story of increasing compositional prescriptiveness in the sense that there were already, at the time of its composition, considerable cracks within its own intense individualisation. For a start, it was part of a larger conception ultimately devised by Le Corbusier himself, a twentieth-century *Gesamtkunstwerk* involving architecture, visual display, music and an audience to be 'digested' in the stomach-like interior of the Pavilion at regular ten-minute intervals. Such were the contingencies of all these technologies in the 1950s that they could not be executed by a single figure: Le Corbusier delegated much of the architectural responsibility to Xenakis; much of the execution and eventual design of the building was in the hands of the builder who had particular experience in concrete structures; Le Corbusier's ideas for the visual display were remodelled and executed by Philippe Agostini; and Varèse (Le Corbusier's personal choice, in opposition to the plans of the Philips corporation) worked independently, under the sole injunction to provide precisely eight minutes of music to match the length of the visual display. In other words, the work as a whole shows a resistance to the supreme rationalisation that Varèse seems to have prized so highly, 'its conception of integral structure as unstructured independence prefigured developments in the modern arts and those later prompted by poststructuralist literary theory' (p. 174).

There were many other signs of this 'decline' in the rational control of musical composition during the 1950s onwards. For instance, this period of the strictest serialism was also the time of aleatoric music, where within certain parameters the performer had free rein to determine the course of events (or rather, often left them to chance). The end of the story may also lie in the irony that works exhibiting the strictest serialism sounded, even to some relatively informed listeners, no different in kind from those that were the product of chance. With the demise of tape music and the development towards computers there has been a tendency to return to the sense of a live performance by allowing for more chance factors or spontaneous decisions, and by involving performers to a greater degree in the interpretation of the music.[17] A contrary approach is adopted by Brian Ferneyhough, where the notation is rendered so specific and complex that there is a degree to which the music is actually unplayable. This problematic relation between notation and performance thus becomes an essential part of the music's identity.

The seeming obviousness of the story might be conditioned by the specific experiences of those concerned in musical production, thought and scholarship, for whom the ever more precise conventions of notation must be extremely noticeable and, consequently, influential. Umberto Eco, writing outside the music profession, sees the history of music – as of western culture in general – as working in precisely the opposite direction to that theorised by Weber and Adorno, from more restricted possibilities of meaning and interpretation towards increasing openness, culminating in the 'work in movement' of the twentieth century. Musical works (precisely those from the 1950s by Stockhausen, Berio, Pousseur and Boulez) allowing – indeed demanding – the complicity of the performer in their constitution and interpretation are his prime examples of the 'open work'.[18] Rather than seeing these as a definite break with the tradition of increasing authorial control, as I have so far suggested, Eco sees this stage as the culmination of a long historical progression, one that mirrors changes in the sciences and the prevailing world view. While writings of the Middle Ages admit multiple meanings, by the interpretative standards of the day, these meanings are far from being indefinite or infinite and, indeed, are governed by 'the laws of an authoritarian regime which guide the individual in his every action, prescribing the ends for him and offering him the means to attain them' (Eco, *The Open Work*, pp. 6–7). In the Baroque era, Eco observes a move away from the 'static and unquestionable definitiveness of the classical Renaissance form'; its visual art 'induces the spectator to shift his position continuously in order to see the work in constantly new aspects, as if it were in a state of perpetual transformation' (p. 7). Here the observer is actively encouraged to play a part in the creation and understanding of the work. Nevertheless, even this activity was to a certain degree governed by convention, and Eco sees a further emancipation with the notion of 'pure poetry' developing towards the necessary vagueness and infinite suggestiveness of Mallarmé and the openness of Kafka and Joyce (pp. 7–11).

Eco even considers the strictly serial works of Webern as more open than their predecessors, in the sense that there is a greater amount of 'information' and hence, ambiguity, that such works present to the listener (pp. 62–3, 95–6). From here it is a small but significant step to the 'work in movement', one where the performer (and, by extension, the listener) are required to organise and order certain aspects of the musical discourse.

Eco's explanation of this story of increasing openness verges on the glib: Mediaeval closure reflects the fixed, hierarchical conception of the cosmos; Baroque openness and dynamism reflect a new scientific awareness, in which attention is shifted from essence to appearance and to the psychological preconditions of the viewer; this fits neatly into the Copernican view of the universe. The radical openness that arose in the late nineteenth century with Mallarmé's plans 'for a multidimensional, deconstructible book . . . obviously suggests the universe as it is conceived by modern, non-Euclidean geometries' (p. 14). Even the supposedly strict world of serial composition is to be compared with Einstein's universe, where the observer, like the listener, must come to terms with the infinite number of ways of perceiving the whole system. In the realm of the musical performance of 'works in movement' every performance is 'complementary to all possible other performances of the work' (p. 15). Eco's macroscopic view of art history may provide a useful foil to the local history of performance and its notation, but he might be too facile in equating the variability in meaning of an artwork with the range of interpretative choices open to the musical performer. By separating the concept of openness of meaning from openness of performance options, we might be able to see them not as unaccountably contradicting one another but as part of a reactive process. Thus the increasing precision of notation may be one of the means musical institutions and composers developed to counteract the fear of the increasing openness of artistic meaning; what cannot be fixed in the abstract – indeed what may seem to be increasingly out of control – can perhaps be more closely defined in the particular, notated details. After all, the concept of an individual genius producing individualised musical works brings with it the contradictory notions of exquisite specificity and infinite potential for meaning. Thus we might consider the extreme specificity of much twentieth-century notation as a last-chance effort to preserve the identity of a musical work from the threat – indeed the inevitability – of indeterminacy.

If this is indeed the case, then perhaps we should be wary of equating the increasing complexity of notation purely with the technicalities of performance, something which seems substantiated by the variability of recorded evidence. In other words, the notation of performance details may have a function over and above (and occasionally contrary to) the simple prescription of actual, practical performance. This will be a thought that underlies much of the remainder of this chapter. I will examine several possible relations between notation and performance – alternative 'stories' – which are undervalued by the 'story' of notational progress, working towards the general point that we should be wary of treating notation as it has so often come to be regarded in the late twentieth century – namely, as a transparent recipe for performance, one that is indeed almost interchangeable with performance itself.

NOTATION AS PURPOSELY INCOMPLETE

My first alternative account of the historical relation between notation and performance – not a 'story' as such – briefly considers some cases that the first model would tend to undervalue, such as those in which the notation is *purposely* incomplete. Thus this is the case of a composer or scribe leaving details imprecise not because he lacked the notational machinery but because certain details of the piece were variable from one performance to another; imprecision was thus a positive advantage. Here, then, there is not the desire to aim for the perfected, unique and definitive work, even if, as Adorno would be quick to point out, there were signs of a unifying rationality within the compositional fabric. Most obvious is perhaps the notion of the figured (or, more often than not, unfigured) bass of the Baroque era, something that implies both a standard of harmonic correctness in realisation and a supreme adaptability to performing circumstances and the style to be projected. We should note the implications of a handbook such as Niedt's *Musicalische Handleitung zur Variation*, in which a whole suite of pieces (from prelude to gigue) can be generated in notation or performance from a single bass line.[19] With such a supremely practical theory as figured bass – spanning as it does the disciplines of composition and performance – one can readily see how flimsy is the notion of an individualised piece. With one seeming flick of the interpretative switch, that which seems essential to one piece (i.e. its bass line and implied chords) can become the basis for an apparently new piece.

One interesting, yet contentious, case of purposely incomplete notation is the issue of musica ficta and recta, particularly in music of the fifteenth and sixteenth centuries. In this era, if we are to believe Reinhard Strohm, there really was a move towards authorial distinction and the perfection of individual works.[20] Yet many significant local inflections of pitch were left unnotated. The degree to which each performing community made consistent choices from the general conventions of musica ficta is moot. Karol Berger suggests that many accidentals added in performance should be considered part of the 'musical text' (whether notated or not), so that they were often omitted more for notational convenience than to facilitate a wide arena of variability. On the other hand, he notes that some cases can be interpreted in several ways according to the conventions, thus allowing for considerable leeway in the performance.[21] As Anthony Newcomb remarks, in an examination of lute intabulations chronologically close to original motets by Gombert, 'the . . . variety of possible behavior seems to have been a source of delight rather than dismay . . . Perhaps the process of devising a way out of these puzzle-passages was itself considered a source of delight, another intellectual game for the members of academies of the time and a test of a musician's *virtù*.'[22] Sometimes the uninflected notation may have been designed so that the application of the conventions of ficta engendered startling results going beyond the pitches customarily included in the gamut, the most famous example being Willaert's experimental duo, *Quid non ebrietas*.[23] Here there is a definite sense of the notation being designed as a puzzle that the informed performer tries to solve.

Perhaps Margaret Bent's analogy between the application of unnotated accidentals and the conventions of figured bass in the Baroque era is useful in alluding to a variable practice with its boundaries of correctness.[24] In fact, the paucity of the notation was doubtlessly useful in allowing adaptability between variable performance circumstances, rather than frustratingly ambiguous.

NOTATION AS 'FITTED SUIT'

Another area in which notation may have been left purposely vague or at least plain was Italian opera from its inception until well into the nineteenth century. The musical text was often prepared extremely quickly and may have gone through as many versions as there were productions (if not performances). The notation thus had to be designed from the outset with adaptability in mind.[25] Moreover, many elements of performance, most notably the singer's ornamentation, would have been determined by the individual performer and were thus redundant in the notation.

Mozart's notation, however, often looks highly developed and very specific regarding details of ornamentation and expression. Nevertheless, it is increasingly emerging that much of Mozart's operatic writing was conceived with particular singers in mind, that to him his skill lay in making 'an aria to fit the singer like a well-made garment',[26] rather than in creating fixed sequences of immutable arias. So strong does Patricia Lewy Gidwitz consider the influence of singers to have been that if an attributed aria is at odds with what is known of the attributed singers she 'is tempted to disbelieve the extramusical evidence that links a particular singer with a role and perhaps look for another, more likely, candidate'.[27] Daniel Heartz sums up the situation with two apposite examples concerning the influence of Adriano Ferrarese, a splendid *seria* singer with negligible acting abilities: the dressing-up song from Act 2 of *Figaro* (fashioned for Nancy Storace) is replaced by a 'little waltz song which stands completely outside the action'. The following year, Mozart writes a part specially for her in *Così fan tutte*; the character Fiordiligi sings 'Come scoglio' – like a rock immovable – which must have summed up exactly what she looked like on stage.[28]

These examples lead to another, more complex, conception of notation, one in which the notation may look detailed and often prescriptive (particularly in a modern, scholarly edition), but where, in fact, it represents only one of several versions of the piece. The piece, as it stands in a 'Fassung letzter Hand', may represent only the performing situation for the final version, the ghosts of the performers for whom it was latterly refashioned masquerading in the light of later reception as the composer's ultimate intention.[29] Thus detailed notation, complete with many refinements relating to performance, does not automatically suggest a work that was conceived as a perfect whole from the start, however much it may be co-opted by the ideology of the supremely controlling composer: 'In as dynamic a form as early nineteenth-century Italian opera, it is almost always impossible to isolate . . . self-contained categories of authorial intention.'[30] As Roger Parker goes on to state, with regard to Donizetti: 'it is rare that one can call any version of a Donizetti opera the "finished" work. One has the impression that most operas were simply suspended, awaiting new revivals, new performers to reanimate the composer's creative faculties. Only with his disablement and death does the story reach a first conclusion; an unequivocal barrier.'[31]

Opinions about Handel's operatic practice vary: did Handel conceive of the works as potentially variable from the start, as suggested by Reinhard Strohm, or is the first (autograph) version in a sense the 'true' work, as Steven Larue argues? It is certainly clear that Handel went to great lengths to recast roles for later singers and this clearly resulted in changes to the whole that he could not have anticipated at the first compositional stage.[32] Much might depend on how intentionality is construed and the priority one gives to different stages in that intention: if we take the 'formal cause' approach to intentionality we might agree more with Larue, while if we take the inferential approach that I advocated in chapter 3 we might tend more toward Strohm's perspective. Nevertheless, regardless of the status of the 'original', all agree that the original cast of singers had a profound influence on the way the opera was conceived in the first place.

It is not only in Italian opera during the eighteenth and nineteenth centuries that the performers had a considerable influence on the way the music was composed. Alan Armstrong has shown how Meyerbeer's composing of the title role in *Le Prophète* was strongly influenced by the tenors he had in mind. Indeed the singer 'in many ways wielded the greatest power in the creation of Parisian operatic works'.[33] Meyerbeer first conceived the role for the virtuoso dramatic tenor Gilbert-Louis Duprez. The singer's varying vocal condition resulted in several changes, even before Meyerbeer began the music. The composer also seems to have made contingency plans for passages that might have proved too demanding for the singer. By the time of the much delayed premier in 1849 (eight years after Meyerbeer finished the initial composition) Duprez was no longer suitable for the part and was replaced by Gustave Hippolyte Roger, a singer with far less vocal talent than Duprez in his prime. Not only did Meyerbeer rewrite some of the more difficult passages, he considerably reduced the role for the prophet, complaining of the 'difference between an opera that comes from one's head . . . and the one that one sees at the theatre' (Armstrong, 'Gilbert Louis Duprez', p. 164). Nevertheless, as soon as the opera met with great success from its opening night, the composer seemed entirely happy with the 'mutilated' score and did not even restore missing pieces to the published version of the work. Here, then, the textual 'enshrinement' of the piece, as conditioned by its first vocal forces, came as a result of the early (and, importantly, successful) reception and not the composer's intention. Or, rather, the composer's intention changed in accordance with the public success.

NOTATION AS EXAMPLE

There is a further subset of the category in which the notation presents only one possible version of the piece. In this the notation does, in fact, offer precise performance directives, but perhaps with no single

performer in mind, and rather by way of example than prescription
(José A. Bowen uses the term 'sample').[34] Here the danger of applying
anachronistic notions of the perfected, immutable work is particularly
acute. One prime example might be Monteverdi's sample realisation of
the vocal part to 'Possente spirito' in the commemorative publication
of *Orfeo* (1607). Modern singers may often admit that they will follow
this version because they cannot ornament so well themselves, but they
would be mistaken to think that Monteverdi's suggestions should be
followed to the letter because the composer wished it to go no other
way: 'The florid version provided by Monteverdi indicated to the singer
that the aria was one that required ornamentation, and furnished a
model, though one which the singer was by no means bound to follow.'[35]
Indeed, some seventeenth century composers offering elaborated versions of simple lines often seem positively embarrassed by their suggestions, encroaching, as it were, on the territory of the performing experts.
Michael Praetorius refers to his remarkably sophisticated diminutions
in *Polyhumnia caduceatrix* (1619) as if he were merely adding a fashionable
accessory: 'your humble servant has somewhat diminished the Chorale
in the vocal parts in the current Italian fashion'.[36]

Many accept that Corelli's ornaments in the Amsterdam publication
(1710) of his Violin Sonatas, op. 5 (1700), are examples rather than hard-
and-fast prescriptions. These sonatas enjoyed an unparalleled reception
in the eighteenth century and, almost from the start, they were seen
as a forum for improvised embellishment. Ornamented versions of certain slow movements (and, occasionally, other movements besides) exist
well into the middle of the century.[37] As Neil Zaslaw has observed, each
version shows the stylistic characteristics of its originator and, as the
eighteenth century progressed, the notated ornaments became denser;
this might reflect both a slowing of tempo, but also a sense that each generation tried to outdo the previous one (Zaslaw, 'Ornaments for Corelli's
Violin Sonatas', pp. 100–1). Zaslaw presents a convincing case for the
authenticity of Estienne Roger's claim that his edition of 1710 presents
ornaments for the adagios of the first six sonatas 'composed by Corelli
as he plays them' (Zaslaw, 'Ornaments', p. 102). He suggests that the
ornaments presented in print represent: 'minimal, all-purpose examples that could work for many types of violinists in a variety of venues.
These would have been intended primarily for inexperienced players
who needed to be shown what was wanted in this type of music, not
for virtuosos, who would be well able to take care of themselves in that
department' (Zaslaw, 'Ornaments', p. 109).

Zaslaw bases this assertion on the assumption that there was a fundamental difference between manuscript and published notation, the former catering to the local, the latter to the general and public, indeed, almost the universal. I do not believe that this distinction is self-evident in this period of notational history – a manuscript might contain elements of the general as much as a print might allude to the local[38] – but, in either case, it would seem that we go against the original sense of the music if we perform Corelli's often lavish ornaments literally. Thus it is rather ironic to discover from Peter Walls' survey that while four of the most expert modern performers of Baroque violin are fully capable of improvising their own ornaments for those slow movements not ornamented in the Roger/Corelli print (sonatas 7–11), they take the notated ornaments as more or less fixed. Although they are sometimes prepared to amplify Roger/Corelli's graces, they are loath to add ornaments where the print presents unadorned portions of the original line.[39]

Much that could be said about the status of Corelli's ornaments – as examples rather than hard-and-fast prescriptions – may also be claimed of Mozart's solo piano lines. As Robert Levin reminds us: 'Mozart's virtuosity as a pianist was prized above his composing, and his abilities as an improviser stood above both in the public's esteem.'[40] To Levin, Mozart's variants of rondo themes 'provide invaluable examples of spontaneity captured on the page' (Levin, 'Improvised Embellishments', p. 224). He lists several situations that seem to call for elaboration in Mozart's scores: when an orchestral ritornello following a piano statement contains more decoration than the original piano line; passages that are designed to be repeated; passages where melodic and rhythmic activity suddenly slacken (particularly in slow movements); passages where only the 'top and bottom notes are delineated without the necessary connective arpeggios' and recitative passages in slow movements of piano concertos (p. 230). In the latter category, Mozart once referred to that fact that there was 'something missing' in a passage from K451 and promised to supply a reworking of the deficiency together with the cadenzas (p. 232). This suggests that some of Mozart's notations may be considered incomplete – hurriedly sketched by the composer–performer – and that he would have provided a finished version had he had the time. But this is surely more a tendency than a clearly defined policy. Perhaps Mozart considered different components within a piece to have a different level of 'fixity'; as Wye J. Allenbrook suggests, the development sections of concertos – consisting mainly of arpeggios – perhaps represent a specific arena of improvisation, something which belies the entire notion of Classical 'development'.[41]

Another contentious case of the possible ornamentation or alteration of notated lines concerns the Lieder of Schubert. As Walther Dürr has noted, Johann Michael Vogl was well known for his free alterations of Schubert's Lieder and even induced the composer to make notational changes.[42] While there was sometimes 'friendly controversy' between singer and composer, Dürr believes that most disputes would have been over not whether improvised embellishments were permitted but where they should be applied. Dürr sees Vogl's performing versions as so central to the Schubert tradition that he sanctions their inclusion in the appendices of the *New Schubert Edition*. They are not to be reproduced literally in performance but rather present a model of improvised 'non-essential' alterations.

By positing a distinction (still used in Schubert's day) between the categories of 'wesentliche' ornaments (essential, indicated by the composer) and 'willkürliche' ornaments (non-essential, the province of the performer), Dürr can allow Schubert's notated works to survive in their individualised glory (p. 127). Yet by suggesting that Schubert was actually influenced by Vogl's ornaments he seems to admit that what is by nature inessential, can influence the essential; the 'work itself' preserved in the main text of the new edition is perhaps not as impervious to the variations of the appendix as Dürr would like to admit. David Montgomery, fighting a rear-guard action, considers things to have gone too far in Schubert performance:[43] he admonishes historical performers for deviations from the text (including most forms of rubato) and he summarily dismisses Schubert's relationship with Vogl: 'In light of further evidence concerning Schubert's smooth and straightforward piano playing, it seems most likely that he merely tolerated Vogl's liberties because the singer was an important advocate for his music.'[44]

In all, it is hardly surprising that the notion that Mozart's notation might be incomplete and that some apparently 'finished' passages in both Mozart and Schubert might have been varied have met with far more resistance than have similar suggestions regarding Corelli.[45] This music as it is notated has simply acquired too privileged a place in western culture for it to be considered in any way mutable. Mozart's identity as a virtuoso performer has been subsumed by his expanding posthumous identity as a composer, a composer with the authoritarian persona of Wagner, late Verdi, or even Stravinsky. Yet, even well into the nineteenth century, major composers such as Chopin and Schumann quite clearly viewed their notation and performance markings as offering examples of the way the piece might go rather than fixed prescriptions.[46] The very subjectivity that was essential to Romanticism is so often stifled by the work concept that arose at the very same time. As Montgomery's position regarding Schubert shows, it is indeed difficult to grapple with the received view of such pieces as eternally fixed and 'classical'; the more one allows the music to be varied, the more the very essence of what makes this music so supremely admired is destroyed. Yet while the undefiled notation may have been essential for the survival of such music, it may also contain the echo of Mozart the dazzling performer or of Schubert's 'friendly controversies' with Vogl. Even without necessarily changing one note, the score can be considered as much the record or echo of performative acts and dialogues as the blueprint of a 'work'.

One final example of the category of notation that appears complete but may have been exemplary rather than mandatory is provided by the entire field of liturgical organ music. The exemplary nature is most obvious in repertories with a pedagogical intent such as the *Fundamenta* of Conrad Paumann (perhaps together with several other elements of the late fifteenth-century Buxheim collection).[47] However, the stakes are higher for a collection such as Bach's 'Orgelbüchlein', something with a wide range of purposes such as providing music for the liturgy, examples for students, theological interpretation or as an exercise in perfecting small-scale pieces of music. It is unlikely that Bach, who seems to have been unable to copy any manuscript without adding corrections or improvements, regularly played these pieces in precisely their notated form. Furthermore, given the amount of improvisation required by most Lutheran liturgies of the time, they must surely be only the notational tip of an enormous improvisational iceberg.

Similar things could be said of the French Classical organ repertory of the seventeenth and early-eighteenth centuries. Like Bach's notated music, this music must feature among the most precisely notated material of the age with an increasing prescriptiveness regarding registration, ornamentation and other performance markings. Yet, as Bruce Gustafson remarks, '[t]he organ music that does come down to us represents models of an improvisational art by famous masters'.[48] The complexity of the French liturgy was such that the organist might have been required to provide over 100 versets each day, clearly far more than was available in printed sources of the time and certainly more than could have been practical in manuscript form. In Italy too, the organ played a major role in the liturgy and, as Frescobaldi notes on his title pages to both the first book of toccatas and the *Fiori Musicali*, the pieces are designed in a sectional form so that the organist can break off whenever necessary.

All the composer–organists mentioned so far went out of their way to notate their music as precisely as the conventions of the day allowed (although Frescobaldi outlines in his prefaces many striking features of performance practice that could hardly have been notated). Even if we were to allow that these composers might have insisted that their pupils played these pieces as closely to their notated forms as possible, their nature changes once we understand that the same pupils would have been required to improvise their own pieces after these models, just as did the composers themselves. In other words, a perfected 'example' is not to be confused with an autonomous, perfected 'work'. David Fuller sees the various versions of harpsichord pieces by Chambonnières, however detailed their specification of ornaments, as reflecting a state of 'hetero-textuality'. There is no single line of development towards a perfected final version; the differing versions lie side-by-side, akin to different performances by the composer. The apparent specificity of the notation may be more an element of style (e.g. a sense of subtlety, attention to detail) rather than reflecting an ontological imperative (see p. 93 above).

In all, there is no particular sense of historical progress in all these categories of notation that is purposely incomplete or provided by way of example. Indeed diverse historical periods may have several points in common. The challenge to understand the relation between the notation and the musical practices with which it was associated is as present in the fields of Mozart performance and nineteenth-century Italian opera, as it is in those of musica ficta and continuo realisation.

NOTATION AS A RECORD OF PERFORMING TRADITION; NOTATION AS DESCRIPTION

A third approach to the history of notation is, to some degree, the opposite of the first, which tended to see notation as the starting-point and controlling manifestation of the work and, consequently, the prescription for future performance. In this case, then, the notation comes as a *result* of a performing tradition, it is 'descriptive' in the formulation of Stanley Boorman.[49] Even if it is meant to prescribe later performance, the history of how it got that way is surely significant. This type of notation surfaces even in a composer as late as Olivier Messiaen. One of his most refined and notationally complex organ works is the *Messe de la Pentecôte* (1951). According to the composer himself, this was the product of over twenty years improvising at the church of Sainte Trinité and the energy expended on its notated composition was such that the composer ceased to improvise for several years subsequently.

[My] improvisations went on for a rather long time, until the day I realized they were tiring me out, that I was emptying all my substance into them. So I wrote my *Messe de la Pentecôte*, which is the summation of all my previous improvisations. *Messe de la Pentecôte*, was followed by *Livre d'orgue*, which is a more thought-out work. After that, as it were, I ceased to improvise.[50]

This seems like a classic modernist dilemma of a composer achieving such a perfection and abstraction on paper that his creative urges as a performer were effectively stunted. This work might represent the ultimate clash between the final chapter of the usual story of notational progress with a tradition that allowed more of a fluid interplay between composition and performance.

There is an increasing number of studies of music before 1500 showing that notation can often come not only at the end of the compositional process rather than the beginning, but also after a considerable number of memorised performances have taken place. With the researches of Helmut Hucke and Leo Treitler, most agree that the Gregorian repertory was stabilised in memorised performance before it was notated, and that when notation first came into use the activities of remembering, improvising and reading continued side-by-side. According to Hucke, 'the propagation of Gregorian chant in the Empire and the distribution of manuscripts with neumes are not the same phenomenon; they represent two different stages in the spread of chant'.[51] He further observes that the oldest chant manuscripts were simply too small to sing from and may instead 'have served as reference for the cantor and as a control against deviation from the true and venerable tradition'. As Leo Treitler shows with regard to the Old Roman tradition, notational variants reflect variants that already existed in the improvisatory system.[52] But this variability was more an element of the values held within the Old Roman tradition than a reflection of the nature of memory; the greater uniformity of the Gregorian tradition – also memorised – was the result of a different value system and correspondingly not conditioned by the fact of notation. With this in mind, Treitler concludes that early notation was always conceived as a matter of choice, and not through ignorance, carelessness, lack of skill, primitiveness or underdevelopment. The notation often provides more information for music that was less familiar to the original performers, resorting to a less informative system for the more familiar aspects of the repertory; it would also serve musicians who were not well versed in the tradition.[53]

Craig Wright has proposed that much of the early polyphonic repertory of Notre Dame was performed without notation because there is a total absence of sources (and, more significantly, references to them) before 1230.[54] Anna Maria Busse Berger has gone a long way towards substantiating this view. She stresses the importance of memory in general education and particularly in the art of verbal composition and notes the closeness of literate Parisians of the age, who extolled the virtues of memory.[55] Rather than excusing the cross-references and citations between works in the Notre Dame repertory, she suggests that reference and citation, when done consciously, was a positive virtue in literary composition (where one was encouraged to draw on a large memorised 'warehouse of wisdom'). Not only performance, then, but composition itself was intimately connected with memory, the art of invention being the compiling of a collection from one's memory archive. If the end-result was written down, this was usually done by dictation (i.e. not by the author) and the product was by no means a finished, immutable piece of music.

These findings suggest that we should not compare sources in order to discern a single, authentic, original that was written down with the direct sanction of the composer. Not only is the notion of 'composer' rendered ambiguous in a culture that prides itself on the borrowing and adapting of models, but we should be wary of viewing the notation as the ideal embodiment of a piece. We should, rather, see it as a mnemonic aid and work backwards towards an original that existed only in the minds of its original performers and composers.

Rob C. Wegman has attempted to highlight the specific era, around 1500, during which the distinction became possible between composition as an object and improvisation as a practice.[56] He notes that before this time, performed music was conceived primarily in terms of event rather than object. The fact '[t]hat a given musical event might be based in notation was an accidental circumstance: it did not affect the aesthetic criteria by which the event itself was to be judged' (Wegman, 'From Maker to Composer', p. 434). Even if Tinctoris applied the word 'compositio' to music that was written out, this could be just as much a counterpoint exercise as a fully fledged composition in the modern sense, with all parts relating equally to one another. Conversely, compositional skill *per se* was recognised regardless of whether the piece concerned was written out or not. Tinctoris encouraged singers to relate to one another, rather than only to the tenor, thus minimising the distinction between extemporisation and the notated *res facta*.[57] In all, Wegman suggests that fifteenth-century notation does not necessarily reflect the compositional status of the piece; it serves the purely utilitarian purpose of providing instructions for performing counterpoint and it does not necessarily represent a compositional conception. A composer differed only from the co-ordinating tenor to the extent that he converted such co-ordinations into mensural notation – moreover, these two roles could have been performed by one and the same person.[58]

As compositions became conceived more as notated objects – a notion which Wegman observes as spreading to the general consciousness during the sixteenth century – composers developed increasingly esoteric notation in order to preserve a sense of secrecy, professional demarcation and protection (p. 470). However, as I will emphasise later, the recognition of the profession of composer from the last decades of the fifteenth century, a recognition that depends on the notated *res facta*, does not automatically imply that such notation contains precise and limiting directions for the performer; it took on something of a life of its own,[59] obliquely to its function as providing instructions for the performer. Performers, on the other hand, continued to improvise at all degrees of the spectrum of compositional refinement, and, in some locations, were still memorising enormous liturgical repertories, well into the seventeenth century.[60]

The concept of notation coming towards the end of the compositional process is surely valid for several cases and types of repertoire after 1500, in other words, after the time when a composer became defined as someone who fixed his own music in notation. This applies specifically to composers who were well-known performers, such as Corelli. If we accept that Roger's notation of Corelli's own ornaments is authentic, such notation surely comes after many performances rather than before. Likewise, Bach's *Musical Offering* originated in an improvisation before Frederick the Great and certain parts of it (most probably the 3 part Ricercar) are notational improvements of a performance. Most nineteenth-century composers who improvised come into the same category; indeed many of Schumann's piano works 'often seem not even to progress toward a single final version but rather to swing between various distinct alternative versions'.[61] Composers who rely on both the melodies and the expressive gestures of folk music also, in a sense, notate something that already existed in performance as, of course, do most composers of liturgical organ music from Paumann to Messiaen.

NOTATION AS AN ALTERNATIVE EMBODIMENT OF MUSIC

My final category – perhaps the most contentious – draws on all the other approaches but focuses on those cases in which the notation reflects a work that is generally regarded as 'complete', in some respect, on paper, but in which the composer, in fact, allowed, expected, or himself made deviations in performance. This is to be distinguished from the category in which the composer produced an exemplary notation which the performer could alter at will, in that a certain perfection or 'finish' was expected in the notation of the music for its own sake, while its performance entailed a different set of conventions which may, at times, have gone against the perfection of the notated music.

Rob C. Wegman makes this notion explicit for the notation of Renaissance polyphony: 'the notion of contrapuntal "correctness" . . . may have more relevance on paper than in the actual practice of extemporizing counterpoint (and hence perhaps more to us than to many singers and listeners in the Middle Ages)'.[62] Contrapuntal correctness on paper may itself be a symptom of the newfound primacy that the sixteenth century gave to that which was written, the 'male principle of language', according to Michel Foucault. It may well have been accepted in the music profession that the 'sounds made by voices provide no more than a transitory and precarious translation of it.'[63] Perhaps the most significant example of this distinction between what is written and what is heard in performance is the choral music of Palestrina, in which the notation presents an extremely refined and perfected treatment of dissonance, line and rhythm (one that has become the paradigm for contrapuntal study). However, there is a considerable amount of evidence to suggest that in performance some – if not all – singers improvised around these lines, often negating the contrapuntal 'perfection'. Graham Dixon draws attention to the numerous primers in vocal ornamentation in the late sixteenth century, Bovicelli providing a lavishly ornamented version of Palestrina's *Benedicta sit sancta Trinitas* in 1594, the year of the composer's death. Furthermore, one of the leading exponents of vocal ornamentation, Giovanni Luca Conforti, was himself a member of the papal chapel.[64]

Conforti's ornament treatise *Breve et facile maniera d'essercitarsi* is designed to provide (with less than two months work!) the novice singer with the skill a famous singer might have acquired through years of practice and listening to his peers. Conforti hardly ventures into the laws of counterpoint (although, as the title suggests, he does seem to wish to give the reader skills for basic ornamented – but presumably unnotated – composition). Knowledge of the correct consonants on which passage-work can be inserted is apparently not necessary, Conforti merely marks with a cross those passages which work over suitable consonances.[65] The method is formulaic in the extreme: those who wish to insert runs need only decide which notes to ornament and then look for ornaments for similar pitches and note values in Conforti's systematic examples (treating, as they do, each ascending and descending interval in turn with countless examples in a wide range of note values). The only rule the singer is exhorted to follow is that dictated by the ear.

Much of Dixon's view of Palestrina performance rests on the assumption that most of his music was sung with single voices, thus enabling singers to perform embellishments with relatively little danger of ungainly clashes. Noel O'Regan has somewhat modified this view by showing that many parts of the Mass Ordinary were sung with more than one voice to a part, solos being reserved for particular sections. He points to an extremely varied and flexible practice for the performance of non-concertato music: multiple voices for four- to six-voice Ordinaries and some motets; single voices for the divided choirs of polychoral music; one-per-part singing for trios and quartets in masses, some motets, hymns and magnificats.[66] O'Regan also notes that Dixon fails to see the connection between the practice of ornamentation and another – often ignored – practice of performing motets: that in which one or more parts are abstracted from polyphonic motets with the organ substituting for the missing voices. This was accepted practice in Rome long before Viadana's famous publication of sacred concertos in 1600.

While there is no consensus as to what degree of ornamentation was practised in polyphonic performance of the music of Palestrina and his contemporaries, ornamented performance with organ was clearly an acceptable manner of performance at the time (O'Regan, 'The Performance of Palestrina', p. 151). Furthermore, given such group improvisatory practices as *contrapunto alla mente*, which were regularly applied to offertory chants and magnificat antiphons,[67] it may not necessarily be the case that the hypothesis for ornamented performance relies on the assumption of one-per-part performance. If Palestrina's motets were embellished almost to the point of being unrecognisable in the versions with organ accompaniment, the possibility of simultaneous heterophonic embellishment might not seem so extreme. Certainly Conforti's elaborations of psalm formulae in his *Salmi passagiati* (1601) and *Passagi sopra tutti li salmi* (1607) suggest that austerity was not a feature of even the simplest liturgical genres.

In short, it seems that much of the supreme refinement of Palestrina's compositional technique was designed more for the eye than the ear and that only to reactionary contemporaries such as Artusi did the eye version become mandatory for the ear; this is the view of Palestrina that has taken hold throughout most stages of his subsequent reception. The distinction between compositional practice and performance at the time of Palestrina can be inferred, somewhat negatively, from Artusi's famous polemic against the imperfections of modern music. Artusi suggests that some of the small *accento* ornaments that modern composers introduce into their music have arisen because 'singers do not sing what is written, but go ahead "carrying the voice" and sustaining it in such a way that, when they perceive that it is about to produce some bad effect, they divert it elsewhere, taking it somewhere where it seems it will not offend the ear'.[68] The ear has been corrupted by sensuous excess, so that it has become acceptable for composers to write music incorporating such 'errors'.

There are several other examples in music history of music that, in its notated form, has – or has acquired – a particular 'purity' that was violated in its early performance. Corelli provides an interesting parallel to Palestrina, a century or so later. We can be as certain as possible that Corelli produced Dionysian performances of at least the slow movements of his violin sonatas. What is fascinating about the comparison between the original edition of 1700 and ornamented versions in the 1710 print is that the 'plain' version does not look incomplete and contains its own logic of sequence and motivic consistency; the ornamented versions often undo the 'finish' by obscuring the melodic sequences and subverting the supreme rationality of the texture with unpredictable, irrationally divided runs. It is not unlikely that Corelli and his contemporaries embellished other movements too – particularly binary dances.[69] We know less about the performance of the trio sonatas and concertos, but it is difficult to conceive that they were played entirely without adornment.

Nevertheless, Corelli's reputation (at least as it stretches into the nineteenth and twentieth centuries) has been made not through his performance but through his notation, a notation that, like Palestrina's, is unusually Apollonian, implying beautifully finished, sonorous pieces of music. The Apollonian view was evidently an 'authentic' view of the age, one epitomised by Roger North's comment of 1728 that 'Upon the bare view of the print any one would wonder how so much vermin could creep into the work of such a master . . . Judicious architects abominate any thing of imbroidery upon a structure that is to appear great, and trifling about an harmonious composition is no less absurd'.[70] It is this view that has most strongly coloured Corelli's subsequent reception, one that would prefer to ignore the seeming contradiction between Corelli the Apollonian composer and Corelli the Dionysian performer.

Bojan Bujic sensibly suggests that we should not project our 'modern notion of performance as a logical continuation of the process of composition' on earlier music in which there was a strong separation of the categories of notated composition and performance.[71] But, I would suggest, we should exercise precisely the same caution in that very period when the two were considered coterminous. Many composers in the nineteenth and twentieth centuries may have fixed details in the notation simply because this was something increasingly expected in the publishing world. Schumann may have notated details against his better judgement and natural reluctance to provide a definitive version.[72] Even in the twentieth century composers who were themselves expert performers often seemed to treat their performances as ontological categories entirely different from their notated composition. László Somfai's work on Bartók is particularly striking, showing that Bartók the composer followed the twentieth-century tendency towards notational precision while allowing himself considerable freedoms as a performer.[73]

Messiaen again provides a good example of a composer obsessed with notational perfection that may be disregarded in performance, with a piece such as the 'Introit' to the *Messe de la Pentecôte*. Here the rhythmic notation is particularly complex and esoteric, apparently the fruit of twenty years of improvisation (as discussed above). In performance of the 'Introit', though, the composer seems to have 'reverted' to the improvisational mode, largely ignoring the letter of the rhythmic notation.[74] Why then did he not notate the piece in simple values, with a rubric along the lines of 'molto rubato'? Presumably because it was the 'look' of the piece that counted; it had a particular identity on paper which – at least to the composer – was not to be followed literally in performance. Brian Ferneyhough makes the disjunction (or perhaps – rather – counterpoint) between the work, its complex notation, its possible performances, and the listener's perception of the difficulty of the music, one of the essential metaphysical issues of his music.[75]

The ultimate significance of this final category – notation that is 'complete' for its own sake and that is not necessarily to be followed literally in performance – is that it can be applied to many more repertories and compositional styles; indeed, it should perhaps be tested, at least, for virtually any music we encounter. To what extent did each composer take delight in the composition and notation of the music on paper and to what extent was this independent of the practicalities of performance? In Palestrina's era this may have had something to do with a perfected theoretical system of dissonance that could be realised in notation. At the turn of the twentieth century it might have had more to do with details of performance marking, rendering, as it were, the work more individualised on paper, more precisely defined for copyright purposes. This move was facilitated, if not necessitated, by the number of markings available and the improving technologies of notational reproduction. My approach is thus an antidote to perhaps the most significant change in the history of performance – the mass production of recording and broadcasting that has become ubiquitous since World War II. Only in this age, I contest, has it been possible for performance virtually to reduplicate notation and vice versa; only in this period has exact compliance with notation been widely seen as a virtue, since it is the first time that such a notion has become truly verifiable.

PART 3

*Historically informed performance within
the culture of the late twentieth century*

5

Historical performance at the crossroads of modernism and postmodernism

Until recently, historically informed performers were in no doubt about the nature of their enterprise, 'This is my historical (or old) violin', they would say, and, if they also played conventional instruments, 'This is my modern violin.' But all this was challenged by Richard Taruskin's contention that much of what goes on in HIP is in fact *modern* performance, that the urge to perform in an 'historical' fashion and – particularly – the musical results, bear all the traces of musical high modernism. The movement apparently shares much with Stravinsky's attitude to performance and covertly continues general tendencies evident since the middle of the twentieth century: a privileging of text over performance, and an increasingly strict, geometrical approach to rhythm.[1] On the whole, Taruskin sees 'modernism' as virtually synonymous with musicological positivism, objectivism and the retreat from personal commitment and human involvement in musical interpretation. He suggests that the 'postmodern' will provide some solution (whether 'historically informed' or not) by reintroducing the human element, breaking down grand claims for truth and allowing more freedom in performance.

It is the aim of this chapter to explore the relation of historical performance to modernism and postmodernism in more detail. For, although Taruskin's claims have usefully precipitated a debate about the place of HIP in late twentieth-century western culture, they do presuppose very specific and restricted definitions of the terms (just as they focus only on certain tendencies within HIP itself). Moreover, it is difficult to reconcile Taruskin's promotion of postmodernism as something that will break down the status of the serious, classical musical work (*Text and Act*, p. 17), leading to a post-authoritarian approach to performance (p. 47), with his complaint that many HIP performers devalue and decanonise great musical works (p. 138) and forsake the authority of a conductor.

Here I attempt something of a genealogy of HIP, placing it within the various debates on modernism and postmodernism in the hope of

highlighting something of the complex interaction of cultural and historical forces involved. Some of the things I suggest will go against the grain
of the more usual presuppositions about modernism, postmodernism
and HIP in general. For example, I believe that while modernism is undoubtedly the correct label for the literalistic and mechanistic approach
to HIP, there are also certain elements in the modernist approach to
history that might both explain some of the more inspiring aspects of
HIP and still be of benefit for its continuing dialogue with history. On
the other hand, the extraordinary surge of interest in HIP, from the late
1960s onwards, coincides and resonates with many of the theories and
descriptions of postmodernism. Indeed the HIP phenomenon, at least
since becoming a major cultural and commercial force, cannot be understood without reference to the 'postmodern condition'. But to suggest
that the postmodern styles of art we experience at the outset of a new
century are historically necessary and the only 'true' conception of the
times is to fall into a totalitarian historicism which soon condemns everything out of tune with the prevailing ideologies. Indeed the coexistence
of multiple value systems seems endemic to the late twentieth century
and only in this sense could the postmodern be defined as a necessary
condition.

Some of the most succinct definitions of modernism and postmodernism within recent musical culture come from Georgina Born's study
of the Parisian research centre, IRCAM.[2] Born associates modernism
with a variety of new aesthetic movements dating from the late nineteenth and early twentieth centuries, all linked by their common reaction
against prevailing classical and romantic currents. Its formalist bias carries with it an interest in technology and science, the futurists being the
most extreme modernists, embracing ever-new sounds from the modern
world (pp. 40–1). Associated with this is an unprecedented interest in
music theory and the concept of a theoretical text preceding the act of
composition. While many modernists might be politically neutral they
have often sought to shock official establishments and bourgeois audiences and have thus engendered an association between modernism and
radical politics. Their main imperative is towards progress and constant
innovation (p. 43), keeping ahead of current tastes and subverting the status quo. What is particularly complex about modernism, in Born's view,
is its oscillation between the seeming opposites of rationalism and irra-
tionalism, objectivism and subjectivism (p. 44), intensifying two strands
of nineteenth-century art, positivistic naturalism and late romanticism.
Finally, modernism's ambiguous relationship with popular culture stems

from the fact that both flourished simultaneously and that modernism's move towards formalism and abstraction has taken it progressively away from a direct association with popular culture. In fact, popular culture has become the 'other' of modernism, ignored, reviled or, occasionally, envied and appropriated.

At a glance, these features of modernism would seem to sit rather awkwardly in relation to HIP; to be sure, the latter has often been a re-action against prevailing currents and tastes in performance, and it has often attempted to shock the establishment (see p. 8 above), but it hardly seems to embrace technology, progress or the new for its own sake. In-deed, it has been a decidedly anti-modernist movement, searching for the pre-modern and rejecting many of the 'advances' of nineteenth-century instrumental technology. Moreover, HIP would hardly be a welcome guest within most modernist circles since the typical modernist narrative of art history would discount any reversion to an earlier form of art as 'beyond the pale' of history proper.[3]

Nevertheless, the interest in historical data and 'authentic' musical notations as a prerequisite for performance may well relate to the mod-ernist imperative of negating a more recent past. Most importantly, the development of reproductive sound technology has itself enabled HIP to enjoy immense success, broadening access to forgotten repertories and allowing unstable or nearly unplayable instruments to be heard to their best. In sum, if HIP cannot be directly related to the mainstream of modernism, many of its beginnings and presuppositions could not have arisen outside a modern culture. As the movement has come of age, cer-tain modernist traits, particularly the cult of 'newness', have undoubtedly become rather less relevant. After thirty years of constant publicity, HIP no longer shocks us in the way that even *The Rite of Spring* continues to do.

Born associates postmodernism with movements in literary and archi-tectural criticism that arose in the 1960s and seventies onwards, move-ments that in some degree experienced dissatisfaction with modernism. It might attempt to counter the traditional division between high and low culture by advocating a new sense of cultural pluralism. It might also turn away from modernism's negation of earlier 'languages' of art (e.g. realism, narrative and, specifically in music, tonality), precisely by reap-propriating these earlier modes (as in 'neoromanticism'). As Born notes, both these negations of modernism are themselves ironically dependent on a modernist tendency towards negation. Postmodernism must thus be seen as something that preserves discursive continuities with modernism, some of these continuities being themselves defined by negation (Born,

Rationalizing Culture, p. 46). This view is substantiated by an 'arch' post-modernist, such as Lyotard, who insists that the postmodern is 'modern' to the extent that 'All that has been received, if only yesterday . . . must be suspected'.[4]

Born defines this bundle of postmodern tendencies as 'populist' and links it to a less visible 'vanguardist' position, which rejects 'the predominantly asocial and formalist, pedagogic and elitist cultural politics of modernism' (Born, *Rationalizing Culture*, p. 46), together with the modernist belief in the autonomy of the aesthetic. The 'vanguardist' position preserves the specifically modernist notion of a critical avant-garde that promotes many political movements associated with minorities and cultural diversity; it finds one of its most pervasive definitions in Lyotard's 'postmodern condition', which celebrates the end of the grand modernist narratives (including humanism and Marxism) and heralds an age of heterogeneity, dissent and local traditions (Born, *Rationalizing Culture*, p. 47, and see p. 152 below).

With its doubling negation of modernism's original contempt for past aesthetic conventions, Born's populist postmodernism resonates immediately with many of the ideals of HIP as the latter also moves towards overcoming the distinction between 'high' and 'low' in a number of ways. First, there is the obvious way in which vast tracts of earlier musical repertoire, ignored or simply unknown by the central musical institutions, have been recovered in new editions, performances and recordings. Secondly, there has also been an emphasis on re-establishing local traditions, whether large and national (e.g. William Christie's seemingly single-handed re-establishment of French Baroque musical drama) or more regional (e.g. Jordi Savall's Catalan interests).

Secondly, many HIP performances of works from the western canon seem purposely to have countered the reverential attitude associated with traditional twentieth-century performance: Reinhardt Goebel might perform certain well-known movements by Bach at such a fast tempo that it almost parodies the 'geometricism' Taruskin observes in modernist performance;[5] performances of Beethoven symphonies by Christopher Hogwood purposely aim for the amateur matter-of-factness that he believes belonged to the first performances.[6] This approach seems to link back to the postmodern tendency to break down the division between popular and elite artistic expression (HIP bringing with it, ironically, a new 'elite' body of historicist dogma).

Performers within HIP will disagree as to whether their movement promotes more or less virtuosity than the mainstream but it is obvious that at least the pioneer performers of HIP did not place progressive technical proficiency at a premium (historical spirit, textual and stylistic accuracy were generally more important, see p. 9 above). Certainly, with a greater interest in ornamentation and improvisation, different forms of virtuosity have been developed. But there is an obvious sense in which many historical instruments and their copies were not designed with the same stability and dependability as their more modern equivalents. The benefits and disadvantages of non-equal keyboard temperaments parallel and exemplify a general characteristic of earlier, pre-industrial instruments: it is a system in which certain intervals are acoustically pure at the expense of others, thus preventing a consistent average standard of accuracy across the range (in which, on the other hand, none of the intervals other than the octave would be acoustically pure). The HIP sensibility seems thus to reflect a pre-modern notion of hierarchy, although only the most brazen homology would suggest that this represents a nostalgia for the feudal (see pp. 203–17 below).

Some of these attitudes within HIP – such as those that promote a local culture, or the music of women composers – also seem to approach Born's vanguardist position. There is the common notion that HIP performers are turning their back on the rat-race of mainstream performance, that they are to some degree counter-cultural. They might break down the usual division of labour by playing some part in the making and maintaining of instruments, and by cultivating the historical knowledge of the performing practices. Whether this is ever true in practice is, of course, another matter; a comprehensive course in historical performance is, after all, far from the norm in educational institutions and many players do little more than impersonate the supposed HIPness of their elders, as Michelle Dulak has observed. The increasing professionalisation of HIP is also difficult to ignore with performers ever more likely to adopt traditional concert dress and signing up with professional concert agencies.[7]

Using Born's definitions, then, it would seem that Taruskin's modernist definition of HIP is misplaced. He may be quite correct in perceiving modernist elements, but these are reused and realigned in a way that is typical of the postmodernism that Born outlines. Nevertheless, further reading of both authors shows that they have radically different conceptions of how modernism and postmodernism should be applied to twentieth-century western musical culture. Born sees the Second Viennese School as the central bastion of musical modernism, with serialism 'for some decades the organizing force of musical modernism'

(Born, *Rationalizing Culture*, p. 48). She goes on to identify two rival tendencies of the 1920s and 1930s which – while part of a broader, eclectic modernism – she considers to demonstrate a 'proto' postmodernism. On the one side, there is the neoclassicism of Stravinsky and Hindemith which attempted to reinvigorate the present with materials and principles from earlier centuries; on the other, the appropriation of urban and folk-based popular musics by composers ranging from Debussy and Bartók to Gershwin and Vaughan Williams.

Born's view of the Second Viennese School as the central impetus for musical modernism becomes even more plausible as she begins to describe its hegemonic status for the leading European and American composers after the World War II. During the 1950s many composers sought to extend serialism to all other parameters of composition and became concerned with other tools of rationalism, such as mathematical and acoustical research and technological developments. This period engendered the archetypal modernist union of music theory and composition, often researched and produced by the very same person (p. 53).

Born sees the counterpoint between modernism and postmodernism as beginning around the 1920s and continuing throughout the remainder of the century, 'a continuous and centripetal antinomy, a kind of mobile stasis' (p. 64). Thus she seems to imply that there is no essential break in the late 1960s and 1970s, at the point when the first theories of postmodernism were formulated; to her these are presumably describing and theorising situations, movements and tendencies that, in some cases, had been around for several decades.

Taruskin, on the other hand, tends to follow more the time-line of the theorists of postmodernism and see virtually everything before the 1970s (and much after, to his distress) as symptomatic of modernism. If there is a central tradition of the modern, he believes this to be centred around Stravinsky (something, incidentally, substantiated by Schoenberg's own reference to Stravinsky as 'little Modernsky').[8] Only when composers and performers take note of audience interests and concerns, only when the political nature of music is openly and consistently acknowledged is the tyranny of modernism finally overcome (see pp. 19–22 above).

Already it has become clear that this chapter cannot quickly draw to a firm conclusion by proclaiming the movement of HIP to belong to either a modernist or a postmodernist culture. These terms themselves need to be examined afresh together with the very phenomenon they are meant to illuminate, HIP. And this, the object of study, will in turn influence the way the categories are defined and employed.

DEFINING MODERNISM

'So cold and optimistic, modernism. So sure it will get there eventually' (T. J. Clark)[9]

In the widest possible sense, modernity is a concept that can be traced back to the Renaissance or to the onset of modern rationalistic thought during the seventeenth century.[10] Some see a more definite beginning with the Enlightenment in the latter half of the eighteenth century, a movement that instigated a project of human development and self-realisation that, to some, is not yet complete.[11] Whatever the outer bounds of modernity, modernism, as a specific cultural movement is usually dated to the last decades of the nineteenth century, thenceforth dominating much of the twentieth century (at least so far as cultural ideology is concerned). 'Modern' in this sense implies particular defining characteristics and 'does not merely mean "the most recent"'.[12]

While T. J. Clark sees the roots of modernist art in the French Revolution itself, he suggests that it also stopped with the Revolution and began again at subsequent times of revolution (Clark, *Farewell to an Idea*, p. 52). To him 'modernity' is a slow, agonising recognition of contingency in the order of the human world, a progressive movement towards 'disenchantment' (that expression first formulated by Max Weber)[13] which engenders desperate attempts to create order (often with totalitarian regimes). Material and economic factors progressively rule human affairs, thus rendering tradition and its rituals redundant; so modernism is the desperate response to the very visibility of Adam Smith's 'hidden hand', revelling in its own technique as a surrogate for truth (Clark, *Farewell to an Idea*, pp. 7–8). The utopian element of modernism lies in its doctrinaire insistence on showing us the contingency of our beliefs and comforting modes of representation, but at the same time pointing towards some future natural order – a totality – that is ever on the verge of discovery.

Thus, if modernism by its very nature turns its back on history, it still carries with it a sense of historical destiny, of a process yet to be completed.[14] Zygmunt Bauman suggests that all residents in modernity are nomads who intend to settle but who are ever frustrated just as the final corner is turned, aspiring residents 'without a residence permit'.

If the pre-moderns tended to go round the same tracks time and again, the moderns always followed new tracks, but tracks that they had laid only momentarily before.[15]

Much recent musicological literature tends to view modernism as a consistent dogma based around objectivism, positivism, geometricism, depersonalisation and the separability of the aesthetic realm from all other aspects of life. While all these elements have at some point been relevant to modernism, they are by no means the only characteristics and, indeed, stand diametrically opposed to other elements of the movement. Moreover, if this modernist caricature is applied to the HIP movement there is unlikely to be more than the most superficial association since the depersonalised and autonomous view of art is fundamentally anti-historicist. Some of the more extreme modernists, Marinetti and Le Corbusier, for instance, were quite strident – to say the least – in their negation of history or the historicist stance. Modernism also tends to stress technique at the expense of the representation of 'reality', idea or mood, and thus lays a tremendous premium on competence and high technical achievement (Danto, *After the End of Art*, p. 7). This again runs against the 'traditional' HIP view that virtuosity is not the prime aim of musical performance and that, indeed, a more amateur or 'routine' approach may not be without its advantages.

Thus, it would seem, HIP is fundamentally opposed to this caricature of modernism, however much it might borrow some of the cultural trappings of the movement (such as playing in time). Taruskin cleverly suggests that HIP is, in fact, more modernist than historical, that its pretensions to historicism are merely a smoke screen for a thoroughly modernist aesthetic. But, however true this may be, it does not account for why the smoke screen of history came to be applied in the first place; why do the 'modernists' of HIP need the excuse of history? It would follow that either some sense of history must belong to modernism after all or that HIP belongs elsewhere. Perversely, it seems to me that both of these may be true: an historical sense is central to some forms of modernism and the antiquarian, positivistic side of HIP belongs precisely to an attitude – born of Romanticism – that many early modernists sought to overthrow.

While – as I have suggested already – few generalisations about modernism can be made, Born's sense of the oppositional nature of modernism is crucial. In opposing whatever went before (even other forms of modernism) it presupposes a fundamentally negational and dualistic form of thinking. As Michael Levenson observes in the field of Anglo-American literature:

The effect of such a dualism is to suggest a thorough historical discontinuity. Victorian poetry has been soft; modern poetry will be hard (Pound's terms). Humanist art has been vital; the coming geometric art will be inorganic (Hulme's terms). Romanticism was immature; the new classicism will be adult (Eliot's terms). 'We have got to clean out of history', wrote Lewis. 'We are not to-day living in history.'[16]

However fragmented or alienated a modernist artwork might appear, this fundamentally dualistic mentality ensures that there is some sort of ultimate unity. Thus most modernist endeavours will claim to represent something universal or potentially unified at some higher level. In this sense, the common HIP belief that the sounds of one era will have exactly the same aesthetic effect in another does suggest a form of universalism. The movement is modernist to the extent that it puts its faith in the materials at hand; they are where truth lies and will thus transcend the superficialities of historical culture. But, on the other hand, universalist thinking is common to virtually all western cultural models before postmodernism and this phenomenon in HIP may be just as much a Romantic characteristic as a modernist one.

MODERNIST CONCEPTIONS OF HISTORY

To rescue the relation between modernism and HIP we have to trace the historicist element within modernism itself. First, the more familiar, anti-historicist, stance in modernism is significant specifically for its negation of a previous interest in history; it is, in other words, dependent on history in the first place. The anti-historical moment (at least so far as positivist history is concerned) is usually associated with Nietzsche's essay 'The use and abuse of history' (1874). Paul de Man has made this central to his argument that 'history' is the most fruitful antonym for 'modernity', the necessary member of the moderist dyad.[17] Although Nietzsche's negative views of history – an interest in the past that inhibits life in the present, a concern only with origins – drew a large following, he does see room for certain kinds of history, particularly those which show the eternal and stable element in both past and present, namely the metaphorical relations suggested by myth. As I have suggested already, Nietzsche's use of history as a means of debunking religion was part of a general pattern of disenchantment that modernism, as a whole, reflected (see p. 49 above). Most significant for the purposes of this discussion, though, is his belief that history is a unity woven by the historian as dramatist (Longenbach, *Modernist Poetics of History*, p. 6). It is with this sense of history as a creative act and as something that shares certain elements with the present that many of the early modernists most concerned themselves. The prevailing mode of history against which they were reacting usually rested on the concepts of linear teleological progress, a model which, incidentally, continued to survive in much twentieth-century historical writing. Although modernist thought retained a sense of the universal and even of the overall system of history, this was not to be seen as akin to a beautifully rounded, and satisfyingly concluded, novel.

The historicist strands of early modernism were also reacting against another aspect of previous historiography: the scientific and 'neutral' approach to historical data, reflecting the ideology and methodology of positivism. This – symptomatic of the general domination of scientific positivism in the latter half of the nineteenth century – presupposed that historical facts spoke for themselves and that the historian could adopt the neutral pose of observer. Here, in essence, lies precisely the same problem that many today would associate with the more literalistic elements of HIP: namely, the insistence that historical data relating to performance are both sufficient and unambiguous, and that, once the letter has been followed, both the original meanings and the original experiences of the audience effortlessly follow. There is almost the scientistic presupposition that the presumed identity of sound will precipitate precisely the human chemical reactions of the past.

All this relates to the interesting notion of the roots of HIP lying in nineteenth-century positivism long before the later positivist turn after World War II. Moreover, the very development of the historical sense – on a large scale – was a feature of Romanticism, so that the concept of HIP must ultimately rely on a residue of Romantic sensibility (that movement against which so many HIP performers believed they were revolting).[18] Recent studies of nineteenth-century attitudes to performing earlier music show the early development of the historicist strain. José Bowen traces this specifically to Mendelssohn and, with the growing respect for the authority of the composer, also in such vanguardist figures as Berlioz and Wagner.[19] Furthermore, the mid-nineteenth century saw the birth of the collected edition, something which strove both for epic completeness and – so far as the science of musical editing had developed – fidelity to the 'original'. In a sense, historical positivism and purity seem to lie as a *prima prattica* behind the *seconda prattica* of the unfettered Romantic imagination, just as Palestrina and Bach were worshipped as the historical forefathers of modern music.

The new historical perspective of modernism, 'existential historicism', to borrow Fredric Jameson's term, receives its first comprehensive theory in the work of Wilhelm Dilthey. For this philosophy, living without history is an impossibility, since the historical consciousness is essential to the human spirit. Historical thinking results in a transhistorical consciousness that both belongs to the present and somehow conjures up a real sense of the past (Longenbach, *Modernist Poetics of History*, pp. 13–14). The historian needs to understand his own historicity and acknowledge that studying history is a specifically creative act. Gustav Droysen (1868) made the seminal point that facts do not objectively speak for themselves so that the historian must attempt to understand them through a specifically subjective consciousness. In Dilthey's famous formulation, the historian needs to rediscover the 'I in the thou'. Dilthey distanced himself from the Romantic sense of spirit as a metaphysical universal reason, by seeing spirit as objectified in the immediate reality and experience of life, and in human communication; each age shows a different 'objectivication' of this spirit. Thus this attitude suggests a coupling of the sense of transcendental spirit with the relativism of positivist historicism. Benedetto Croce further emphasised the modern, up-to-the-minute character of history by stating that 'every true history is contemporary history' (Longenbach, *Modernist Poetics of History*, pp. 15–27).

Both professional historians and literary figures concerned with history tended to distance themselves from empirical science and saw true history as lying in the artistic stance.[20] This point was forcefully articulated by Croce and also, as Longenbach goes on to show, by figures closely associated with literary modernism. Walter Pater believed that the most true and inspiring historicism was to be found in poetry (p. 37) and F. H. Bradley, the philosopher with whom T. S. Eliot was most closely associated, looked to poetry as the best model for historical enquiry (p. 162). This point has interesting resonances with the postmodern stance of Richard Rorty, someone who believes that our model for understanding ethical action should come more from literature than from the abstract ahistorical reason of traditional philosophy.[21] Obviously the most palpable difference between an 'ironist' such as Rorty ('the sort of person who faces up to the contingency of his or her own most central beliefs and desires', Rorty, *Contingency*, xv) and the existential historicists is the shameless certainty the latter seemed to assume, the mystical connection with the past that is guaranteed by the universal world spirit.

There is also a sense that, however much personal spontaneity and passion an existential historian might bring to history, he will soon come to see himself as part of an elite, ruling class of modernism. T. S. Eliot's establishment of a 'classicist' historical sense is the most obvious manifestation of this tendency. This exemplifies one of the typical paradoxes of modernism: it so often begins as an anti-establishment movement but ends up by engendering a new, even more elite, establishment. Postmodernists try to avoid this paradox, particularly by attempting to eradicate the distinction between high and low culture, but even they cannot avoid the establishment of a new canon of theoretical – rather than literary or artistic – texts and a discourse that demands considerable intellectual experience and privilege.

The literary bias of existential historicism is useful in framing a discussion of HIP because it likewise relates to an artistic activity that works in tandem with a specific use of history. The Anglo-American literary figures often crossed the divide between academic discipline and artistic endeavour, just as did the musical modernists of the 1950s, and just as historicist performers attempt to do today. Ezra Pound is a particularly interesting figure in this regard since he was very much drawn to Arnold Dolmetsch's early music movement and even made references to the musician in his poetry and criticism.[22] However, there are some discontinuities here: first, Pound's references to anti-emotionalism, purity, patterned play and 'wide-awake precision' hardly accord, in fact, with Dolmetsch's much more vitalist approach to music making. As Taruskin suggests, Pound may have 'creatively misread' Dolmetsch (p. 145). Moreover, Pound's early literary work suggests that he himself may once have had more in common with the vitalist Dolmetsch. He reacted violently against his training as a philologist, once complaining that academic scholarship makes no difference between the jewels and mud of literature, that everything is treated in like fashion regardless of its quality (Longenbach, *Modernist Poetics of History*, p. 49). His early *Three Cantos* try to relive the experience of history, pouring life into, and drinking the blood of, a dead past. Much of this provides a literary analogue to the theoretical concerns of the existential historicists.

In breaking from his positivist past Pound distances himself from the fact-gathering process by seeking only those facts that 'give us intelligence of a period' – in other words a blatant choice of those facts that confirm or support his particular sense of the past. It was better to go for a flavour of historical style than to cultivate deadly accuracy (Longenbach, *Modernist Poetics of History*, p. 96). Moreover, mixing of historical material from different periods, anachronisms, matter 'Not in the least' according to

Three Cantos I (pp. 110–11), since it is the interaction and breathing of life between past and present that counts. Pound is clearly not inclined to see history in discrete periods to be clearly defined from one another since they all filter into the spirit of the present.

After the publication of the *Three Cantos* in 1917 Pound himself began to react against existential historicism, becoming more interested in objective fact than personal inspiration or even a strong sense of authorial presence (pp. 143, 150); the misreading of Dolmetsch may be evidence of this same process. This also paralleled his move away from the social utility of art, away from an interest in humanity and democracy and more towards the strident futurism of Marinetti (Levenson, *A Genealogy of Modernism*, pp. 74–6). Now art was to set itself in direct opposition to both society and artistic tradition.

Meanwhile, it was Eliot who brought existential historicism to its most enduring, classical phase. Eliot maintained the relativist stance while believing that the critic with the greatest awareness of all the systems together came closest to being able to understand the whole (Longenbach, *Modernist Poetics of History*, pp. 165–6). Both his theoretical work and poetry pursue the contradictory aims of a strong authorial personality and the sense of individual subjects melting into one another to accomplish a greater unity (pp. 205, 209). So strongly does the past weave into the texture of the present that the past is itself changed by a new work in the present. Thus, for Eliot, tradition provides the key to 'the painful task of unifying' (p. 225), something which the individual is unable to accomplish alone.

There could be no doubt that Eliot would have disapproved of HIP in most of its manifestations, since he saw traditionalism (itself a Romantic throwback) as the best way of capturing the past in the present. This is most aptly shown by his reaction to a performance of Stravinsky's *Rite of Spring* in 1921 (Levenson, *Music, Art, and Metaphysics*, p. 195, Longenbach, *Modernist Poetics of History*, p. 198). To him the music was an excellent example of the present boldly gripping the past by using (as Debussy would have put it) all the modern conveniences:

[Stravinsky's music] did seek to transform the rhythm of the steppes into the scream of the motor horn, the rattle of machinery, the grind of wheels, the beating of iron and steel, the roar of the underground railway, and the other barbaric cries of modern life; and to transform these despairing noises into music. (Longenbach, *Modernist Poetics of History*, p. 198)

On the other hand, Eliot disliked the dancing in the Rite since it evoked a 'primitive ceremony' in which 'one missed the sense of the present', an antiquarian approach to history that evidenced nothing of the unified system of past and present so essential for Eliot's brand of existential historicism.

Taruskin's use of Eliot's 1919 essay, 'Tradition and the individual talent' as a stick with which to beat the anti-traditionalist nature of HIP certainly served its purpose of creating a more developed discourse about the ideologies of HIP. However, many elements of Eliot's attitudes to art and history seem to be precisely those features that Taruskin criticises in HIP. First, Eliot's desire that the writer abandon concerns with self expression and his 'insistence on order, intelligence and form' (Levenson, *Music, Art, and Metaphysics*, p. 159) seems to encapsulate the modernist traits that Taruskin sees in HIP. Indeed, Eliot's review of a production of *The Duchess of Malfi* (1919) reads almost like one of Stravinsky's tracts on musical performance or something from the Puritan wing of HIP:

For poetry is something which the actor cannot improve or 'interpret'; there is no such thing as the interpretation of poetry; poetry can only be transmitted; in consequence, the ideal actor for a poetic drama is the actor *with no personal vanity.*

...We required only that [Miss Catherine Nesbitt] should transmit the lines, but to transmit the lines is beyond the self-control of a modern actor, and so she did what the modern actor does: she 'interpreted' them. (Longenbach, *Modernist Poetics of History*, pp. 179–80)

In short, Eliot's view of performance, as of history itself, inveighs against the fragmented, limited experience of the individual; he believes that the individual should melt into the larger organic whole of inherited performing tradition.

Already it is clear that Eliot's 'classicist' view of history has developed a long way from earlier modernist conceptions of existential historicism in which the subjectivity of the historian was so highly prized. In many ways, it seems that this earlier historicism, with its loathing of positivism and objectivity, comes closer to the sort of historicism that characterises some of the more imaginative approaches to HIP, from Dolmetsch onwards.

It is not obvious how existential historians such as Dilthey, Croce and Pound might have viewed the various manifestations of HIP towards the end of the twentieth century. In one sense they might provide the theoretical justification for the 'vitalist' style that Taruskin characterises in the traditionalist performances of Strauss and Furtwängler, performances that might seek to capture the spirit of the composer's vision without necessarily complying with many of the historical details. On the other hand, they might relate to certain performers within HIP who do recreate or reuse certain historical objects with a particular subjective flair. This brings to mind figures from the early part of the century such as Arnold Dolmetsch, Wanda Landowska or Violet Gordon Woodhouse, or the more recent 'inspired antiquarians' such as Nikolaus Harnoncourt, Thomas Binkley and William Christie. These figures tend to take several historical elements – instruments, presentation or documented performance practices – and enter into the performance with such total confidence and boldness that we may actually believe we are transported to a past age as if at a seance (incidentally, a popular pursuit at the time of the existential historicists). Such performers may take a variety of attitudes towards historical evidence (ranging from the strenuously compliant to the cavalier) but what unites them is the force of their belief in the 'real' historical presence evoked by their efforts and a corresponding experience on the part of the audience.

The attitude and dilemmas of what I call the 'inspired' or 'mystical antiquarian' are excellently captured in Henry James's posthumous and unfinished novel, *The Sense of the Past* (1917).[23] Beverly Haviland suggests that James's conception of history provides a viable alternative to the triumphalist, Whig interpretation by making us sensitive to the 'incremental, infinitesimal dislocations in continuous relations' that characterise the difference between past and present and that, incidentally, pertain to all relations in general.[24] The story hinges on a problem that was evidently close to the author's heart, how a full commitment to the past can be reconciled with a commitment to, and acknowledgement of, life in the present.

Ralph Pendrel, a young American historian, inherits a house in London of which he takes possession in the wake of a failed romance at home. The story soon becomes one of hauntings and apparitions as Ralph sees his face in the portrait of a presumed ancestor and, after a bizarre encounter with the American ambassador – his lifeline to the present, as it were – he finds himself somehow confused with the ancestor and encountering a family that had rented the house nearly a century before. As if by intuition, he finds that he knows much about the family, and by inspired guesswork – genuinely creative history, this – he finds the portrait of the woman he is to woo in his pocket and recalls precise details about their house in the country. Soon, though, cracks begin to appear in this seemingly perfect assimilation to the past. Ralph somehow fails to conjure up knowledge of the absent younger sister and when she does appear in the final surviving pages, he suddenly recognises that she is somehow aware of the 'modern'. According to James's notes on the remainder of the novel, she is to be the true partner for the histori-cally transplanted Ralph even though she would have meant nothing to the ancestor with whom he has become fused. Through her sense of the modern (and the ultimate sacrifice of her love) he is able to recapture the present and eventually attain union with his original lover, Aurora (ap-parently the only 'happy end' in James's entire oeuvre, Haviland, *Henry James's Last Romance*, p. 29).

The novel articulates several themes that are crucial to the modernist conception of HIP. First, there is, quite simply, 'the sense of the past', a feel for the textures and sensations of the past, something that is somehow latent in modern life for the existential historian. An 'inspired antiquar-ian' in HIP might seek this as a way of enlarging the experience of the present, or in severe cases of the 'syndrome', of escaping it:

What he wanted himself was the very smell of that simpler mixture of things that had so long served; he wanted the very tick of the old stopped clocks. He wanted the hour of the day at which this and that had happened, and the temperature and the weather and the sound, and yet more the stillness, from the street, and the exact look-out, with the corresponding look-in, through the window and the slant on the walls of the light of afternoons that had been. He wanted the unimaginable accidents, the little notes of truth for which the common lens of history, however the scowling muse might bury her nose, was not sufficiently fine. He wanted evidence of a sort for which there had never been documents enough, or for which documents mainly, however multiplied, would never *be* enough. That was indeed in any case the artist's method – to try for an ell in order to get an inch. The difficult, as at best it is, becomes under such conditions so dire that to face it with any prospect one had to propose the impossible. Recovering the lost was at all events on this scale much like entering the enemy's lines to get back one's dead for burial; and to that extent was he not, by his deepening penetration, contemporaneous and present? (James, *The Sense of the Past*, pp. 48–9)

This description of Ralph, ever the artistic historian who by his very passion for history keeps a foot in the present, also shows a disdain for pos-itivistic detail, not least the truism that there are many things documents will never reveal. Indeed, Ralph is almost quite comically vague about some of the details of his new house – it is, rather, his passion that counts: 'He had said to himself crudely and artlessly "It's Jacobean" – which it wasn't, even though he had thought but of the later James. The intensity of the inference and the charm of the mistake had marked withal his good faith' (p. 62).[25] He certainly had questions as to whether all the things in the house had always been there or as to whether they had been acquired by some modern motive for the sake of suggestion; did they make a whole or did they fortuitously harmonise? Yet he was not inclined, as a first priority, to seek the advice of 'an obliging expert' (pp. 67–8).

Ralph's communion with history has a strong religious dimension, a thirst for real presence (which, as the novel progresses, graduates into a full transubstantiation that threatens to engulf Ralph's modern identity). In looking at the portrait of his ancestor hanging over the mantelpiece 'He was like the worshipper in a Spanish church who watches for the tear on the cheek or the blood-drop from the wound of some wonder-working effigy of Mother or of Son' (p. 77). In a typically Diltheyesque twist, the historical presence reflects and becomes the historian's own presence. After his intense contemplation the figure from a picture 'presented him the face he had prayed to reward his vigil; but the face – miracle of miracles, yes – confounded him as his own' (p. 86).

Not only does history become a religious devotion that is quite clearly essential to this modernist construction of subjecthood, there is also a sense of a sexual partnering of past and present (or is it necrophilia?). Ralph's very existence in the present is dependent on 'his deepening penetration' of the past (see above quote from p. 49), but there is also a sense in which his historical double looks forward to a consummation with the future:

I've been ridden all my life, I think I should tell you . . . by the desire to cultivate some better sense of the past than has mostly seemed sufficient even for those people who have gone in most for cultivating it . . . So you can fancy what a charm it was . . . to catch a person, and a beautifully intelligent one, in the very act of cultivating . . . His sense of the present! (p. 101).

In all, this shows us how inspired antiquarianism is part of the very modernist crisis of subjecthood, how a craving for history – establishing one's own historicity – plays a part in establishing the qualifications of a real, existing subject. Even Nietzsche acknowledged this much of the antiquarian mode of history: 'the contentment of the tree in its roots, the happiness of knowing that one is not wholly accidental and arbitrary but grown out of a past as its heir, flower and fruit, and that one's existence is thus excused and, indeed, justified'.[26] There may be something of this need to establish one's own presence in a disorienting world that lies behind the impulse for HIP, whatever the approach one might take to factual evidence. Like all forms of spiritual and conjugal immersion, there is always the danger that the balance can go too far in the direction of the 'other', resulting in precisely the loss of one's presence that one had so feared in the first place. In the case of Ralph's house, the historian tries to retain his awareness that he, as the future, is necessary to make the past speak:

It had determined clearly, on the apprehension then interchanged, to have as little to say to the future as an animated home, of whatever period, might get off with. 'And yet I am the future', Ralph Pendrel mused, 'And I dream of making it speak.' (p. 46)

The American Ambassador provides an important lifeline to the present, as James notes (p. 286), and he ultimately intends the novel to end with Ralph rescued from the past:

saved from all the horror of the growing fear of *not* being saved, of being lost, of being *in* the past to stay, heart-breakingly to stay and never know his own original precious Present again; that horror which his conception of his adventure had never reckoned with. (p. 288)

James also intends that certain modern features stay with the historically transported Ralph: he is slightly too refined, too rich, too 'clever' and has teeth that could not have been so well maintained a century before (pp. 289–91). The author states that, throughout he seeks to 'cling thus to, I work thus admirably, what I have called Ralph's insuperable and in-effaceable margin of independence, clinging taint of modernity' (p. 316).

The Ambassador's arrival at Ralph's door somehow brings him back to the present and to union with Aurora Coyne (pp. 343–51). The fact that Aurora had gone back on her resolution, in Book I, not to go with Ralph to visit the 'old world' after having suffered unspecified sorrow there, is extremely interesting in that it relates to a sense of geographical distance which parallels the historical distance with which Ralph is so obsessed. He is redeemed back into the present by his lover's ultimate acceptance of the 'old world' and her apparent dissatisfaction with the 'new' in New York. A magnanimous acceptance of historicity by those around him thus seems to be all it takes to rescue him from his antiquarian prison. Ralph (and presumably Henry James himself) is clearly frustrated by the denial of history in his home environment. With his English ancestry, James was especially sensitive to the anti-historical culture of America, perhaps its greatest cultural difference with Europe (see p. 173 below).

James makes the association of the vertical–horizontal (historical–geographical) axes explicit very near the beginning of the book. Ralph's inheritance of the house was to him a way of impressing Aurora with the history of his name, something that would balance its spread in the present: 'He was glad, at this hour, that his name, by common consent . . . cast a fine sharp traceable shadow, or in other words that his race had something of a backward, as well as of a not too sprawling lateral reach' (p. 3). The diachronic bias of the historian is balanced throughout much of the book by the geographic, synchronic perspective of 'old' and 'new' worlds, namely England and America. The former is totally defined and conditioned by its history while the latter tries to efface all historical traces from its culture: in telling Aurora about his ability to communicate with the past she replies 'It's very wonderful, you know, your having arrived at that, your having guessed it, in *this* place, which denies the old at every turn and contains so few such objects or surfaces' (p. 34). Later, on his voyage to Europe, he senses that past in the same way the discoverers of America must have sensed the future: 'He had sniffed the elder world from afar very much as Columbus had caught on *his* immortal approach the spices of the western Isles' (p. 58).

In all, James's historical trauma is almost certainly brought on by his experience in a rapidly modernising America. Moreover, this sense of disorientation may be similar to that which has since been experienced throughout the western world, and particularly in Europe in the years after the Second World War. With the near completion of modernisation and the hegemony of the media and information technology, the 'American problem' of the evaporation of historicity, that loss of the sense of being historically situated, has perhaps spread eastwards. This – the completion of modernisation, which removes all traces of the archaic – is precisely what Jameson defines as the *postmodern*, which is effectively the Americanisation of the entire western world (and much of the rest besides, see p. 163 below).

Thus an historical revival such as HIP may in part be an attempt in a postmodern world (i.e. one which I shall provisionally define as having largely completed the task of modernisation) to restore the sense of history that is otherwise lacking, just as Henry James did in the American context over half a century before. Another phenomenon of the last three decades of the twentieth century is the tremendous growth in non-western musical traditions and the assimilation of their performance practices in both America and Europe. It cannot be fortuitous, I believe, that HIP and ethnomusicology flourish at the same time; a sense of cultural disorientation is assuaged by trying to establish something certain about the past and by trying to assimilate an entirely 'other' culture. The conjunction of the two perspectives is latent in the musicological writing of Peter Jeffery and also in the attitudes of those performers who assume a 'transhistorical humanness' that links their study of history with their own performing activity (see p. 43 above). The impossibilities latent in these vertical and lateral perspectives may be surprisingly close: documents and other records will never bring back the past 'as it really was' in the same way that the observation of, and attempted assimilation within, a culture into which one was not born or raised, will never provide us with the 'true' experience of the native. Ralph's very attempt at understanding and explaining what he discovers in his own 'living history' simultaneously 'estranges him from his context rather than integrating him into it' (Haviland, *Henry James's Last Romance*, pp. 33–4). After all, 'his doubts and omissions appertain to his past, theirs to their future',[27] his psyche is orientated in the opposite direction to those of his ancestors. In all then, I maintain that James's modernist crisis of history is an important precursor of the crisis that has precipitated the flowering of HIP, a phenomenon born of a typically modernist concern with the loss of one's historical and subjective depth, and one that is itself now a feature of a postmodern situation. Our irreversible loss of the experience of the past is not necessarily without its advantages though. As Arthur C. Danto claims of the postmodern (or, as he prefers to call it, post-historical) condition, while we cannot relate to the art of previous eras exactly as those who lived then could, we can make their life-forms ours in a way that they never could. For we now have '[t]he sense in which everything is possible [which] is that in which all forms are ours' (*After the End of Art*, p. 198).

James also gives us a concept of history that is in many ways more subtle than that based on the obvious connections between epochs. By bringing out the dissimilarities between eras with complex differences that are small in themselves but interact in countless ways, he gives us a sense of how the process of events work, a metonymical rather than a metaphorical connection between past and present, one concerned with contiguity and difference rather than similarity (Haviland, *Henry James's Last Romance*, pp. 10–11).[28] The multiple strands we begin to perceive connecting us to the past thus represent part of the infinite number of strands that together constitute the profound difference between past and present. This acts as a corrective to conceptions such as the triumphalist Whiggish history that sees the great events of the past leading up (by resemblance) to a more perfect present. Indeed, it also provides an alternative to more recent 'New Historical' accounts that – almost in a neo-modernist manner – tend to generalise (and also isolate) the multi-layered conceptions of a particular era (synecdoche) or show interesting cross relationships between seemingly diverse elements (chiasmus). Whatever service New Historicism might give us in creating new histories of displaced 'others' its very methodology will constantly make new exclusions. James's metonymical approach offers us a sense of the texture of an era, in which seemingly insignificant details contribute to our sense of difference. Moreover, in an era like ours that fears the erosion of its links with the past, this web-like historical process might give us a sense of the way our present has been woven out of countless contiguous historical strands, unconnected in themselves but now crucially connected by our very own subjective historical position.

In a similar way, HIP has a customary concern for historical differences that are often dismissed as irrelevant by Whiggish conceptions of eras linked by a great tradition. Instead it offers us an imagined slice of the past in which familiar gestures and parameters are heard in a slightly different balance, one that may change when we move from the music of one era to another. Not only does this alert us to the countless differences between various pasts and the present, it also offers us a valuable insight into the way our very present is constructed and how it is linked to the past in a series of infinitesimal steps. From this point of view, the tables are turned: HIP, in its very modernist break with the conventional continuities between past and present ('tradition') offers us a new sense of the *contiguous* connection with our past, one that is recognisable through the very plurality of its differences.

FROM THE MODERN TO THE POSTMODERN

If modernists show a remarkable diversity of ideology and approach, even on the level of conscious debate, such diversity is that much greater in the case of postmodernism. Indeed, diversity and a plurality of local, group consensuses might together be one of the only secure defining characteristics of postmodernism. While the most literal sense of the term seems to describe something both coming after and distancing itself from modernism, many theorists try to show, like Born, that its origins may date back almost as far, if not further.[29] Many also see considerable continuities with modernism, or a reworking and recoding of modern styles. Indeed, one of the most plausible conceptions of postmodernism is that it represents not so much a turning away from the modern as a sign that modernisation has been successfully completed. T. J. Clark suggests that, with the final defining moment of the collapse

of the Berlin wall, we live in a changed world in which artefacts from
the not-yet-completed era of modernism are now more difficult to read,
in the light of its completion: 'Modernism is unintelligible now because
it had truck with a modernity not yet fully in place.'[30] Thus that which
we may perceive as the failure of modernism for our present needs is,
rather, the success of a modernity that renders strange the process that
strove towards it. If postmodernism represents a state of full 'disenchantment', the myths and utopias of modernism – its very resistance against
the process of disenchantment of which it itself was a part – must look
strangely archaic.

Anthony Giddens suggests that the reason the fully modernised world
is so profoundly different from any previous world is that much of the
world has a unitary framework of experience (basic axes of time and
space, and, one could add, global technologies), yet, paradoxically, it
is also one containing 'new forms of fragmentation and dispersal'.[31]
Perhaps it is this fragmentation in the wake of triumphal rationalisation
that is so unexpected in our present age, something that modernism
never quite predicted. On the assumption that the success of HIP is an
example of this fragmentation within western musical culture, much of
the remainder of this chapter will be concerned with the causes and
nature of this pluralist condition.

Perhaps the most tangible change to be associated with the closure
of modernism is the end of the Cold War, something that clearly facilitated the spread of the unitary framework afforded by technology and
communications.[32] Even more important is the strong evidence that the
Cold War (at least on the western side) acted as a life-support system for
late modernist art. Abstract Expressionism provided a contrast to the traditional and narrow culture of socialist realism while showing the virtues
of a free society that could accommodate art that is counter-cultural,
radical and otherwise controversial.[33] This archetypal ideological support also, conversely, ensured that the bourgeois myth of the separability
of art and politics was prolonged in a particularly intense manner during
the post-war years (Cockcroft, 'Abstract Expressionism', p. 89).

Some writers acknowledge that while a change has undoubtedly taken
place 'postmodernism' is the wrong label to apply. Arthur C. Danto, for
instance, associates the term 'postmodernism' with a specific style of art
('camp'), one that is not especially significant in the long term, although
Danto would be the last to have much time for notions of 'significance'
and 'long term' in themselves.[34] Instead he uses the term 'contemporary'
to describe the wider cultural phenomenon of art that does not need to

adhere to the modernist canon, that 'has no brief against the art of the past, no sense that the past is something from which liberation must be won' (p. 5), and that – by its very nature – cannot be defined by a single style (p. 15). He also uses the term 'post-historical' to describe that art which does not conform to a specific historical narrative of progress (i.e. that which goes 'beyond the pale of history' by adopting styles that before would have been considered irrelevant or trivial to the 'true' course of history). Thus in his definition, HIP, with its intense – and often indiscriminate – cultivation of history, would exist precisely because it is 'post-historical'. Karol Berger also stresses the continuities with modernism, suggesting on the one hand that 'we are the postmodern sort of moderns' in acknowledging 'a plurality of coexisting life forms and partial, local stories that make sense of these life forms' (p. 7), and on the other hand that, in preserving some sense of the need to discriminate and make distinctions of value, we are modernists (p. 241).[35] In other words, in the messy reality in which we have to live there is inevitably a competition between different values and life forms, one that cannot simply be wished out of existence. Thus Berger senses a danger in that the term 'postmodernism' could deceive us into thinking that crucial moral choices are merely of a piece with choices between brands of car or styles of coffee.

The term 'postmodernism' certainly becomes irksome through overuse and indiscriminate application. It often seems to promise false hopes or to work as a term of unjustified abuse. Yet I would agree with Fredric Jameson in believing that it is still a useful tool if we are ever called on 'to name the system', that it explains more of the contemporary situation in the developed world than it darkens or confuses.[36]

DEFINING THE POSTMODERN

If postmodernism is to be considered as something more than just another strand of modernism it is unlikely to represent a symmetrical opposition to the latter. Condemnation of whatever has just come before is, after all, one of the most stable characteristics of the modernist stance. Neither modernism nor postmodernism should be viewed in isolation and an awareness of the constant interaction between the two might prevent us from settling into the complacency of continual celebration or condemnation.

There is also the issue of whether postmodernism refers to a specific style or form of cultural production (as Danto sees it), to a general attitude to cultural discourse and academic procedures (perhaps beginning with the era of poststructuralism), or to a much wider cultural phenomenon involving both lifestyle and economics. The first category is arguably the most limited and time-specific, and is often characterised by a playful, ironic style that, to a modernist, would be profoundly trivial and superficial. The second relates to how we treat issues such as history or the canonicity of artworks. Both the conscious historical attitudes of figures within HIP and the type of historical thought that HIP makes possible or plausible might relate or contribute to this wider cultural discourse (as I have attempted to do in the preceding chapters). The third category is undoubtedly the most significant for the purposes of our genealogy of HIP, suggesting as it does a fundamental change in the global situation of which the other two categories are symptomatic. On the other hand, postmodernism is problematic from the point of view that it is simply too all-embracing. Like Anselm's Ontological Argument for the existence of God, once the concept has been mooted, everything can be taken as evidence for it, and, conversely, to suggest that something is *not* a symptom of it, is to question its very existence.

It is with Charles Jencks's successive definitions of postmodernism within architecture that we may have one of the most succinct and consistent formulations of the first category, of postmodernism as a style or cultural product. The central element of Jencks's postmodernism is his concept of 'double-coding', which in its simplest sense refers to the combining of some historical allusion with something from the present.[37] This finds an obvious analogy in HIP in those performances that purposely combine the old with the new – the Hilliard ensemble performances with saxophone, the avant-garde productions of Peter Sellars and Mark Morris that employ period instruments in the pit, or groups specialising in Mediaeval or women's music coupled with popularising or New Age elements (see p. 40 above).

On the other hand, most 'straightforward' proponents of HIP will show no obvious sign of double-coding; some such performers may even consciously adhere to an antiquarian mind-set that simply seeks to ignore the present. But, regardless of the attitudes within the movement the reasons for its success in the late twentieth century might actually witness a form of double-coding, albeit in a much weaker sense than Jencks would intend. The supremely modern advances of technology and media expansion bring what were hitherto considered inadequate sounds (at least in the setting of a large concert hall) to a public that listens to the music in an astonishingly wide range of local situations: 'Now we can hear *Aida* on the patio and the St Matthew Passion in the shower', to quote Richard Taruskin.[38] There is thus a double-coding both in the means of production and (to depart even further from Jencks's original conception) in the reception of the music. As I have already suggested, this is not so much evidence of a decline in the historical awareness of art as an attempt to add something historical to the all-pervading presence of technology, a way of giving depth and difference to a lifestyle that threatens to become all too standardised (see p. 40 above).

Jencks, from the time of his earliest discussions of the postmodern, connects it with an arrest of the culture of progress and avant-garde extremism, returning partially to tradition and promoting a much closer communication with the public (Rose, *The Post-Modern*, p. 101). Postmodernism in this sense could be considered the optimistic description for the end of linear progress that is so pessimistically observed by modernists (such as Robert Morgan, see p. 10 above). While the turning back from modern 'advances' has an immediate resonance with HIP it is important not to see too many close analogies between an architectural conception and the performance art of music. After all, the tradition of which Jencks speaks is immediately latent in existing architectural examples and many more documentary descriptions and representations of buildings. Literally none of the performances to which HIP aligns itself exists (unless one is referring to the early years of recorded sound), so it can hardly be returning to tradition in the purest sense. Moreover, the issue of tradition is particularly complex in the context of musical performance. Many would consider 'returning to tradition' to mean a reversion to the romantic/modernist 'mainstream' rather than the reinvention of lost practices.

Of all Jencks's descriptions of postmodernism it is perhaps in his call for communication between the architect and the public (i.e. the closing of the gap between artist and customer) that he comes closest to the most pervasive definitions of the movement. Not only is the gap between critic and audience closed (cf. Taruskin, *Text and Act*, p. 20 above), but also that between artist and audience and between professional and amateur. Benjamin relates the steady effacement of the distinction between an artistic producer and the public to the enabling effects of mechanical reproduction.[39] Much of this resonates with Dreyfus's observations of the culture of HIP, at least as it stood at the beginning of the 1980s (see p. 9 above), and also with Kay Shelemay's ethnography of the Early Music Movement, which suggests that the movement, at least in Boston, had its roots in amateur culture with a 'push toward professionalism'.[40]

Jencks's concern for 'communicating with the public' matches some aspects of HIP, but not others. On the one hand, HIP, with its initial indifference to the purely virtuosic, obviously allows the potential for more public involvement in music making (witness the growth in amateur early music groups); moreover, some of its practitioners seek to overcome the traditional formality of concert performance and communicate more directly with the audience. There is also the issue of a public more interested in 'alternative' forms of culture, in music that may not make grand spiritual and metaphysical demands on the listener, music as background, or music that supposedly recreates a state of timeless contemplation. On the other hand, there is a sense in which HIP makes claims for a superior, specialised form of knowledge in a manner which is just as elitist as that of the modernist mainstream, also a sense in which its practitioners insist that the public hear new/old modes of interpretation whether it wishes to or not. Here, HIP, in at least its earlier manifestations has retained a modernist 'shock of the new'. In conclusion, though, it is clear that HIP has capitalised on the pervasive postmodern call for a breakdown of traditional barriers, even if, in practice, it has often produced new forms of stratification.

Another feature of Jencks's theory is his emphasis on pluralism, suggesting that a versatility in several styles increases the architect's palette: 'if the architect were trained in four or five different styles, then he could control the way his forms communicate with much greater effect' (Rose, *The Post-Modern*, p. 104). This is a complex issue: does Jencks's pluralism not carry with it the danger that the pluralist architect will have actually less commitment to any style at all? A subconscious, culturally confident adherence to the 'mainstream' style of one's age and community might give way to a dazzling superficiality that serves all with equal indifference. On the other hand, it may be that this is precisely what the postmodern condition entails – an ever-changing flux of styles and cultural allusions that harms no one in a potentially dangerous and overcrowded world. There is no doubt that HIP displays a pluralism along the lines Jencks suggests, although each individual specialist may only work in one particular style and very few have been able to master the 'four or five' Jencks prescribes (Norrington, Harnoncourt and Gardiner being obvious exceptions). The overall picture of HIP is of a wide palette of performing styles, each appropriate to a particular composer, style or age; even within one particular style there is often more divergence than may have been evident before the advent of HIP. Nevertheless, some scholars of recent performance do perceive stylistic similarities across the entire field of HIP (see p. 15 above), and – the extreme divergences evident by the 1990s notwithstanding – there does indeed seem to have been an 'early music vernacular' that can render diverse recordings of the same repertoire virtually indistinguishable.⁴¹

Jencks's 1986 definition of double-coding (Rose, *The Post-Modern*, p. 107) suggests that the combination of modern techniques with some form of traditional building enables postmodern architecture to communicate both with the public (which is presumed not to appreciate modernist architecture) and with a specialist minority. This may be his way out of a superficial or populist view of the postmodern, by advocating a construction that appeals to the general public without losing some level of specialist excellence. Nevertheless, it is clear that a distinguished modernist mainstream persists in architecture that is increasingly at odds with the historicising tendencies of both postmodern architects and preservationists (see chapter 6, pp. 184–7 below). A similar sort of increasing split has emerged between the HIP artist and the professional musicologist, just as there has – on a much greater scale – between the musicologist and the composer. Perhaps it is a 'rule' of the postmodern world that the breaking down of one particular boundary engenders the further isolation and splintering of yesterday's avant-garde. The pluralist flux is not necessary always a happy one.

In the face of both criticism and in the wake of more architectural experiments, Jencks has both refined and limited his theory of the postmodern. His opening distinction of the postmodern from the modern accords extremely well with the objectives of HIP: 'For Modernists the subject of art was often the process of art; for postmodernists it is often the history of art' (Rose, *The Post-Modern*, p. 119). For instance, in traditional western performance, the conservatoires will insists on the learning of basic technique and then an exhaustive study of the repertoire (as defined by the current state of concert and competitive performance). In HIP, to the extent that there is any formalised education (and many of the most famous practitioners did not embark on a specific 'early music' course), the emphasis is clearly on the historical conditions of the repertory, performance and instrument.

The second category of the postmodern – that pertaining to cultural discourse – is most famously outlined by Jean-François Lyotard's attempt to identify a systematic change in human thought. In contradistinction to Jencks's eclectic historicism, Lyotard's postmodernism retains something of the avant-garde charge of modernism.⁴² He sees postmodernism as reflecting a state of culture resulting from transformations in the game rules for science, literature and the arts (Rose, *The Post-Modern*, p. 55) and it is most evident in an 'incredulity towards metanarratives'. The latter – to him a specifically 'modern' phenomenon – are to be seen as grand narratives (e.g. the historicism of Hegel, Marxism, capitalism or even 'progress' per se) which serve as the presuppositions behind any kind of discourse. Danto's conception of 'The end of art' is a significant parallel to Lyotard's conception of the death of grand narratives; far from meaning the end of any art activity whatsoever, it refers to the end of the *narrative* of Art, in which an ongoing story demands a sequence of necessary stages (Danto, *After the End of Art*, p. 4).

Lyotard's postmodernism sees a fragmentation of the large, totalising narratives into 'flexible networks of language games'. He has been severely criticised for assuming that adherence to local language games is going to preserve us from terrorism any more than adherence to modernist metanarratives will (see p. 22 above). Indeed, the undermining of a binding concept of truth and a diminution of the moral responsibility of the subject might well lead to a situation even more dangerous than before. Nevertheless, Lyotard does seem to have faith that the postmodern world of knowledge will lead to a healthy democratisation of society: the computer, for instance, will become the potential means of opening up all information and data to the public at large.[43]

Lyotard's theory seems well substantiated by changes in the political world. While modernity had promised a new world order that would finally eclipse the quaint differences between cultures, postmodernity sees a sudden resurgence of local and ethnic identities and the reinvention of traditions. To many, these are now the only way of finding order and of recapturing a sense of cultural grounding, 'the long roundabout of modernity has brought us to where our ancestors once started. Or so it may seem.'[44] The world of diverse communities, happily returning to whatever traditions give their life significance is a cause for celebration for anti-foundationalist philosophers such as Richard Rorty. Others, such as Zygmunt Bauman, remind us that just as the quest for designed perfection in modernity often dealt with difference in ways that ultimately led to genocide, postmodern tribalism could lead to heterophobia, countless small-scale practices of separating, banishing and exiling (Bauman, 'Parvenu and Pariah', pp. 32–4). Moreover, the strong beliefs in diversity and relativism threaten to become the secret police of the critical mind and ultimately leave us powerless in the face of intolerance. Bauman's solution is to suggest that we acknowledge some of the continuing principles of modernity, most notably the general hope of making things better than they are, something that a large proportion of the diverse communities can share.

Whatever its political implications, Lyotard's concept of the local language game does describe something of the condition of musical performance since the advent of HIP and other experimental approaches to composition and performance. Instead of one central western tradition (one that admittedly has contained considerable variety) the historical imperative has produced at least one more, based on entirely different conceptions of what a good performance may be. This new tradition itself has itself split into many more, producing musical results ranging from the ultra-objective to the neo-Romantic. Within these further strands, those that doubt that performance can be securely based on the value-neutral accumulation of objective facts would count as veering most towards Lyotard's postmodern since they are sceptical of the 'grand narrative' of objective knowledge. Then there are the many musical movements other than HIP, including experimentalism, minimalism, performance art and an increasing flexibility of the boundaries between 'classical' and 'popular' musics. As Patricia Waugh has suggested, 'we are living in a period where the multiplication of value systems has produced a major crisis of legitimation (which, of course, is part of Lyotard's definition of the postmodern condition)'.[45]

Jameson would probably account for the HIP phenomenon within his concept of the 'group' and the micropolitics surrounding it, something which provides a social equivalent of Lyotard's language game. To him the proliferation of small groups results from the confluence of increased democracy, the supposed freedom of the market and the proliferation of the media (the latter being crucial to HIP).[46] No longer does postmodern society countenance 'the older kinds of solitude' (misfits, solitary rebels and antiheros striking a blow at the 'system', Jameson, *Postmodernism*, pp. 321–2); such figures, who were previously seen as harmless eccentrics (the Dolmetsch phenomenon in HIP comes to mind here), have now become 'leaders' of accredited groups, organised and classified with 'the appropriate experts' (p. 322). Moreover, each new group creates its own new markets that help solidify its identity. As Terry Eagleton ironically puts it, 'Postmodernism is thus a grisly parody of socialist utopia, having abolished all alienation at a stroke.'[47] The ideology of groups is a direct corollary of the 'death of the subject': 'the aesthetic attack on originality, genius and modernist private style, the waning of "charisma" in the media age and of "great men" in the age of feminism, the fragmentary, schizophrenic aesthetic' (Jameson, *Postmodernism*, p. 348). Again this seems to correspond directly to HIP in its conductorless, anti-heroistic mode. If there is any one thing that links critics of HIP, Left, Right and Centre (Adorno, Scruton and Taruskin, to be precise), it is their revulsion at the group mentality – Adorno's 'resentment listeners' – at those who seem to revel in a pious form of eccentricity.[48] Certainly, it is easy to share their distaste for the pious, the complacent or the smug, but there is also the danger of a certain nostalgia for conformity.

Lyotard's sense that the postmodern work and text will have more of the character of an *event*,[49] resonates with some aspects of pre-modern performance – the unattainable goal of many HIP practitioners – which was often more event-based than work-based.[50] Lyotard's consequent reduction of the agency of the artist also seems to describe those in HIP who have privileged historical style over the uniqueness of any particular work or composer. Thus HIP often draws more attention to itself and the problems it has raised than to the greatness of the more canonical works it may perform. This tendency may sometimes be enervating in the context of works that were conceived in an age of individual genius, but it may also be beneficial for music written according to other values (see p. 101 above).

Jameson provides a rather different fate for what used to be the autonomous work within modernism. Works now have more of the nature of text (Jameson, *Postmodernism*, p. xvii), or rather, the language of the work has been replaced by a sense of 'text' and textuality, which tends to underplay the organic or the monumental (p. 77). Everything we encounter in daily life is to be read as a text and what used to be considered a single text or work is to be seen as an immense collection of various intersecting texts. In other words, works are no longer viewed in isolation but participate in a much wider process of intertextuality, what some historians would call the 'thick context'. Jameson's emphasis on textuality certainly recalls many recent developments in musicology which have moved away from treating pieces as transhistorical wholes and, of course, it resonates with the attitude of HIP towards greater interest in variable sources, performance contexts, wider performing conventions and the influence of instrumental technology. If the aim within HIP is towards defining a work more closely, policing its limits of variability, adding historical factors to its unique identity, and, above all, finding closure at a certain point in the inquiry, then this attitude will fall more in the modernist direction. If, on the other hand, it serves to destabilise a work that is otherwise considered a timeless, unique component of the repertory, and is somehow open-ended and ever-amenable to new levels and angles of inquiry, then it will lean more towards the postmodern. It is quite possible that any particular proponent of HIP may display a combination of both these attitudes. But, if Jameson is right, the increased emphasis on the work as the intersection of a bundle of texts is itself part of the postmodern mindset.

THE POST-INDUSTRIAL AND THE SIMULACRUM

Moving now to the larger conception of postmodernity as a basic change in cultural and economic circumstances, one concept often associated with postmodernism and clearly related to HIP, is that of the post-industrial.[51] Certainly, the Arts and Crafts movement, as an early manifestation of a post-industrial tendency, coincides and intersects with the early attempts at HIP by Arnold Dolmetsch (see chapter 6, p. 209 below). Arthur Penty's call in 1917 for a return to a decentralised, artisan society based on small workshops seems to associate the post-industrial with the pre-industrial, just as postmodernism – in its more modernist guise as a sense of negation – often resonates with the pre-modern (Rose, *The Post-Modern*, pp. 21–5). This was also central to William Morris's Arts and Crafts movement and written up in his 1891 allegory *News from Nowhere* (see p. 184 below). More recent definitions of the post-industrial, particularly those of Marshall McLuhan and Daniel Bell, have tended to focus on the growth in technology and the concept of the 'global village' and the general move from heavy industrial production to service industries (Rose, *The Post-Modern*, pp. 26, 31–2).

Jameson suggests that the move to new technologies has had a profound effect on our capacities for artistic representation. While machinery in all its forms provided an exciting visual (and sonic) image for most forms of modernism, more recent technology is far less tangible:

Such machines are indeed machines of reproduction rather than of production, and they make very different demands on our capacity for aesthetic representation than did the relatively mimetic idolatry of the older machinery of the futurist moment, of some older speed-and-energy sculpture. (Jameson, *Postmodernism*, p. 37)

Rose, however, cautions against defining the post-industrial as part of the postmodern, since the increasing dominance of technology is a direct result of late modernity and the forces of modernisation (Rose, *The Post-Modern*, p. 27). Moreover, old forms of modernisation continue alongside the newer ones, which are themselves continuations of the earlier forms. Thus, to Rose, the post-industrial fits only into a concept of the postmodern that sees it as more of a continuation of modernity than as a distinct break; to her it is perhaps a 'necessary' but not a 'sufficient' cause in the development of the postmodern (Rose, *The Post-Modern*, p. 129).

However, if Baudrillard is correct in observing a distinct change in mentality, where many cannot distinguish reality from a presentation or creation of the media, then it does seem that there has been some form of definite break within modernity, however continuous the technological progress. Something of this change of consciousness was already grasped by Walter Benjamin: the proliferation of copies (he is talking mainly about the visual arts here) means that the 'aura' of the original begins to wither, authenticity and power now residing in multiples. Hillel Schwartz develops this position by suggesting that it is not the aura of artworks that withers but the assurance of our own liveliness.[52] Far from leading to a replacement of the original by the copy, Schwartz believes that the very concept of the original is enhanced, that we arrive at a new experience of originality through the world of copies (*The Culture of the Copy*, p. 212). However, it is becoming increasingly difficult to distinguish a creation from an imitation to the extent that a pilot will experience the same trauma using the simulator as when he is flying a plane (p. 268). Schwartz notes the conflation of the concepts of preservation and restoration in the reconstruction of historic sites which choose that which authenticates over the 'authentic'.

Both Baudrillard and Jameson find Plato's conception of the 'simu-lacrum' essential to this new mentality, namely the concept of an identical copy for which no original exists (Jameson, *Postmodernism*, p. 18). This re-lates to the culture of the image in contemporary society in which media icons actually come to define themselves by the image that has been created for them. As Walter Benjamin suggested, the artificial build-up of the film personality outside the studio is a direct response to the film medium's 'shrivelling of aura', as a form of mechanical reproduction that takes us away from the 'authentic' presence of the actor (Benjamin, 'The Work of Art in the Age of Mechanical Reproduction', p. 231). Jameson also relates the simulacrum specifically to the sense of historical recon-struction in period films, something which 'endows present reality and the openness of present history with the spell and distance of a glossy mirage' (Jameson, *Postmodernism*, p. 21). Much of this is part of Jameson's belief that the late twentieth century has lost its historicity and has a growing sense of the remoteness of its historical background. As I will try to show, the concept of HIP as a simulacrum of a lost historical past is the most convincing way of relating the movement to the conditions of a postmodern age, as something that is indeed an 'authentic' representation of a cultural situation.

Although HIP ostensibly turns its back on the achievements of modernisation it seems to relate to developments in technology at virtually every turn. Schwartz notes that Dolmetsch was working in precisely the era that the phonograph, player piano and sprocketed film were developed (Schwartz, *The Culture of the Copy*, p. 374–5). Not only might Dolmetsch's movement have been a conscious retreat from such progress, it may well have been inspired by the new conceptual possibilities arising from such developments: piano rolls were, after all, the waxworks of music and the production of a plausible copy may well have led to a renewed interest in the original. The performance that was already lost could somehow be replayed. A similar relationship may operate in the more recent age of the commercial success of HIP: the sound of old instruments and a variety of performing formats – not necessarily practicable in large concert halls – are more than adequately captured by the new recording and broadcasting technologies. Not only does the culture of recording influence our attitudes to live performance, there is also a sense in which our experiences of the two media are becoming ever closer to one another. This blending of original and copy may work particularly well for HIP, since it might condition us to distinguish less sharply the difference between the modern 'reconstruction' (of HIP on CD) and the absent original performance in history. In other words, listening to a CD, as a copy of a live performance, might enhance the sense of the (now lost) actual performance in the studio as authentically representing an absent original. If stereo comes so close to reproducing the real experience of music, the time may be coming when music can only 'be imagined in terms of the model stereo provides', and such a model could presumably include the imagination of an actual historical performance.[53] HIP thus lies directly at the crossroads of the modern and postmodern. A thoroughly modern development leads to a new mind-set that could be defined as postmodern, the pyrrhic victory of the modern itself.

HIP clearly also belongs to the post-industrial to the degree that the latter may show an affinity with, or re-admittance of, the pre-industrial. This is evident in the remarkable growth in the number of instrument makers reusing ancient crafts in both America and Europe (see also p. 191 below). The period from Dolmetsch to the last decade of the twentieth century has been characterised by an ever-increasing interest in historical methods and the precise duplication of existing historical instruments. This shows a clear departure from the division of labour customarily associated with industrialisation (and, soon after, modernism), in that the (post?)modern instrument maker will design and oversee all stages of the production, including research and procurement of materials. Jencks makes a similar call for the pre-industrial within the context of postmodern architectural production, something that seems almost a cottage-industry with closer communication between smaller architectural offices and their clients (Rose, *The Post-Modern*, p. 104).

The same move away from the division of labour is evident in the attitudes of many musicians who take an interest in the choice of instruments, the historical sources of the music and performance style and the interpretation and presentation of the music in public. Ironically, several performer-composers in pre-modern history seem to show a tendency in precisely the opposite direction: e.g. Lully's firm direction of his players, treating them as cogs in a large machine; Bach's desire that instrumentalists should specialise – and so excel – on only one instrument, thus taking only one job within the larger production of performance.

Nevertheless, it is clear that 'industrial' control of a large body of performers reaches its peak with the performance aesthetic of Stravinsky and the authoritarian control of Toscanini, something that could lead to a monotonous uniformity of performances and performers. Bach's complaint that performers had to master several national styles at once has been turned on its head by HIP, where performers, in theory, at least, seek to recover stylistic differentiations between different repertories, eras and nationalities, however much the result might be coloured, and sometimes standardised, by unconscious modern conceptions of interpretation.

POSTMODERNISM AND THE LOSS OF HISTORICITY

Jameson begins his study of postmodernism with an interesting assertion relating our present condition to the 'attempt to think the present historically in an age that has forgotten how to think historically in the first place' (Jameson, *Postmodernism*, p. ix). With a world of completed modernity, capital seeping into all areas of culture, history has lost its active charge as something grounding present traditions or promising a better future. This leads to a sense of 'historical deafness, an exasperating condition (provided you are aware of it) that determines a series of spasmodic and intermittent, but desperate, attempts at recuperation' (p. xi). This relates to his notion of the simulacrum, the desire for a copy of an original that has ceased to exist, that is unknown or somehow in-accessible, or that never really existed in the first place. In some ways the problem of eroded historicity – if it is indeed a problem – is exactly that which Henry James suffered and expressed through his character Ralph Pendrell (see p. 143 above) a century before, but now spread to western culture as a whole. James identified a specifically American problem of isolation from history, something that drove Ralph to such desperate and supernatural measures. The historicity that Jameson affirms is so difficult to reclaim today is primarily 'a perception of the present as history; that is, as a relationship to the present which somehow defamiliarizes it and allows us that distance from immediacy which is at length characterised as a historical perspective' (Jameson, *Postmodernism*, p. 284).

By implication though, Jameson's 'de-historicised' present must have a degree of immanence and immediacy that was not so possible before. Moreover, however nostalgic one may be for that historical perspective of the present, there is no means of recovering it precisely as it was. Perhaps postmodern contentment – if there were any – would approach that of Nietzsche's cows, happily grazing off the present moment. Yet Jameson is surely correct to sense that we retain a residue of historical thought, one that cannot simply be wished out of existence. The antidote to this sense of being historically marooned generally takes one of the various forms of *historicism*.

Jameson explains the postmodern state as a historical reality that is specifically the cultural reflex of late, multinational capitalism (p. 49). Thus it cannot be one optional style that can be chosen at will, neither can it simply be repudiated or celebrated. Any objections to postmod-ernism therefore go hand in hand with classical objections to capitalism itself (p. 343). Not only does multinational capitalism represent a system from which we have no recourse to distance ourselves, but the system cannot be grasped in any way as a whole. This 'reality' of economic and social institutions that cannot be conceived as a totality is where Jameson situates the 'postmodern sublime' (p. 38). In this situation the unevenness of modernism, in which archaic elements still persisted, has been swept away (pp. 309–10).

This suggests that definition of the postmodern – by T. J. Clark and others – as representing the state achieved with the completion of mod-ernisation. Thus there is a sense in which the postmodern (as Lyotard also suggested) must be more 'modern' than modernism itself.[54] In this state of completed modernisation the very sense of the word 'new' loses its resonance, something which presumably strikes a fatal blow at historicity. Furthermore, even the word *modernisation* becomes a mis-nomer in a world in which everything is already 'modern'.

The omnipresence of multinational capitalism goes hand in hand with the spread of new technologies, although Jameson seems to retreat from Baudrillard's contention that technology is the 'ultimately determining instance' of contemporary life and cultural production. Rather, the new technologies provide a 'representational shorthand' for understanding the incomprehensible network of power in late capitalism (Jameson, *Postmodernism*, pp. 37–8). It is presumably as if the 'virtual reality' evoked by new technology provides a metaphor for the intangible 'reality' of multinational capital. In an interesting twist, Jameson suggests that 'late capitalism' should perhaps be renamed 'infantile capitalism' in that ev-eryone born into it takes it for granted and, having known nothing else, is not aware of the friction and resistance that gave birth to the system in the modern age. The 'infantile capitalist' experiences a life of 'roller skates and multinationals, word processors and overnight unfamiliar postmod-ern downtown high rises' (p. 367).

With the roots of historicity severed the historical urge returns in the form of a blind historicism, in other words, a historicism that is somehow detached from our present condition. Not only is a 'true' connection with our history unavailable, it will ever be out of reach by virtue of our state of total modernisation. In an interesting reworking of the modernist histor-ical dictum that history is always created afresh in the present, Jameson suggests that it is possible not only to generate history out of the present, but also 'to endow today's fantasy projections and wish fulfillments with the force if not of a reality, then at least of what grounds and inaugurates realities' (p. 376). To an earlier human subject, aware of his historical being and able to think 'historically', postmodern historicism, with its omnipresent and indiscriminate appetite for dead styles and fashions will seem more like a caricature of historical thinking (p. 286). This seems to sum up precisely the feeling a mainstream musician, brought up on the 'traditional' performing conventions which one believed to be handed down from generation to generation, will feel towards the HIP musician who seems to create history, convention and tradition out of thin air.

In original postmodern art this detachment from history means that an artist can recover a style or idiom as if it were an *objet trouvé*, detached entirely from its original meaning and significance (p. 174). This phe-nomenon, which semiologists might refer to as the ultimate free play of signifiers no longer attached to what they signified, also ties in with Jameson's observation of the general waning of affect in the postmodern world, corresponding to the decline of the subject and the end of the concept of a unique, personal distinctive style (pp. 10, 15). Jameson uses the word 'nostalgia' cautiously for the omnivorous, even libidinal historicism of the postmodern, for there is nothing of the 'pain of a properly modernist nostalgia with a past beyond all but aesthetic retrieval' (p. 19). It is a curiously detached sense of nostalgia, one that is more of a choice than a necessity, and one that is set in motion by historicist details of presentation (such as in period films) that immediately 'program the spectator to the appropriate "nostalgia" mode of reception' (p. 20). This might suggest then, that the contemporary audience for classical music almost expects historical details in the presentation of the music at the same juncture that performers and scholars have sought to inaugurate them. Precise details of periodicity are thus expected across the range of the arts and, in cases of the mixing of style or periods in 'double-coded' productions, a specifically postmodern energy of stylistic conflict and cross-reference arises, something that could never have been evoked by the multiple temporalities of, say, a Mediaeval cathedral that was built over several centuries. Existing historical styles could be modified and built upon in artefacts right up until the mid-twentieth century without any real sense of conflict, specifically because the older styles could be viewed as part of an historical continuum extending from past to present.

On the one hand, then, postmodernism might reflect an unravelling of much that modernism (and indeed Enlightenment thought) held dear. On the other, there is the precisely contrary reaction, an increase in intensity that desperately tries to reclaim that which modernity has lost for us. This is evident in the revitalisation of smaller states and national groupings: 'little legacies supplant greater ones; minority roots matter more than the mainstream', according to David Lowenthal.[55] Most striking of all is the number of religious revivals that seem to parallel the numerous historical returns in postmodernism. The loss of tradition and continuity with the past and the sense of depthlessness in the new social orders find their compensation in that specifically postmodern phenomenon of fundamentalism. As Anthony Giddens has remarked, modernity may have undermined the sureties of tradition, but these have not been replaced by the expected 'certitude of rational knowledge'.[56]

However antimodern a fundamentalist revolution might be (Jameson specifically notes that of Iran, pp. 386–7) it still relies entirely on the infrastructure of late capitalism; fundamentalists try to recreate what they believe to be a purer and more authentic past with the new technologies and media. Jameson examines the roots of theological modernism in

the nineteenth century, the relativising stance that increasingly sees the
necessity of an allegorical interpretation of scripture in a modernising
age. While peasants at the time of the English civil war had a life experience not too distanced from that of characters in the Old and New
Testaments, this was no longer a possibility in the wake of the industrialisation of the nineteenth century (pp. 389–90). With the unevenness
of the age of modernisation the differences with the past, and also the
continuities, are readily evident. But, in the postmodern age, all residual
elements connecting us with biblical times are effaced and fundamentalism reappears as a simulated relationship with the past, the most striking
effect being 'the denial of any fundamental social or cultural difference
between postmodern subjects of late capitalism and the Middle-Eastern
subjects of the early Roman Empire'.

Not all proponents of HIP are 'fundamentalists' of the movement,
but there is clearly an eerie resonance here between the redisciplining
of religious practice according to historical details and a similar revolution in musical performance. The details become important at precisely
the moment that the past becomes ineradicably alien, when we can no
longer intuit any direct connection with it; all data that survive from it
can become equally familiar to the postmodern ventriloquist. In other
words, an inescapable historical deafness is balanced by an incorrigible
factual verbosity.[57] Moreover, the belief in the power of historical details is curiously detached from whatever we believe they empower us
to do or experience. This sense obviously borrows something from the
modernist detachment of the aesthetic realm from 'real' life, but it now
happens in the postmodern context where both the real and the aesthetic
are infinitely fluid and no longer work in productive tension. And, just
like religious revivals, HIP shows a broad range of churchmanship: the
Calvinists, following the letter of the document with the confidence of
the elect, but allowing little to the imagination; the charismatics who
find inspiration in history for their intense, fanatical performances; or
those who insist on the detailed observance of countless historical niceties
which may lead both to performances of subtle, detailed observance and
to those that seem to negate anything profound in the music.

In all, Jameson's theory of the postmodern is extremely productive as
a means of understanding the phenomenon of HIP. Not only does it explain larger historical processes but it also relates it to other phenomena
of the postmodern world without being dependent on the notion of a
specific postmodern style. But, of course, the notion of a post-Marxian
historical process retains much of the concept of the totalising 'grand

narrative' that Lyotard sought so hard to distance from the postmodern condition. Jameson would respond that 'the notion that there is something misguided and contradictory about a unified theory of differentiation also rests on a confusion between levels of abstraction: a system that constitutively produces differences remains a system; nor is the idea of such a system supposed to be in kind "like" the object it tries to theorize' (p. 343). In other words, the very idea of theorising any phenomenon brings with it a system, a grid that helps us map what we experience. From this point of view, the theory is not successful to the degree of its truth content but as to whether it *works* for the task at hand, whether it enables us to tell a convincing story.

Furthermore, however cynical it might sound to suggest that the historicist imperative behind HIP is basically a compensation for a waning historicity, there is not necessarily any choice in the matter. The historicist urge of HIP is perhaps 'authentic' for our times (but, I would now suggest, authentic within postmodernism rather than in Taruskin's modernism) and brings with it new intensities and resonances that are relevant for us in a way that would not have been available to the 'original' performers in history. History provides us with 'an atmosphere, a mysterious misty vapour', which Nietzsche insisted was essential for all living things.[58] If this was once provided by an awareness of historicity – the sense of historical rootedness – this now has to come from the historicist synthesis of the countless differences within the past itself.

HIP AS A EUROPEAN PHENOMENON

While I suggest that Jameson's theory of the postmodern explains something of the background for the HIP phenomenon there is one area where substantial modification is necessary. This brings us back to the horizontal American–European distance that, for Henry James, balanced the vertical distance between past and present. Jameson might be right in describing postmodernism as primarily an American phenomenon, 'the first specifically North American global style'. There is also a sense in which multinational capitalism found its origins in the unfettered capitalist system of America, however much it has continued to spread in Europe and many other areas of the world.

Yet there is a side to Jameson's postmodern that rings true for America but not necessarily so well for Europe: 'What was once a separate point on the map has become an imperceptible thickening in a continuum of identical products and standardized spaces from coast to coast' (p. 281).

Certainly this standardisation has affected Europe strongly too, but here the individuality of places and survival of historical artefacts is positively deafening compared with America. However much Jameson might suggest that surviving monuments 'become glittering simulacra of the past, and not its survival' (p. 311), European settlements show their past through the very peculiarities of their geography; the old part of town cannot simply be razed or – in a typically American fashion – moved to a more convenient location.

So the European experience might be particularly complex: the standardisation and repetitive nature of multinational capitalism, the shining, depthless surfaces of postmodern artefacts work side-by-side the historically conditioned geography. Modernisation – in Jameson's sense, at least – will never be truly complete unless all the ancient sites are rebuilt or their historical nature somehow effaced. Moreover, the individual and collective memories of some remarkably long-standing European settlements are perhaps far stronger than many theorists of postmodernism may realise.

A weakened historicity may still survive in Europe and there one is often led to believe that many objects are 'originals' and not simulacra. Yet there is perhaps the nagging feeling that we may not always be able to tell the original apart from the simulacrum, something elegantly illustrated by the ambitious rebuilding projects – beginning in Poland, but now spread throughout Europe – since the mass destruction of World War II (see p. 174 below). The technology is now there to rebuild virtually any monument in Europe, and to rebuild it better than ever before.[59] Perhaps the trauma of two world wars has also had something to do with the tendency to arrest the visible past just at the threshold of modernity. Here reconstruction of the past is not just a choice, as it is in the pluralistic and increasingly flexible culture of America, it has become an imperative.

This brings us full circle in the debate over modernism and postmodernism. HIP may well have come to fruition within the jagged unevenness of post-war European culture and thus carries with it the very essence of modernist angst. The history it has always tried to recreate is just there, fading on the distant horizon, and the tools of a postmodern mindset, media and imagery bring it the richest nourishment. The last chapter retraces some of the ground covered here, but more in relation to the material effects of 'the postmodern condition', namely, the culture of restoration and heritage that has sprung up throughout the developed world in the final decades of the twentieth century.

6

'A reactionary wolf in countercultural sheep's clothing'? – historical performance, the heritage industry and the politics of revival

A cursory history of revivals in older repertories and performance practices reveals a surprisingly consistent pattern. If there has been some revolutionary or otherwise 'artificial' break with the past in recent memory,
there is almost inevitably a reaction that seeks to restore a past practice
evoking some supposedly simpler or purer life. This phenomenon is central to the most spectacular musical revival of the nineteenth century, the
restoration of an entire repertory, performance practice and lifestyle by
the monks of Solesmes. Katherine Bergeron relates this to the wider sense
of loss felt in France after the Revolution and throughout the turbulent
twists and turns that ensued. Viollet-le-Duc's meticulous and imaginative restoration of Notre Dame – recreating every stage of the building's
history in order to redress the violence of a single revolutionary era – was
clearly symptomatic of the urge towards restoration. But it was soulless
without the concomitant restoration of its liturgy and music, according
to Prosper Guéranger, the founder of the Solesmes community.[2] The
musical restoration was thus integral to a wider culture of restoration,
just as the latter was a reaction to a particular historical situation. There
is also a pattern here which is immediately congruent with HIP in the
late twentieth century, in which the restoration of an object (whether a
building, instrument or forgotten musical text) is closely followed by a
desire to revive its wider context and the practices with which it was originally associated. The revolutionary age had exposed the vulnerability
of ancient buildings and the threat to one's own historicity – that sense of
historical and geographical cultural roots. Reciprocally, the recovery of
forgotten repertories and the regeneration of ancient genres was a potent
way of giving the past a semblance of life, since actual performance
achieved an immanence that even architectural restoration could not
approach.

Nineteenth-century France provides many other examples of musical
restoration that – like the various political restorations – all might relate

to the Revolution and its aftermath. Indeed, Katherine Ellis has shown that many of the seeds of the HIP movement – cultivating not only the music of the past, but also its manner of performance – were sown in France. As early as 1804 Geoffroy was stressing the maintenance of earlier performance traditions as essential to the future success of early music.[3] Napoleon himself advocated a restoration of liturgy and its associated music in 1801 and Alexandre Choron's *Institution royale de musique classique et religieuse* (1817) had the multiple aims of restoring both the best music of the past and the traditional liturgical use of music. His historical concerts of vocal music from the age of Josquin to Handel began in 1822 and lasted until the July Revolution of 1830, this musical restoration thus corresponding precisely with an era of monarchical restoration.

The vast historicist movement in Germany, symbolically inaugurated by Goethe's 'conversion' to Gothic architecture in the closing decades of the eighteenth century, was undoubtedly connected to the desire to ground the emerging – but disturbingly disparate – German nation in history. In England, the pattern of restoration was set, in particular, by the fate of the monarchy. As the first country in the modern era to undergo a traumatic and bloody revolution, the culture of restoration in 1660 was particularly potent. Cathedral worship and court music were re-founded with a particular nostalgia for the past that influenced both the repertory and the re-establishment of performance forces. Perhaps it was this spirit of restoration, experienced nowhere else in Europe for over a century to come, that led to the founding of specifically historicist performing organisations in the eighteenth century – e.g. *The Academy of Ancient Music* (1726), The *Concerts of Antient Music* (1776) – together with retrospective publications like William Boyce's three-volume *Cathedral Music* (1760).[4] The English early music movements of both the late nineteenth and late twentieth centuries thus seem to fit into a pattern that stretches back at least three hundred years, one moreover that expanded immensely with each successive century. 'Restoration' here had gained a particular cultural resonance and – perverse though it may seem – actually became an element of 'tradition'.

But, such patterns notwithstanding, does the 'trauma thesis' for the origins of restoration culture really explain everything about the late twentieth-century phenomenon of HIP? Certainly the burgeoning of authoritative collected editions from 1950 might come in the wake of a war that had threatened to destroy virtually all the manuscript sources of western music. It eerily echoes a similar phenomenon precisely a century before, following two unsettling years of revolution. But while World

War II must play a part in the desire to preserve repertories old and new on an almost indiscriminate basis, it is more difficult to associate it directly with the imperative to restore actual performance practice (unless on the rather dubious point that antique instruments were also among the arte-facts destroyed or threatened by such an unprecedented land war). In all, given the breadth and extent of the recent HIP phenomenon, it is undoubtedly too complex to be explained by a single trauma or by the neuroses of individual nations. If Raphael Samuel and Peter Borsay are correct to include brief references to the HIP phenomenon in their de-tailed surveys of heritage movements in Britain,[5] the musical movement needs to be seen in a context that is not only culturally and nationally, but also politically, complex.

The wave-like pre-history of HIP and the complex cultural inter-change inherent in its commodified form in the late twentieth century render simple assessments of the movement grossly inadequate. A com-mon story in its favour is that based on the notion of progress, particularly the advances in knowledge and scientific technique, an ideology consis-tent from the Enlightenment era up until modernism. As scholarship into early performance 'advances' we learn more about the 'true' his-torical identity of the music we love or rediscover, everyone accepts such advances as advantageous for performance and assumes the results will be better. The negative story usually runs along the lines that unimagi-native scholars obsessed with objectivity and positive evidence bludgeon weak-minded performers into submission and force sub-standard prod-ucts on to an unwitting audience. Dreyfus has already shown some of the problems with both these stories: the idea that musicology and perfor-mance progress together, hand in hand, is belied by the considerable rift that has been emerging between mainstream musicology and HIP. The latter both threatens to take over some of the expertise of the musicologist and uses historical evidence in unpredictable and 'unscholarly' ways.[6] And the view that it is all the fault of the 'producers' of HIP ignores the considerable – and necessary – financial support coming from the con-sumers themselves. If we examine HIP as part of a wider phenomenon we may begin to understand how it is a much more complex process in which the buying public is deeply implicated, responding both to the benefits and to the traumatic disorientation engendered by modernisa-tion and modernist culture. As Eric Hobsbawm aptly puts it in regard to invented traditions in general: 'conscious invention succeeded mainly in proportion to its success in broadcasting on a wavelength to which the public was ready to tune in'.[7]

In Taruskin's case, in particular, the critique of English groups is part of a thinly-veiled attack on the perceived smugness of British scholarship and culture, the notion that such people are colonial aristocrats at heart, using bogus history to enforce a naturalising class system on an innocent modern world.[8] As we shall see, his viewpoint is shared by many critics of the heritage industry in general, and it is impossible not to acknowledge a grain of truth in his suspicion. On the other hand, the refutation, or rather, the modification, of this view might be found within the wider discourse on heritage and national history. Although the weight of the arguments both in this chapter and in the general literature relate to the British situation in particular, the very fact that similar 'heritage phenomena' can also be observed in the United States, continental Europe and Far East suggests that it is wrong to explain them in purely nationalistic terms. As David Lowenthal observes, different nations have different motives for exploring and preserving their past, but these represent 'a cluster of trends whose premises, promises, and problems are truly global'. And these global issues, however refracted nationally, relate to common phenomena of 'increasing longevity, family dissolution, the loss of familiar surroundings, quickened obsolescence, genocide and wholesale migration, and a growing fear of technology.'[9] The notion that restoration of any kind belongs to a specifically reactionary ethos, turning its back on recent 'advances' in politics and social structure, rests on the assumption that there is a consistency of meaning, that signifiers are securely bound to what they signify, that an artefact or interpretative gesture from the past has precisely the same effect today as it had when it was first devised. Indeed, as I hope to show, the recycling of what is perceived to be the 'past' in a radically different social and political environment is not necessarily without its advantages for the world in which we are situated.

Far from signifying a consistency of practice, meaning or belief, the very urge to restore something from the past comes from a recognition that the past is 'a foreign country', according to Lowenthal.[10] Indeed, this sense of difference between past and present is essential to the very conception of 'modernity'. Before the late eighteenth century most of those who contemplated the past assumed it to be like the present, believing that both were woven from identical threads of a consistent human nature and condition; history was thus primarily a source of useful examples.[11] But as the past ceased to be exemplary and thus to be imitated and improved in the present, relics became more important as 'emblems of communal identity, continuity, and aspiration' (Lowenthal, *The Past is a Foreign Country*, p. xvi). In short, preservation began to provide the comfort of a continuity that imitation could no longer supply (pp. xxiv, 384). Moreover, if history was no longer controlled by destiny or time- less human nature, then every past epoch became important for its very uniqueness and unrepeatability (p. 391). While this desire to preserve the past is of relatively recent vintage, the idea of using a past to correct a more recent decline dates from – indeed is definitive of – the Renais- sance itself, a time in which the concept of the 'modern' could first be articulated, through a tripartite awareness of the present in relation to a discredited immediate past and a corrective, model antiquity (p. 86). Thus, even if modernist movements and preservationist movements are fundamentally at loggerheads they come surprisingly close in their radi- cal dissatisfaction with the present and their desire for an imagined past or future utopia (see chapter 1, pp. 8–10 above).[12]

Not only have subsequent cycles of revival progressively replaced cre- ative imitation with preservation, but the distance between the age of the object and the time of its revival has become ever shorter. The restora- tion movements of both nineteenth and twentieth centuries coincide with rapid accelerations in industrialisation and technology; as the public be- comes aware of the increasing pace of change its attachment to relics of the past seems to become ever more intense and indiscriminate.[13] As Gavin Stamp describes the British situation in the twentieth century: 'the interval between creation and revival is diminishing. Around 1900, the gap could be measured in centuries; in the 1990s it is but a few decades . . . Soon, perhaps, conservation will catch up with the present, so nothing will be unfashionable and there will be no battles to fight'.[14] So long as the pace of change was virtually imperceptible as it was before the industrial revolution, it was much easier to see the past as more or less like the present. Thus, although the late eighteenth century saw many developments in musical instruments, many older models persisted and it was quite common for music up to a century old to be performed from manuscript or printed parts dating from the time the music was written.[15] Historical consciousness thus depends on the perception of difference and change.

Another reason for the acceleration is the fact that as soon as an object or building becomes obsolete so far as its original function is concerned, it becomes an object of preservationist fervour; the faster the rate of obsolescence, the quicker things qualify for preservation. While in the early 1960s a housing expert might suggest that even a good house had a natural life of eighty years, by the 1980s Victorian houses became highly desirable, the very features which before condemned them as dust-traps now being valued as 'original'.[16] Raphael Samuel notes the remarkable instant historicisation in pop music, where older sounds are recycled or otherwise reused on a regular basis, the concept of 'retrochic' being 'systematic, built into the technology of recording, the tastes of the public and the life-cycle of a hit' (Samuel, *Past and Present*, p. 90).

It is perhaps no accident that this era of the accelerating cycles of fashion – in which revivals are readily perceptible and anticipated – coincides with an unprecedented increase in ecological consciousness. As we begin to perceive the limits of the earth's resources a culture of recycling becomes vital for our future survival. This culture seems to parallel the cycles of arts, politics and even science, as the notion of linear progress becomes less obviously advantageous. In an age in which even national parks represent a form of simulation in the face of potentially unchecked urban growth, '[w]hat all the acculturated receive is not culture, but *cultural recycling*'.[17]

The apparently indiscriminate editing, performing and recording of virtually any repertory that can be counted as 'Early Music' is by no means an isolated affair. From the late 1960s onwards there was a general move away from preserving elements of the past merely on account of their perceived quality, scarcity or sumptuousness, but rather towards preserving anything that was representative of any particular epoch, that gave a sense of continuity or, quite simply, was to be seen as 'old'.[18] As Lowenthal notes 'Preservationists in Metroland fight as hard to save Edwardian half-timbering and thatched roofs as they do any surviving originals, and 1930s mock-Tudor has begun to take on the sacred aura of the long-ago look it sought to copy' (*The Past is a Foreign Country*, p. 319). The outcry in England over the demolition of a 1930s Firestone factory in 1979 could not have been greater had the threatened object been a prehistoric monument.[19]

Our urge to preserve everything from the past is surely also the corollary of our urge to know everything *in toto*. And this thirst for knowledge itself results both from our unprecedented facilities of data storage and retrieval and from our increasing sense of impotence in the face of the ever vertiginous complexity of causality. It is 'the hysteria of causality, corresponding to the simultaneous erasure of origins and causes' that, for Baudrillard, gives rise to 'the obsessive search for origin, responsibility, and reference . . . the hypertrophy of historical research, the frenzy to explain everything, attribute everything, footnote everything'.[20] Paul Crowther draws a more optimistic message from the urge toward detailed historical knowledge; it helps to fill out our existing sense of shared experience with one another, restoring a dimension of intersubjective significance that is otherwise threatened in the postmodern world of appearance and image.[21] There is also a sense that, insofar as we are experiencing complete and successful modernisation, the past no longer seems to represent a primitive version of our present state, just as the provincial or peripheral in our own world ceases to be provincial or peripheral as it is embraced by the modern. Rather the past presents an infinity of alternative worlds that we can attempt to understand without condemning them at the outset.[22]

Given that the urge to preserve and retain virtually everything is one that has accelerated in recent years, HIP could *never* return us to the mindset of the past it recreates. Furthermore, the newfound significance of that which was trivial when it was first created is perhaps the most crucially enduring difference with the past 'as it actually was'. Lowenthal is surely wrong to suggest that *history* strives for a comprehensive view of the past while *heritage* relies on a 'modicum of knowledge . . . the less explicit the better' (*The Heritage Crusade*, p. 134). It is surely just as often the case that heritage movements pay attention to details considered trivial both by the original creators and by the broader historical sweeps of academic history.

THE GROWTH OF THE HERITAGE MOVEMENTS

This is no place to give a comprehensive genealogy and history of heritage movements but it is worth noting how the same phenomena are evident in many different western cultures albeit with idiosyncratic national characteristics and temporal dislocations. While Michael Hunter sees some fledgling protection measures in the Italian Renaissance itself and pioneering codes in seventeenth-century Sweden,[23] systematic preservation is an invention of nineteenth-century Europe. Measures to protect antiquities date from 1807 in Denmark and 1818 in German states. Although Napoleon instilled a sense of preserving classical buildings with his decree for Rome in 1809, it was the 1830s that saw a particularly vigorous movement in France and a preservation law was passed in newly independent Greece in 1834.[24] Hunter relates this to the concurrent growth of both centralised and local governments and also to a larger consensus of public opinion that had not existed before the popularisation of the past and the broader spread of both education and leisure ('The Preconditions of Preservation', p. 25). What had been decidedly

minority, antiquarian pursuits in the eighteenth century became a mainstream historicism in a century that remembered the destructive force
of the Enlightenment realised in the French Revolution (p. 27).

The effectiveness of preservation measures in the Netherlands from
the end of the nineteenth century is particularly striking: by 1918 monuments were protected by a state office and since then there has been
a secure co-ordination of central and local government protection, together with the activities of numerous voluntary organisations. With
a general belief that the reuse of old buildings is more effective than
replacement and a restoration budget proportionally higher than other
countries, the Netherlands was perhaps the dominant force in twentieth-
century heritage movements before the boom in Britain from the 1970s
onwards.[25] The parallel with the role of both these two countries in the
early music movement is unmistakable: the Netherlands was among the
first in institutionalising an early music culture from the 1950s onwards,
and British (or, rather, London-based) early music became a mainstream
commercial culture in the 1970s (1973 marking the advent of both the
Academy of Ancient Music and the journal *Early Music*).

Lowenthal's outline of the causes of the nineteenth-century heritage
phenomenon centres on large-scale changes: the unprecedented pace of
change in the wake of revolutions, the Industrial Revolution, and the
concomitant urbanisation. He also proposes less visible elements, such
as the growing awareness of individual identity and attachment to one's
own past. More tangible were specific events that triggered a particular
country's sense of endangered heritage: the Victoria and Albert Museum's purchase of a rood loft from a Dutch church in 1869 precipitated
the foundation of the Netherlands' official preservation body and the
threat of a US purchase and removal of Tattershall Castle in 1913 inspired a preservationist sense in England in the early twentieth century
(*The Past is a Foreign Country*, p. 394, *The Heritage Crusade*, p. 24). Germany
founded a national art collection fund in 1903 specifically to counter the
speculative threats of the US (Hunter, *Preserving the Past*, p. 8).

What is clear in Britain, particularly at the time when the concepts
of historicism and heritage first peaked in the 1870s, is the tremendous
institutionalised resistance to these concepts. A proposal in 1845 tried
to mimic the French preservation laws of 1837 but failed outright.[26]
Sir John Lubbock's Ancient Monuments' bill of 1873 was resisted
for so long owing to the laissez-fair sentiment of Victorian England,
that before long it was called the 'monumentally ancient bill'. It was
eventually passed in 1882 in a severely diluted form that allowed public

involvement in the preservation of ancient monuments, but only with the owner's consent.[27] In other words, much of the opposition came from the threat to an ingrained sense of property rights, an issue equally strong in the US, where it continued to endure throughout the twentieth century. While preservation laws and organisations follow quite steadily after 1873 – William Morris's *Society for the Protection of Ancient Buildings* in 1877, the Ancient Monuments Act of 1882, the *National Trust* in 1895[28] – Baldwin Brown's seminal report on the care of ancient monuments in 1905, still stressed how much the United Kingdom lagged behind the continent in its preservationist measures.[29] Even in 1927, after measures had been passed to inventory all significant buildings before 1700 in the three mainland UK countries,[30] Sir Lionel Earle could still state that Britain had weaker preservationist legislation than any European country except the Balkan states and Turkey (Hunter, *Preserving the Past*, p. 9). At the turn of the century, even early seventeenth-century buildings could be demolished on account of their lack of antique value and in 1919 there was a serious proposal to demolish nineteen city churches, many of them by Wren.[31] Nevertheless, a 1913 revision of the 1882 act was considerably more stringent, reflecting a much wider sense of the public interest and coinciding with a decline in the power of the aristocracy that was to accelerate later in the century (Champion, 'Protecting the Monuments', p. 44). Thus the resistance to a relatively enthusiastic preservationist movement in Britain had both ancient and modern reasons that distinguished it from the rest of Europe: the extraordinary survival of a landed aristocracy, on the one hand, and on the other, an advanced liberalised industrial economy that sponsored progress at any cost.

In the USA, too, the move towards a culture of restoration was slower, but for different reasons. First, there was clearly an anti-historical impulse accompanying the foundation of the new republic, a belief in an 'immutable covenant, unswerving principles, and immunity from time's corrosion', a sense of a unique exemption from secular historical processes that endured in one form or another well into the twentieth century (Lowenthal, *The Past is a Foreign Country*, p. 109). Major thinkers such as Thoreau advocated the abandonment of anything from the past, particularly the habits of old England, and even the initial enthusiasm for classical authors and architecture declined during the nineteenth century; 'Democracy, anti-intellectualism, materialism, and faith in progress made the classical past useless and derisory' (pp. 112–13). Lowenthal notes a conflict of two moral imperatives in the American psyche: together with the urge to abandon the past and its models, citizens were enjoined to revere the Founding Fathers. In almost direct contradistinction to the process in Europe from the Renaissance to the twentieth century, Americans revered a more immediate past while disdaining anything more distant (p. 122).

Although something of the anti-historicist urge has continued to survive in American culture, much was changed with the trauma of the Civil War. Now, as in Europe, a dissatisfaction with the present led to a nostalgia for the past in many forms; moreover, with increasing industrialisation and immigration from many more distant cultures, the British roots of the republic became more attractive, gaining a sense of old-world decency in the face of uncertain new influences (p. 121). Almost directly contemporaneously with Europe, and Britain in particular, the last two decades of the century saw a proliferation of genealogical societies, antique collecting and 'period' decor, 'The party of Memory for the first time began to outvote the party of Hope', according to Lowenthal (p. 122). Arnold Dolmetsch's arrival on the east coast in 1905 was soon to establish Boston and New York as the principal American centres of early music.[32] Yet, the older anti-historicist sentiment still strongly persisted, if the late work of Henry James is anything to go by. Both *The American Scene* and the unfinished *The Sense of the Past* show his deep-seated concern for the anti-historicist element in American culture during the early years of the twentieth century.[33]

The second wave of the heritage industry – far more intense and still with us – originated directly after the Second World War. Even during the war there were some systematic efforts, especially in Italy and Germany, to create an inventory of historic buildings. Moreover, a Harvard-based group tried, unsuccessfully, to guide the allied bombing campaign away from precious buildings. Typically, Britain lagged behind much of Europe in this respect although, by the end of the war, its forces were better informed.[34] On its own turf, the listing acts of 1944 and 1947 – producing the first systematic account of the nation's historic buildings – were devised in direct anticipation of a massive rebuilding programme in the wake of war-time destruction. The lists would simply inform developers of what should be preserved, incorporated or avoided in their schemes (Saint, 'How Listing Happened', p. 121).

The notion of the total restoration of a lost heritage, the accurate simulacrum that can deceive even recent inhabitants, was born in Poland where the Nazis had purposely sacked cities such as Warsaw in order to demoralise the population. The centre of Warsaw was rebuilt exactly as it had been in absolute defiance of this devastation, a move that some of the inhabitants found almost as unnerving as the 'authentic' destruction (Lowenthal, *The Past is a Foreign Country*, pp. 46, 290–1). Here, the pattern of restoration following violent trauma parallels Viollet's multi-layered restoration of Notre Dame over a century before, but now with greater fidelity to a closely remembered original and with all sense of new creativity effaced.

The Polish reaction was somewhat exceptional for its time although many German city centres were rebuilt with varying degrees of fidelity to the originals. Western European planners who had not experienced such a degree of cultural trauma saw such measures as perversely nostalgic.[35] To many, the large bombed sites gave an opportunity to get rid of unpleasant memories, a sentiment not unlike the traditional American urge to promote the new at the expense of a painful recent past. The late 1940s and 50s were the years of extensive public building projects undertaken with limited resources, while the boom of the 1960s saw much more private enterprise and the peak of modernist architecture, in its most predatory mode.

It was not until the 1970s that Poland's defiant anti-modern stance became more fashionable, thus precisely that decade when HIP began to gain mainstream approval.[36] Recession, energy crises and inflation dramatically slowed the demand for development and conservationist sentiment became attractive from a number of standpoints.[37] Rapid change no longer seemed to evoke a sense of freedom when it happened so quickly. Urban modernisation had brought discomfort, congestion and depersonalisation, and the erasure of the past could inspire a genuine sense of grief.[38] This could even be experienced in America where everything may often be supposed new and infinitely renewable.[39] Moreover, as Hewison has observed, 'The effect of modernisation was not just that everything had changed, but that everything had become more and more the same, as architectural and scenic differences were ironed out under the weight of mediocrity and uniformity' (Hewison, *The Heritage Industry*, p. 39). In short, while the modern movement had responded to the need for new kinds of building, together with new techniques and materials, architectural modernism was both arrogant and naïve in its claims to be able to reshape the urban environment.[40] Arthur C. Danto also relates the 1970s to a fundamental change in attitudes towards art and its history; it marked the beginning of what he would term a 'post-historical' approach to art in which 'absence of direction' was becoming a defining trait.[41]

By the 1980s the 'Polish stance' became so prevalent that when major restoration work was done on Italian historical buildings, the reconstruction would be masked by a 1:1 scale photographic image of the pristine facade: 'Tourists were greeted by the ghostly sight of a city square framed almost entirely with billowing reproductions of the real thing', remarks Maxwell Hutchinson, who believes that '[h]istory in our cities is becoming the reproduction furniture of our urban landscape'.[42] European conservation conferences were spawned by the Council of Europe from the mid-1960s onwards. It was this body that also defined a crucial watershed with the European Architectural Heritage Year in 1975. The Amsterdam conference of that year resulted in the European Charter of Architectural Heritage that was seminal in making conservation an official element of European policy. What distinguishes it from many earlier forms of legislation is the fact that – as its very first principle – it covers lesser buildings, entire ensembles within villages together with their natural or artificial settings, in addition to the major monuments, since 'if the surroundings are impaired, even those monuments can lose much of their character' (Appleyard, *The Conservation of European Cities*, pp. 295–6). Just as early music groups of precisely the same period began performing and recording entire repertories of forgotten *Kleinmeister*, the charter asserts that 'entire groups of buildings, even if they do not include any example of outstanding merit, may have an atmosphere that gives them the quality of works of art'. Moreover, the combined architectural heritage is seen to help us understand how the past is relevant to contemporary life – as if its reclaimed historicity is somehow good for our health.

And health indeed becomes the next major topic of the declaration: the combined architectural heritage facilitates 'a balanced and complete life' in the face of rapid change, 'Otherwise, part of man's awareness of his own continuity will be destroyed.' Education inevitably plays an important part in the declaration, since the preserved heritage will obviously have little meaning without a guided interpretation and explanation. Although the document evidences a profoundly anti-modernist turn, there still remains the formalist belief in the value of the combined past as a whole, the destruction of any part of which affects that inherited unity. Later on we read that if modern buildings are to be constructed they must be designed to match 'the existing context, proportions, forms, sizes and scale', together with a use of 'traditional materials'. As the French minister of culture was to assert in 1979: 'The national heritage is no longer merely a matter of cold stones or of exhibits kept under glass in museum cabinets. It now includes the village wash-house, the little country church, local songs and forms of speech, crafts and skills.'[43] The value of the past now clearly lay in the *ensemble* of its surviving elements, not in its individual autonomous components.

Next in the Declaration come the economic arguments: heritage is an asset that – far from being a luxury – actually saves community resources, another about-turn from the post- (and, indeed, pre-) war doctrine that mass building projects were the most economical way forward. Heritage, quite simply, now belongs within the culture of environmentalism and re-cycling; the declaration puts great emphasis on the fact that this heritage is in danger from all forms of ignorance, neglect and 'misapplied' tech-nology and economics. Together with this comes the idealist pre-modern argument that old towns and villages, through their very design and evo-lution favoured social integration in a way entirely thwarted by more recent planning. The past is thus not only a refuge from the inhospitable present but actually redresses social injustices that are perceived as mod-ern developments. The concept of 'integrated conservation' means that restoration projects are to proceed with social justice as a primary aim, together with concern for the needs of the poorer inhabitants. More-over, traditional crafts should be fostered, thus creating 'new' forms of employment that would have been inconceivable only a few years before. It may well be that the renewed interest in craft also relates to the culture of personal renewal at both physical and mental levels; in direct oppo-sition to the notion that increasing age brings increasing decrepitude and isolation from the industrial workplace, the craftsman mentality ro-mantically suggests a lifecycle that brings increasing understanding and wisdom.[44] There is a sense that this reaction to the division of labour so ubiquitous since the Industrial Revolution will not only benefit the individual, but also improve society in general: 'Integrated conservation cannot succeed without the co-operation of all. Although the architec-tural heritage belongs to everyone, each of its parts is nevertheless at the mercy of any individual.' This ideology of conservation was taken up especially vigorously by the Communist-led municipalities in Italy, such as in Bologna where particular attention was given to the preservation of the old town.[45]

There is no doubt that this declaration foresaw the direction of Euro-pean urban planning and preservation over the remaining years of the twentieth century. It had very strong parallels in the New World too, such as Australia's Burra Charter of 1979. Nevertheless, it is debatable whether its intentions for social justice were ever fulfilled. In the unrestricted

market economy that was shortly to ensue, neighbourhoods traditionally labelled as 'slums' were indeed newly valued and revitalised, but all
too often together with a rise in value that unashamedly encouraged gen-
trification. This development is symptomatic of the political complexities
that bedevil the entire heritage phenomenon in general, in which liberal
causes are easily converted to conservative ends and vice versa.

Exactly the same issues surround the early music movement, which
shares so many characteristics with the ideals of the 1975 declaration: a
concern for lesser repertories in addition to the greater; an antiquarian
desire for the complete preservation of virtually anything from the past,
and the notion that this is somehow better for our health; an environ-
mentalist bent in which nothing is wasted; a quest for greater education
and knowledge; a promotion of the individual as craftsman, with a working knowledge of all the stages of production (revitalising amateur music
culture on the one hand, and dispelling the notion of the professional
musician as a mere cog in the broader process, on the other); and, finally, the sense that this emphasis on the individual – herself aware of a
large number of historical and contextual factors – will contribute to a
healthier community in general. It is clearly this last issue that so easily
flips into the conservative ideology of individual enterprise and profit.

While the late twentieth-century heritage phenomenon is a global
phenomenon (Samuel, *Past and Present*, p. 307), there are particular issues
that single out both Britain and the United States, just as there were a
century earlier. Given the weakness of the existing preservation legislation
compared with much of the rest of Europe, the British destruction of both
country houses and vernacular architecture (such as the lesser Georgian
buildings of Bath) happened on an unprecedented scale during the 1950s
and early sixties. The national stock of country houses was reduced
by 10 per cent,[46] and the general demolition of pre-twentieth-century
buildings far exceeded anything that German bombing had achieved.
Amery and Cruickshank, in their book *The Rape of Britain*, asserted that
the destruction between 1950 and 1975 outweighed the loss of heritage
in the entire nineteenth century.[47] Government planning and the work
of private developers happened on a scale greater than elsewhere in
Europe during the 1950s and 60s. But, as the sixties progressed, the
perceived failure of cheap modern housing projects, both socially and
architecturally, was particularly acute. It was dramatically symbolised by
the partial collapse of the Ronan Point tower-block in 1968.[48] Building on
earlier public outcry at the destruction of such prominent monuments as
the Euston Arch in the early 1960s, the preservationists of the 1970s were

particularly effective at sensationalising the wanton destruction of British heritage. Adam Fergusson's *Sack of Bath* (1973) included contributions by prominent figures such as John Betjeman, together with photographs by Lord Snowdon that dramatised the scale of the destruction of the context that originally surrounded the surviving nobler buildings.

An extremely influential exhibition 'The Destruction of the Country House' was mounted at the Victoria and Albert Museum in 1974 by Marcus Binney, John Harris, Peter Thornton and Roy Strong:[49]

> The hall of destruction was lined on two sides by giant columns frozen in the moment of collapse, with blown up photographs of lost houses pasted round the column shafts. On the opposite walls were hundreds more photographs of lost houses laid row above row like brickwork. All this was accompanied by the doomladen voice of John Harris reciting the roll of the fallen houses, county by county, as if they were names on a war memorial, grouped by regiment. (Binney, *Our Vanishing Heritage*, p. 15)

Out of this came Binney's *SAVE Britain's Heritage*, an organisation that manipulated the necessary media in order to alert the public well in advance of any demolition of heritage. By the late 1970s well-known architectural historians and other prominent figures staged sit-ins in order to thwart the efforts of demolition men and the activites of *SAVE* and other preservation societies received wide coverage in the national press, both right and left. Moreover, in the year of its founding, European Architectural Heritage Year, 1975, *SAVE* could effectively play the economic card by demonstrating that nearly three-quarters of the housing demolished by the Greater London Council between 1967 and 1971 was in good enough condition to have been rehabilitated at far less expense (Binney, *Our Vanishing Heritage*, p. 191). The Labour administrations of the late 1970s soon found themselves under siege, both for their continuing punative taxation of embattled inheritors of country houses and for their mismanagement of the Mentmore Towers affair, when the government failed to secure for the nation the purchase of an extremely important collection housed in a major Victorian mansion.[50]

All these very prominent explosions of interest benefited from extremely skilful publicity.[51] It was precisely this newly charged culture of heritage and preservation that provided a wide public support and thus economic basis for the successful foundation and early flourishing of many London-based early music groups during the 1970s. These could capitalise on a number of advantages already in place: the large number of instrumentalists in the capital; a healthy recording industry; a public broadcasting system already devoted to earlier repertories; and the surviving indigenous choral tradition, itself easily recyclable as part of the national heritage.[52] By contrast, it is quite striking how little HIP activity took place in England before the 1970s. Admittedly, there were successful groups such as *Musica Reservata*, and the charismatic presence of Thurston Dart and David Munrow, who enlivened earlier repertories with their historical reconstructions. But most performers of 'standard' Baroque and Classical repertory in 1960s Britain remained oblivious to the small but significant body of HIP performers on the continent, such as Nikolaus Harnoncourt and Gustav Leonhardt.[53]

By the 1980s, the heritage phenomenon was alive at every conceivable level of society, to the extent that Hewison could assert pessimistically in 1987 that a new museum was opened every week, representing 'the imaginative death of this country' (Hewison, *The Heritage Industry*, p. 9) and threatening to turn the entire island into 'one big open air museum' (p. 24). Perhaps the greatest irony of this situation is the fact that, as industry declined and operations such as mines closed, the original workers were often rehired as museum attendants or actors re-enacting what they had originally done for their work (p. 104).[54] By the end of the 1980s the 'living history' movement moved from being an eccentric fringe activity to become a central element of national culture.[55] Re-enactments became a commonplace at heritage centres with subjects ranging from the most privileged aristocratic lifestyles to the romanticised squalor of Wigan Pier. The urge to revitalise music of the past, whether familiar masterpieces or obscure discoveries, through the supposed reconstruction of its original performing practice would thus seem virtually inevitable in this atmosphere.

The concept of historical re-enactment owes much to the idea of the open-air museum which sprang up in several north European countries during the closing years of the nineteenth century.[56] It was America, however, that provided the major commercial impetus, beginning with John D. Rockefeller Jr's project to recreate Colonial Williamsburg in 1927 and Henry Ford's Greenfield Village of 1929. The latter was a nostalgic attempt to show how far the American people had progressed but also, conversely, to capture something of the world before it lost its innocence to Ford's motor car. The Plimoth Plantation set up in 1956 also established the concept of live interpreters mimicking the habits and speech of the first Puritan settlers (Stratton, 'Open-air and Industrial Museums', pp. 157–8). America's heritage industry was also driven by its technological superiority. Well before World War II and the Polish experience of facsimile restoration, Americans had perfected the art of reproducing ancient scenes, sometimes by importing original structures from other locations, albeit often with a bizarre blindness to context. In the field of music, the effects of this culture reverberated in the imaginative Mediaeval reconstructions of Noah Greenberg and Thomas Binkley from the 1950s onwards, and was still felt at the tremendously successful reconstruction of a seventeenth-century French equestrian ballet at the 2000 Berkeley Festival. While Britain had a tradition for fanciful re-enactments stretching back to mock battles in Elizabethan times,[57] there was often a resistance to American-style re-enactment at tourist sights. However, the trend grew rapidly in the 1970s onwards (Stratton, 'Open-air and Industrial Museums', pp. 169–73) with a plethora of wartime 'Experiences' and a growth in role-play by costumed 'interpreters'.

Lowenthal observes that many involved in such re-enactments actually begin to assume the persona of their predecessors: officers began to eat separately from the common soldiers in a film about the Napoleonic Wars and those who were unfortunate enough to become 'British' soldiers in American Civil War replays became victims of vicious assaults from the spectators (*The Past is a Foreign Country*, pp. 300–1). In America the bicentennial year of 1976 was a major impetus to the spirit of historical re-enactment, the American devotees actually splitting into 'British' and 'American' types, with the former characterised by their kill-joy quest for historical correctness and the latter wearing their makeshift uniforms with more sense of spontaneous fun (p. 295). Thus Julian Barnes might not be so far off the mark when he portrays the 'actors' hired to portray historical figures in his satire on English heritage, *England, England*, as actually becoming their personages: the smugglers start to smuggle, the wreckers to wreck, Robin Hood and his Band become outlaws and 'Dr Johnson' becomes Dr Johnson, assuming the worst aspects of his personality as well as the best. In the end, the island's CEO, Martha Cochrane senses that the doctor believed himself to be more 'real' than she.[58]

Umberto Eco sees America as impregnated with a culture of hyper-reality that is often ignored in critical discourse but nonetheless affects many wider elements of the culture.[59] The successful illusion of authenticity is often far more important than objective accuracy: a facsimile of the Manhattan purchase contract is in English rather than the original Dutch and thus exemplifies the perfect 'fac-different' (*Faith in Fakes*, p. 11). Eco also observes division between those millionaires on the east coast who either build in patently modernist style or restore an older building, and those in the west who – given the relative lack of older remains – create European buildings and neighbourhoods in accurate scale and material (p. 25): 'the Absolute Fake is offspring of the unhappy awareness of a present without depth' (p. 31). Only advanced technology makes the Getty Museum's large-scale reconstructions of context possible as it does the reliable crocodiles at Disneyland who conform so successfully to one's expectations of crocodile behaviour that the real thing comes as something of a disappointment (p. 44). America's particular contribution to the heritage phenomenon is thus not just the skilful preservation of the past, but more importantly, its representation. In the apt words of Hillel Schwartz: 'Living Museums tend to choose that which *authenticates* over that which is authentic'.[60] One of the most striking examples of this is the case of President Johnson's decision to recreate his birthplace on its original site in 1964; on his death, certain officials sought to render it more faithful to what the original house must have been like, but subsequently it was again restored to the state in which Johnson had wished it to be left as 'the nation's only presidential birth place to be reconstructed, refurnished, and interpreted by an incumbent chief executive' (Lowenthal, *The Past is a Foreign Country*, p. 348).

In all, the case of America adds a further layer to the European causes of the heritage industry which, to recapitulate, consist in a pattern of reaction to trauma and a reaction to the changes wrought by an all-too-rapid modernisation of the urban landscape, together with an ecological mistrust of infinite progress. America – technologically and economically the most consistently advanced nation – experiences an even more rapid potential for change in which the restoration of a sparser history blends with the creation of a history that it never had, to the extent that the distinctions between reality and 'hyperreality', and between the original and the 'fake' are virtually effaced. Baudrillard relates 'the debauchery of signs' and the thirst for simulation specifically to the '"diabolical" power of change', and 'immoral energy of transformation' which is actually an indication of the success of the American culture of virtually unrestricted free enterprise and a sure 'sign of its vitality'.[61]

Yet I would hesitate to claim that these causes of the heritage phenomenon and the subculture of HIP are entirely sufficient, since what one may take as the causes of the phenomenon partially depend on the sides one takes in the debate; the perception of causes must be part of a larger value judgement. The three basic areas of debate concern, first, the belief that an all too eager concern for heritage betokens a lack of confidence in human society and progress, a failure to envision a better future; secondly, the idea of the heritage phenomenon as a form of sloppy and deceitful history; and finally, and perhaps most significantly, the notion that heritage evidences a profoundly reactionary impulse that threatens to recapitulate or prolong the injustices of the past as a direct concomitant of the very act of restoration.

HERITAGE AS CULTURAL DECLINE AND PESSIMISM

I would rather be accused of being over-ambitious than of being lily-livered and retreating into a nostalgic past that never existed. (Lord Foster, 2000)[62]

The pessimistic view of the heritage phenomenon in relation to HIP is most eloquently expressed by Robert Morgan (see p. 10 above). To him, the desire to recycle old instruments and performing practices is the result of a crucial lack of direction and progress in the field of original composition, a cultural loss of creative steam. I have encountered one influential figure in the HIP movement who began his career as a Darmstadt-school composer and took to early music as 'the next best thing' when he lost the dodecaphonic 'faith'; to him, his success in the early music scene brings with it the slight taint of failure.[63] Here we have perhaps the clearest substantiation of Taruskin's claim that HIP is a bedfellow of high modernism, that historical research and performance practice serve ends similar to those in the composition and performance of modernist music. Furthermore, there has always been considerable cross-over – in terms of both audience and performers – between the fields of early music and contemporary music in general. Until HIP began to colonise the nineteenth and early twentieth centuries, the two were, after all, often united in their common aversion to the nineteenth-century 'mainstream'. On the whole though, most figures in the HIP movement distance themselves from high modernism in composition and the culture of musical 'progress'. This is not to say, though, that HIP takes an essentially uncreative attitude to the past, akin to that which Hermann Hesse depicts in Catalania in *The Glass Bead Game* (see p. 73 above). Indeed, Kay Shelemay, in her ethnographic study of musical practices at the 1996 Boston Early Music Festival, notes that a large proportion of the interviewed musicians relished the opportunities for creative improvisations, '"re-inventing" music of the past, a process acknowledged as an imaginative and exciting one'. Moreover, this creative environment has also inspired much fresh composition specifically for HIP musicians.[64]

HIP and heritage tend to mark a break with the more traditional, Whiggish, view of history that sees the glories of the past as steps on the way to a more perfect present. There is no doubt that an interest in the past 'on its own terms' can engender the sense of an inferior present (and this is precisely where restoration movements tacitly share a sentiment with modernism). Indeed, many early leaders in the heritage movement made their antipathy to modernity more than clear. William Morris's *Society for the Protection of Ancient Buldings* asserted that it was no longer possible to treat churches 'as living things, to be altered, enlarged, and adapted as they were in the days when the art that produced them was alive and progressive', any new buildings had to be as simple and unpretentious as possible in order not to damage the existing heritage.[65] Morris's 1891 novel, *News from Nowhere*, was a direct reaction to the modern technology, mass production and industrialisation allegorised by Edward Bellamy's *Looking Backward* (1888). In Morris's utopian future, capitalism is replaced by a romantic Arts and Crafts ideology restoring ancient traditions of life and habitation.[66] Only a few years later, in 1896, it was Morris who encouraged Arnold Dolmetsch to build his first harpsichord, which was exhibited at the Arts and Crafts Exhibition in October that year.[67]

Moreover, it must be admitted that the more broadly the architectural heritage is defined and the more that is consequently preserved (or, significantly, copied and extended), the less room there literally remains for the new.[68] This point is exemplified by the case of Roy Strong, a vehement supporter of English heritage in the 1970s, who by 1983 feared that 'there is too much dead heritage around. The past has swallowed us up' (Lowenthal, *The Past is a Foreign Country*, p. 404).[69] This perspective cannot transfer directly to musical culture, where the amount of 'room' for all forms of music, new and old, is practically infinite; but there might be a sense in that the advent of HIP and other forms of the early music movement have absorbed much of the listening-time and buying-power of the public.

Hewison considers the heritage phenomenon to be a specifically British problem, the sign of a nation uncritically using the past as a means of facing an uncertain future. Indeed, 'far from ameliorating the climate of decline, it is actually worsening it. If the only new thing we have to offer is an improved version of the past, then today can only be inferior to yesterday' (Hewison, *The Heritage Industry*, p. 10). Typical of the examples that most disturb him are the recycling of industrial installations as tourist attractions and the fact that enormous sums of money are made out of such institutions that can no longer profit from their original purpose. He speaks of the redundant miner now producing coal for the tourist as if this were a display of chronic impotence (p. 97); to him, the economic justification for such forms of conservation is a 'result of weakness' (p. 104). In a phrase that comes very close to similar criticisms of HIP, 'Commerce reinforces the longing for authenticity in order to exploit it' (p. 29).

His distinction between 'preservation' and 'conservation' betrays an insistent belief in the purity of origins: preservation is thus the maintenance of an object in its original context and 'in such a form that it can be studied with a view to revealing its original meaning' while conservation changes the original context and meaning, creating 'if only by attracting the attention of members of the public, a new use' (p. 98). The argument proceeds with the view that the arts thus cease to be noble and inspiring and become 'merely' part of the leisure business; as customers of a spurious product, the quality of our life is insidiously debased (p. 129). The impotence imagery continues with the claim that nostalgia is a powerless emotion that can never recover the object of recall (p. 134).

Hewison's standpoint as a historian of museum culture finds a striking parallel in complaints made by architects about the turn away from the modernist tradition during the 1980s. Richard Rogers believes that the architectural heritage should be selectively demolished in order to make room for the new. Moreover, he sees the uncritical exploitation of the past as likewise being the result of crass commercialism: 'Ours is an age of business giants and cultural pygmies'.[70] As Maxwell Hutchinson adds, the heritage industry is boosted by tourism and leisure, even faked attractions bringing in piles of foreign currency (Hutchinson, *The Prince of Wales*, p. 172). Architecture that is 'true' to the present needs to be distanced from immediate commercial concerns and to keep step with the miracles of recent scientific progress. In a formulation that works in almost direct contradistinction to the European Charter of 1975 – which suggested that the restoration of diverse historical neighbourhoods would create a healthier social climate (see pp. 176–7 above) – Rogers claims that 'In architecture, as elsewhere, it is only through the development of the most modern ideas and techniques that we can solve both functionally and aesthetically the problems that confront us such as shelter for all, overcrowding, traffic, noise, smell and the general erosion of the beautiful qualities of land, sea and air' (Hutchinson, *The Prince of Wales*, p. xii).

Most telling in this formulation is the assumption that modern solutions suitable for contemporary problems are also aesthetic solutions.

Hutchinson elaborates this point by suggesting that historicist 'regener-
ators of tourism, heritage and retailing' are 'piecemeal', and that a bold
and true architecture will treat 'the city as a whole and not as the sum of
unrelated parts'. In short, quality, unified architecture represents values
more enduring than the mere sex appeal of 'bimbo architecture' (p. 178).

If there is a consistent pattern emerging from the 'pessimistic' critique
of heritage culture, it is that such pessimism is most easily expressed,
and most sorely felt, from within the ideology of modernism. This, almost by definition, would consign any form of reversion to an earlier
aspect of art as 'beyond the pale'.[71] It upholds the traditions of progress
and historical necessity – 'If history is rewritten, it will never forgive us',
complains Hutchinson (p. 37). Aesthetic progress is seen to be the direct
corollary of scientific progress and research, just as Milton Babbitt of
'Who-cares-if-you-listen'-fame expressed for new music in the 1950s.[72]
Architecture in both the large and small scale is to form a coherent
'whole', something that will clean up the embarrassing mess of history.
Together with the aestheticisation of progress goes the distaste of commercialism, a common feature of modernism since it came to the fore
in the late nineteenth century.[73] However, as Lowenthal observes, the
commercialisation of Heritage can be traced back to the Medieval relic
trade: 'What is novel is the mistaken notion that such abuses are new and
hence intolerable' (*The Heritage Crusade*, p. 101). It is worth noting here
that many modernist attacks on HIP, from Adorno onwards, have emphasised the commercial aspect of the enterprise and the sense that this
contributes to its philistine nature.[74] The very complexity of modernist
art requires considerable expertise, requiring both individual talent and
extensive training. As Clement Greenberg put it, the 'essence of Modernism lies ... in the use of the characteristic methods of a discipline
to criticize the discipline itself ... in order to entrench it more firmly in
its area of competence.'[75] Hutchinson suggests that British architecture,
now seemingly lead by the hopelessly postmodern Prince of Wales, has
become the province of amateurs, populist fundamentalists who render
modern architects dumb (*The Prince of Wales*, pp. 27, 157). His language
comes very close to Pinchas Zukerman's in ridiculing the sheer amateur-
ishness and lack of cultivated tone in all forms of Baroque string playing
(see chapter 1, p. 4 above).

Hutchinson's hope is that 'true' history will soon return and modernism, in a truer, fully developed form, will soon rescue us: 'We simply
cannot go to the Millennium Ball wearing the threadbare rags of postmodernism and neo-classicism. It will be a glittering event' (p. 155).

Modernism faltered simply because it was economically misman-
aged and poorly executed; heritage and postmodernism, on the other
hand, exploit and embrace the commercial climate, thus temporarily
blinding us to the truth of historical progress. We will soon tire of stylistic
diversity as we mature: 'the pluralism of the playground cannot go on
for ever, and already the bell is ringing' (p. 156).

Much of Hewison's and Hutchinson's attack on historicist architecture
and the heritage culture relies on the assumption that this is a particularly
British disease. Britain, the story goes, has always had a profoundly conservative and unenterprising nature, partly in reaction to its own success
in the Industrial Revolution. While the rural idyll was basically a late
nineteenth-century invention, beginning with William Morris and – as
'Bypass Tudor' – dominating the domestic architectural style between
the wars, Wiener suggests that the post-war retreat from technology and
modernisation was a direct reaction to the perceived modernity of Nazi
technology (Wiener, *English Culture*, pp. 66, 77). If the post-war years really
did preserve the myth that England was 'humanely old-fashioned and
rural' this does not take into account the remarkable scale in modern
building projects in this period, something which is surely much more the
proximate cause of the British heritage industry. Moreover, the post-war
attitude to ecology, early music and other folk movements in Germany
itself was exactly the opposite to that which Wiener describes for Britain,
since these had themselves been co-opted by Nazi ideology (see pp. 6,
210 above and below).

Whatever truth may lie in all these assumptions, it is clear that Britain's
post-war loss of nerve has causes quite different from the heritage industry (most significantly, these included the haemorrhaging of international
prestige with the dismantling of the empire). Moreover, the reaction
against modernist architecture and an interest in heritage are equally
strong elsewhere (Hunter, *Preserving the Past*, pp. 13–14). Indeed, much of
the money flowing into British heritage institutions comes from abroad,
Hutchinson noting in disapproval that it is the dollar, Deutschmark and
yen that call the heritage tune in architecture (Hutchinson, *The Prince of
Wales*, p. 172).[76] Furthermore, as Hewison himself acknowledges, there
has been a museum boom in Japan, Europe and North America, 'museums have taken over the function once exercised by church and ruler,
they provide the symbols through which a nation and a culture under-
stands itself' (p. 84). But it may no longer be the case that the concept
of the museum automatically conjures up the sense of closure and of a
past that has been immutably fixed and finished. Arthur C. Danto notes

how contemporary artists treat the museum as a field permitting 'constant rearrangement' and facilitating 'living artistic options'.[77] Another fundamental problem with the modernist argument is that it tends to see the heritage phenomenon and, indeed, postmodernity (or Danto's 'contemporaneity') in general in the same way as it wishes it could see itself: as a consistent whole and embodying a uniform system of values. The critique that historicist architecture is often too uniform, that ancient city centres are all too frequently decked out with the same cobblestones and Victorian light fittings, contains more than a grain of truth, exactly as many of us have observed the uniformity and levelling of interpretation that characterises a large proportion of historical performances (see chapter 1, p. 15 above). But it is surely wrong to assume in consequence that this is the essential 'mainstream' of historicist movements and that any exceptions to the levelling rule are happy accidents. Historicism, by definition, must allow a degree of pluralism, one that will bring with it various fads, both simultaneously and in sequence. History to one person might offer a means of limitation, control and closure, to another, an opportunity for limitless invention. History shows us not only countless ways in which the past was different but also just how contingent the present state of affairs actually is.

The heritage phenomenon and the wider culture of environmentalism and conservation do perhaps demonstrate a loose unity in their new-found recognition that the earth and its resources are finite. As Gavin Stamp suggests, perhaps we should reinforce the cultural pessimism of heritage with a new intelligence;[78] just as we realise that technological and industrial expansion and progress cannot any longer go unchecked, culture and the arts in their historicised modes actually reflect this change of perspective in a way that is simply ignored by modernism. Technological innovation now has to work in tandem with a climate of conservation just as heritage arts apply selective modernisation to techniques and styles borrowed from history. Some have even argued that the arts have themselves exhausted the limited number of combinations that are possible (at least to remain within the band of human apperception and appreciation)[79] so that art in the near future may need to conform more to a cyclic than a progressive pattern.

Another telling distinction evident in the modernist critique is that between work and leisure. Hewison laments that miners employed by the tourist industry are no longer doing 'real' work, Hutchinson believes that postmodern architecture represents a playground from which architects will eventually be called to resume their work in 'true' modernist style, and he notes that Morris's utopia in *News from Nowhere* represents class revolution in which the bourgeoisie triumph, where '[w]ork is a spree, a joy' (*The Prince of Wales*, p. 17). Critics of 'living museums' and other forms of animated heritage have complained that such activities blur the distinction between entertainment and education, just as they dilute the value of 'real' artefacts from the past by simulating an original that never really existed (Samuel, *Past and Present*, p. 259). This attitude clearly lies behind much of the criticism of historical performance, the performances seducing the public into thinking that the hard work of the historian can be replaced with entertainment posing as history. The performers themselves are often viewed as amateurs avoiding the long drudge of the conservatoire and justifying their technical incompetence with an appeal to historical accuracy. Samuel also puts this attitude down to a residue of the 'conspiracy theory' which would hold that tastes are manipulated by hidden elites and the power of the media (p. 264).

On the one hand, this critique is worth heeding: it is quite possible that the public may be turned into passive consumers and that the terrors and injustices of the past may be neutralised by the 'package-holiday' approach to history. But, as Samuel observes, there also lies in this critique a dualistic thinking, presupposing a necessary distinction between work and pleasure, the sacred and profane, high and low culture, fact and fiction. All of these – it might be added – maintain some of the essential distinctions of modernism, together with its concept of the elite expert who stands above the commonplace. There is also the assumption that 'true' art, being priceless, does not need to participate in the commercial world and should stand apart from the unpredictable fads of the free market:

For the aesthete, anyway for the alienated and the disaffected, heritage is a mechanism of cultural debasement. It leaves no space for the contemplative or the solitary. It forbids discrimination and the exercise of good taste. Its pleasures are cheap and nasty, confounding high and low, originals and copies, the authentic and the pastiche. (p. 268)

Looked at from another angle, though, it is perhaps the desire for ceaseless innovation within the modernist impulse that led to the breaking down of these divisions of bourgeois order in the first place.[80] Thus the debasing of the work/leisure distinction, far from being an irresponsible departure from modernist principles, is one of the contradictory consequences of those very principles in the first place. The heritage industry and its musical counterpart are thus predicated on the modernist movement that, in its 'purest' form, deplores their dilution of cultural values. With the decline in primary and secondary sectors and a concomitant growth in the service sectors of western economies in the 1970s and 80s, together with the implications of micro-chip technologies (Rojek, *Ways of Escape*, p. 3), the very concept of 'work' as a fixed category to be pursued in fixed hours was profoundly altered. At the same time, many leisure activities have assumed the seriousness and intensity of 'work', something which is especially evident in the pursuit of fitness and the concept of the 'work-out'. Moreover, this might be symptomatic of a wider tendency to reforge one's self-identity in the wake of the increasing diversity of context and authorities. Designing one's own lifestyle becomes a compensation for the effacement of self-identity within an increasing 'openness' of social life.[81] Leisure becomes a form of 'unproductive labour', in the formulation of Baudrillard, something that, like 'old-fashioned' labour, contributes to one's sense of worth and self-respect.[82] If the heritage industry is indeed to be loosely categorised as 'leisure', the profound changes in meaning and loosening of distinctions mean that it can be at least as 'serious' as any other activity that generates money. The miner paid to dig coal for tourists is not necessarily a creature of lower status than he who produced coal for power in an industry that – through no fault of the worker – can no longer compete with other forms of generation.

Finally, there is the technological issue: preservationists and environmentalists argue that heritage in its widest sense is the only economical way forward in the long run while the modernists suggest that the arts, and especially architecture, must keep up with technological advance in order to be suitable for an increasingly advanced society. But this distinction is simplistic as it stands, partly because the preservationist urge, far from being an antiquarian ignorance of the modern, could not have occurred on such a scale without the rapid progress that forms its 'other'. First, much of the urge towards preserving the past seems to come from a reaction to the increasing pace – and unfortunate consequences – of modernisation and technological progress. This is obvious in the field of architecture where the all-too-swift replacement of housing stock in the 1950s and sixties led, for many, to a shocking sense of loss and disorientation. It is also evident in many individual cases, one of the most striking examples in the musical world perhaps being that highly respected American organ builder of the latter half of the twentieth century, Charles B. Fisk. Trained in electronics and nuclear physics, Fisk began his career working on the Manhattan project, but, largely in reaction to the consequences of this experience, he soon pursued a less uncomfortable

career as an organ builder. By the 1960s, he was advocating building
instruments after entirely historical principles, sensing that the 'imperfections' of earlier styles (such as unsteady winding) gave the instruments
more of a human voice. As Patrick Wright has remarked, nothing has
debunked the concept of progress more than the modern developments
in so-called defence: in our age 'an antique Tudor war-machine certainly
makes a more decorous curio than any Cruise missile'.[83]

But many aspects of the restoration movement are actually enabled
by the tremendous post-war advances in technology. Computer analysis
of materials allows painstaking restorations with surviving materials and
also the synthesis of the missing parts (as in the restoration of the Dresden Frauenkirche). Many instrument builders use computers for their
'historical' design, and scientific methods have long been used for the
analysis of watermarks, inks and handwriting in manuscript study. In
other words, many forms of restoration and recreation have been devised precisely because technology has made them possible, and thus
they evidence anything but an ignorance of modernity. The disastrous
fires during the 1980s and 90s at Hampton Court, Uppark House and
Windsor Castle have precipitated an entire restoration industry in England that has learned through its experience, using technology to save
even the least promising looking remains. Moreover, it has engendered
its own 'traditions' in the recreation of pre-modern methods and crafts;
teams of workmen take their experience from one cathedral to another,
just as their ancestors did in the Middle Ages.

The reason that many have been able to afford musical instruments
created according to 'inefficient' craft-like methods, has been because
of the tremendous wealth generated by new technology and market
investment. Many of the finest organs, harpsichords and fortepianos are
made in America and commissioned by individuals and institutions who
have made their wealth through very 'modern' means. In other words,
it is far from the case that modern life demands 'modern' solutions
and modern arts, it is the very success of the modern, and the obscene
superfluities that it generates in some quarters, that makes a return to
pre-industrial technology and traditional crafts conceivable in the first
place. As Lowenthal suggests: 'The vogue for preservation reflects the
victory of the modern. So complete is this victory that we can afford to
save, reproduce, and redistribute innumerable relics of our now distanced
heritage' (*The Past is a Foreign Country*, p. 406). Heritage in this sense is
a form of conspicuous waste. The state which William Morris predicts
for post-industrial England in *News from Nowhere*, in which little new is

invented and only so many inventions as are felt necessary are used (machinery being hidden and silent),[84] is certainly not an inevitability in the present era, but only now is it a possibility, a lifestyle among many. As John Urry suggests, it is the very modernist notion of time that has caused preservationist groups to cultivate a long-term, 'glacial' sense of time, by way of reaction; it becomes imperative to render as durable as possible countless objects, practices and traditions now that constant change and transformation have become the norm.[85]

In the field of early music, it has been precisely the advances in sound reproduction technology that have made much of the earlier repertory viable again. While many repertories, instruments and playing styles flounder in the environment of the nineteenth-century concert hall, recording can transmit the sound of early instruments designed for smaller rooms and recorded at a much closer range than any public environment would permit (see chapter 5, pp. 148–9 above). In Britain, the BBC has been of seminal influence in broadening the appeal of HIP by, for instance, broadcasting from inhospitable churches that have an ideal acoustic for certain types of music. And, finally, there is Taruskin's contention that much within HIP conforms to a modernist aesthetic in any case, something Samuel also observes in the context of the rehabilitation of older houses. Many of the fittings and other features may indeed return to Victorian styles, yet these features often conceal modern, labour-saving devices and the houses are re-formatted to let in more light and continue 1950s ideals of open-plan living (Samuel, *Past and Present*, pp. 75–6). However much heritage movements may react against the supposed impersonality and alienation of modernism, their existence depends on the success – indeed completion – of this movement. As Hobsbawm aptly puts it, 'novelty is no less novel for being able to dress up easily as antiquity', ancient materials are used 'to construct invented traditions of a novel type for quite novel purposes'.[86]

HERITAGE AS BAD HISTORY

Bo-gus? No, I wouldn't say that. I wouldn't say that at all. Vulgar, yes, certainly, in that it is based on a coarsening simplification of pretty well everything. Staggeringly commercial in a way that a poor little country mouse like myself can scarcely credit. Horrible in many of its incidental manifestations. Manipulative in its central philosophy. All these, but not, I think, bogus. (Dr Max, the resident 'expert' assessing the heritage 'Project' in Julian Barnes's *England, England*, p. 131)

Hutchinson's criticism of Skipton's Victorian market reminds us that historical reconstructions often sanitise the past for modern consumption, that if we really wanted to recreate a Victorian environment there would have to be many inconveniences (as was recently tried on a Channel 4 documentary in England) and we would have to recreate an entire social system that contained many injustices: 'It is a deceitful Disneyland for our children to inherit in which history has been rewritten by the packaging of experiences. Real architecture is real history, not repro' (*The Prince of Wales*, p. 10). Thus, the argument would go, it is much better to understand and learn about that past 'as it really was' without actually trying to recreate it, injustices and all. Partial (or diluted) recreation might rather distort our knowledge of the past and the lessons it has to teach us. Even within preservation movements themselves, there is often distaste at too 'clean' a restoration: the patina of age has been erased from Covent Garden, the scars of its life as a market obscured, and the American reconstructions of heritage sites can purposely render imperceivable the distinction between the original and the fabricated. To generalise somewhat baldly, restoration projects in America have traditionally tended towards making the restored objects or their replacements look as 'new' as possible while those in the 'old world' have often attempted to restore the patina of age. In other words, each culture has tended to assimilate the artefact to its basic historical expectations, the one with fewer historical remains and a culture of the 'new', the other with a rich historical landscape already strewn with relics of the past.

Nevertheless, the example of Covent Garden and the restoration of various shopping centres and railway stations in Europe suggests that the 'American' model of 'clean' restoration has become almost equally as strong in the old world. The desire for cleanness, consistency and accuracy has been described as a modernist strain within HIP, and as such is central to Taruskin's critique (particularly of the English strain). The 'European' model of 'distressed' restoration is also common in America, such as at Colonial Williamsburg,[87] and is equally strong within HIP from the earliest years of the movement as a large-scale recording phenomenon. In the Harnoncourt/Leonhardt complete recording of Bach cantatas, Harnoncourt, in particular, capitalised on the unfamiliarity of the old instruments and the players' relative lack of experience (together with the boys' voices and their lack of a fully formed adult technique) to produce a version of Bach that seemed to restore the wear and tear of history. We hear the works afresh in a version that is, literally, 'distressed', both evoking a foreign past and implying the patina of age.

As performers have become more skilled, the 'rough and ready' approach to HIP has somewhat receded, but the spirit of 'distressed' restoration (as opposed to 'clean' modern restoration) lives on in those performers who have cultivated improvisation or creative departures from musical texts that were once considered inviolable – what Taruskin would perhaps describe as the 'crooked' performers (see p. 18 above).

The distaste at 'clean' restoration not only relates to the blandness resulting from the product but also often reflects the awareness that some deception is involved. But to condemn a form of restoration because it is deceptive can obscure a deeper issue: namely, the fact that 'the people' might actually be aware of the deception and welcome it. The city council of Nottingham faced hostile criticism when it issued a tourist leaflet in 1988 admitting that virtually all aspects of the Robin Hood story were mythical.[88] Peter Fowler observes that tourists insist on believing in the Arthurian connections at Tintagel, even while acknowledging his informed opinions to the contrary,[89] and Lowenthal notes that the authors of a 1994 Swiss exhibition debunking the William Tell legend received death threats (*The Heritage Crusade*, p. 130). This tendency is elegantly described by Umberto Eco in his investigation of the American 'faith in fakes' and forms a major strand of Julian Barnes's satire on the English heritage industry. In other words, it does not make sense to criticise anachronism or historical error on the grounds of ignorance or deceit. Indeed, it might be the bewildering surfeit of surviving historical detail and the growing difference we perceive between past and present that make us willing to retell the past in such a way that gives our present condition more permanence and stability (Lowenthal, *The Past is a Foreign Country*, p. 258).

The pervasive interest in make-believe and the culture of deception in which the consumer is implicated as much as the producer is only one side of the coin. Many aspects of environmentalism and heritage are products of a practice that is in essence profoundly religious, in other words based on belief and mythical traditions rather than hard quasi-scientific 'fact'. Artefacts, from the humblest tools to cathedrals, are restored with loving care and detail as if the restorer were communing with some Host from history who is to be honoured and rendered more present through our efforts (Samuel, *Past and Present*, p. 230). Samuel traces the origins of the religious strand of the heritage movement to the Cambridge Camden Society of the 1840s, a Catholic revivalist movement that transferred the numinous qualities that the Reformation had seen exclusively in the Word of God to ecclesiastical buildings and ornaments.

Although subsequent Victorian preservationist movements were largely Protestant, their work was essentially an amplification of this bias. Even to the atheistic Nietzsche, the essential value of history lay not in its information about the past but in its role in the creation of myth.

Lowenthal ultimately disapproves of supporting heritage faith with historical scholarship, since this smudges the line between faith and fact (*The Heritage Crusade*, p. 250). This distinction is surely false, as he seems to admit elsewhere when he remarks that all forms of history and any enterprise of an historical nature require some form of faith: we have to believe that the past did actually exist in some form and if we adopt an attitude of total scepticism the very writing of history will come to a halt (*The Past is a Foreign Country*, p. 236). This also relates to Kivy's criticism of the notion that it is impossible to guess a composer's intention regarding performance or any other aspect of his music. It is indeed impossible to do this with any sense of certainty, but the same proviso applies to discerning any person's intention at any time. The belief that we can often accurately guess the intentions of others is absolutely fundamental to all forms of human interaction and this is far more extensive and complex than the discerning of a fixed, communicable message or an immutable wish. It is the texture of an infinite sequence of spontaneous and often momentary intentions that we may productively construct, as much for the dead as for the living. Such intentive textures are always unrecoverable in their totality (see chapter 3, above).

As with all forms of practice involving belief, heritage has its fundamentalist wing. In HIP this wing has come in for particular criticism since a concern for accurate historical details above all else – and in the absence of much of the necessary evidence – might indeed lead to a sanitised and uninspired performance. The argument for the precise reconstruction of the Globe theatre in London resonates strongly with some of the more fundamentalist aims earlier on in the HIP movement.[90] If modern features are allowed in the reconstruction:

there is no obvious point at which to stop the slide into modernization. Before long there would be a cry to create other modern conveniences such as a transparent roof against the weather, and the original conditions, and certainly the original acoustics, would be gone forever. The line where the authentic reconstruction of the original ends and modernization begins would be impossibly blurred, and the whole principle of authenticity would be lost.[91]

Such slippery-slope arguments founder on their assumption that human experience is entirely unmediated by the context of history and culture, that an identical acoustical and visual event will produce an identical experience. They also assume that the precise reproduction of historical conditions is a good in itself, regardless of the quality, details and historical circumstances of the dramatic or musical work concerned.

However, it would not do to condemn the obsession with historical accuracy across the board, on the grounds that it inevitably leads to sterile performances. A seemingly perfect copy of an historic instrument – or a reconstructed theatre – is not, by its very nature, going to force the performer to play in a sterile manner (or in a particularly 'authentic' manner, for that matter, as Taruskin has shown). The notion of precise reconstruction is useful provided it is to be seen as a starting point for experimentation, an opening of options that could not have been envisaged, rather than as a form of closure that more strictly delimits the definition of a work or repertoire. Moreover, reproduction of original conditions might help us understand something of the choices and decisions the author had and made, the infinite sequence of interactions with the available media being a considerable part of how the piece was written in the first place (see chapter 3, above).

Related to the fundamentalism of reconstruction is the doctrine of 'anti-scrape' that Ruskin and Morris developed in reaction to the seemingly fraudulent 'restorations' of Gothic buildings in Victorian gothic style (Lowenthal, *The Past is a Foreign Country*, pp. 278, 411). This attitude seems to attach an almost religious significance to the appearance of 'natural' ageing, and witnesses a profound distrust in 'human' intervention. Indeed, were replacement components absolutely necessary, Morris and the *SPAB* required that they be clearly distinguished from the original material so as not to deceive the viewer. Although in some ways this is directly opposed to Viollet's fanciful restorations in France (and, even more directly, to Giles Gilbert Scott's in England), Viollet shared with the English preservationists the desire to show the many layers of history, even though his were recreated in the present. To Walter Benjamin, an object's testimony to the full history it has experienced is essential to its authenticity, something that only became fully appreciated in the 'age of mechanical reproduction'. For as soon as the technique of production allowed objects to be made apart from the traditions and uses for which they were devised there was a withering of 'aura'; the potential for an infinite number of copies weakens the notion of a unique existence.[92] The fact that the nineteenth-century restoration movements were interested in historical texture, despite their fundamental differences, might suggest that it is the *appearance* of historical texture, a patina, that is really essential within the urge for preservation and restoration. The entirely inauthentic 'Bach bows' and 'Bach trumpets' at the outset of the twentieth century probably did more to propel forward the enthusiasm for HIP than the authentic items would – it was their distance from their modern equivalents that gave them their particular charm. In a world of forgeries and fakes, it is usually only experts who can tell the difference (and not infallibly, at that, given disputes over authenticity in the art world). However fanatical the pursuit of 'the original', a successful discovery is seldom going to carry an 'authentic aura' that is instantaneously recognisable by all. Benjamin's concept of aura should surely be applied to a particular type of perception, conceivable only in the wake of an age of reproduction (and when it is first threatened), and thus not inherent in the 'object itself'. Thus, while the ubiquity of reproduction makes us aware – as we have never been before – of the status of the original, our ability to distinguish original from reproduction has become progressively uncertain.

One particularly interesting case in recent years is the restoration of Uppark House in Sussex, England. A disastrous fire left the building gutted, although many of the contents were saved. Following a strictly economic policy (replace only if restoration of the original fixture costs more),[93] the house and contents were restored with painstaking accuracy, yet with the necessary 'distressing' to give the impression that nothing had happened and that history had taken its 'natural' course.[94] In this case, experts, far from making a distinction between old and new, used their expertise to render this distinction as imperceptible as possible. 'Distressing' is perhaps the complement of the cultures of rejuvenation (as in bodily care and fitness), recycling and preservation, a belief that reversibility at every level is essential for our survival.[95] What distinguishes this form of restoration from the two attitudes of the nineteenth century is that it combines Viollet's desire for historical texturing with the English antiquarian revulsion at the trace of its own restorative effort. While Morris saw anything more than basic conservation – the attempt to ensure that fragments did not deteriorate any further – as a form of falsification, the 'Uppark syndrome' fully embraces falsification as a guiding principle of historical authenticity, one that restores the patina of time.

Is this then a cynical exploitation of the evident gullibility of the general public (a criticism that is very familiar from the HIP debates)? Or is it, rather, the acknowledgement that 'falsification' is unavoidable in any historical enterprise and that what really counts is the illusion of authenticity, the reclaiming of historicity, and is something in which we all are complicit? If continuity and ontological consistency are unavailable unimpaired, why not indeed use the most advanced technology to create them? It is perhaps not the case that we prefer things aged by time in themselves 'but the sense of life they impart, from the evidence of their struggle with time'.[96]

Much of the criticism of heritage as 'bad history' comes from professional specialists who sense there is something suspect about a wide populist historicist movement which is subject to few rigorous controls. Moreover, the gulf between these two factions has grown considerably in the latter decades of the modern movement. While there was something of a consensus between architects and preservationists over the sad fate of the neo-classical Euston Arch in the early 1960s, this alliance was quite dead twenty years later.[97] Similar shifts are perhaps evident in the fields of musicology and historical performance. While in the 1950s and 60s many scholars writing on earlier music assumed that a large amount of their work would result in more accurate texts and performances that were more informed historically, the situation changed when HIP became a commercial force in its own right. As Dreyfus has shown (1983), musicologists were all too eager to expose the naivety of taking scanty historical evidence at face value,[98] but pure empiricism was not in fact the driving-force of the movement. The best performer–scholars were using the evidence in ever-changing ways and the real threat they posed was in their revolutionary challenge to the supposed norms of western music. Certainly, this sense of threat is still felt by Peter Kivy, writing as late as 1995, for whom the modern concert hall, with its modern conventions and modern instruments, provides the ideal 'museum' for the greater works of musical art (see chapter 1, p. 36 above).

Yet there are several other reasons for the increasing musicological antipathy to HIP. Driven by its own specialist performers from the 1960s onwards, figures within HIP started to make their own editions and interpretative theories without the help of institutionalised musicologists, thus making the latter effectively redundant in the one area of performance where they felt they could make a difference in the 'real world'.[99] Moreover, the performing figures often had to make imaginative decisions in the face of incomplete evidence and were soon distancing themselves from the objectivism of traditional musicology through the very action of spontaneous performance. The discipline of 'performance practice' thus became very much a suspect activity to the mainstream of musicology and composition. It was a 'soft' discipline that fell between too many epistemological cracks – at least to those who held to strict 'positivist' musicology – and a pursuit of the utmost triviality to those who embraced the newer cultural-studies approach to musicology, who saw their purpose in making music central to the cultural and political debates of the age. Trivial and soft though much HIP research may be, some of the real antipathy must lie in the popularity of HIP in the main and the fact that it is embraced by so many amateurs both at the level of performance and of research.

Samuel draws attention to the frequency with which Heritage is a 'whipping boy of Cultural Studies' and 'a prime example of those tutelary complexes which it is the vocation of critical inquiry to unmask', on account of its tendency to provide a 'clean', unthreatening picture of the past (Samuel, *Past and Present*, p. 260). The uncritical nature of much of the heritage industry is, of course, an all-too-easy target, but it is also the case that virtually any form of historical undertaking constitutes a falsification and a necessary cleansing of the past. The very act of rendering knowable whatever remains from the past requires a form of 'domestication', the historian removing or ignoring elements that do not suit the story at hand and inventing countless details to give depth to the narrative (p. 271). While historians throughout the ancient world and Middle Ages had to invent much of their material, modern historians no longer knowingly forge documents but rather have to fabricate contexts: 'Footnotes serve as fetishes and are given as authorities for generalizations which a thousand different instances would not prove' (pp. 433–4). Lowenthal's three limitations on the possibility of recreating the past – the immensity of the past, the distinction between the lost past and the surviving accounts of it, and the inevitability of presentist bias (*The Past is a Foreign Country*, p. 214–16) – are absolutely essential caveats for any historical undertaking and apply as much to academic History as they do to Heritage.

Moreover, common pitfalls in Heritage work are equally prevalent in 'History Proper'. There is the same sense that the past is somehow 'safe' because it is completed and therefore can be tamed and neatly ordered so as to counteract the uncertainties of the present (Lowenthal, *The Past is a Foreign Country*, p. 62). Moreover, the type of uniformity that Daniel Leech-Wilkinson observed quite early on in the Early Music Debate – namely, that numerous groups, covering many different styles of music, tended to adopt similar mannerisms, totally divorced from historical evidence – is obvious within any particular school or period of history writing.[100] Particular fashionable approaches, expressions or buzzwords are applied by a wide range of contemporaneous historians to virtually any historical

phenomenon. Just as the various rooms of a historic building are restored
back to their own peak periods, giving the impression that the epochs
all reached their peak at the same time (Lowenthal, *The Past is a Foreign
Country*, p. 351), HIP can render each period of performance as detailed
and vital as the next. Exactly the same observation could be made of
the finest academic journal or essay collection; every author will address
each age, work or subject with the optimum vividness.

What perhaps distinguishes the Heritage arts, including HIP, is their
tendency to use the evidence in several different ways simultaneously,
according to what suits the project at hand. In other words, the grounds
for the use of historical evidence are constantly shifting and are hard
to establish with a 'scientific' consistency. In professional history, such
grounds are normally more rigorously and consistently maintained, at
least for each individual study, although the historical contexts might
be equally fabricated. On the other hand, much recent so-called 'new
musicology' has, in fact, come closer to the performative model. Here it
is difficult to substantiate or refute an author's approach simply because
there is no consistent model for relating the narrative to the available
evidence. The history, or cultural criticism, often stands or falls according
to the rhetorical flair of the writer concerned.

If it is true that Heritage shares with professional history elements
of make-believe and fabrication, there are also significant differences
underlying the professional historian's contempt. First, there is a type of
literary snobbery that sees true knowledge as residing in books, which
demand active reading rather than merely offering the passive pleasure of
television. An interest in objects, scenarios and practices may even arouse
a puritan distrust of graven images (Samuel, *Past and Present*, pp. 262–7).
Professional history not only tends to fetishise the written record but it
also tends to be practised in complete detachment from the material
environment. If there is any more retrieval work still to be done there
are always 'lower level' workers such as archivists and librarians to do
it; it is the job of the sophisticated historian to interpret and link the
'raw' information (p. 269). This attitude has been evident in musicology
since, at the latest, the famous dispute between Edward Lowinsky and
Joseph Kerman in the 1960s, the former accusing the latter of a form
of professional elitism and of expecting the facts to be served up to the
critic on a silver platter.[101]

Finally, there is the notion that History and Heritage are competing
in their control and sovereignty over the past, recreating or describing
the past 'as it actually was' with equal enthusiasm, but in different ways

(Samuel, *Past and Present*, p. 270). It is not surprising, given this competition for power, that there must be some degree of envy on the part of academic music historians when the slippery history of HIP often gains so much more public interest and media exposure. But, as Samuel suggests, it is quite possible for academic History to profit from the variety of perspectives offered by Heritage: the former's narrow preoccupation with words can be tempered and enlarged with a new-found appreciation of looks, colours and palettes (p. 274). In the musical field, the enquiry into historical performance can offer valuable information on the kinaesthetic experience of performance in different styles, or the combination of several historical elements in dramatic production. Of course, this activity is never going to reproduce an historical reality, nor is there any way of recognising this were it actually to have been achieved. Moreover, enormous elements of cultural context are entirely unretrieveable. But exactly the same problems bedevil any historical endeavour whatever; all are equally 'bogus' in their different ways. While Lowenthal acknowledges Samuel's viewpoint that heritage and history both involve some degree of fabrication, he attempts to make an essential distinction between the two (*The Heritage Crusade*, esp. p. 119). History examines the past on it own terms for it very difference with the present, while heritage unashamedly appropriates the past for present purposes. However, his view that 'objectivity remains a holy grail for even the most engagé historian' (p. 109) seems severely to limit the definition of history to the narrower positivist traditions of both nineteenth and twentieth centuries. It runs the risk of implying that history proper is devoid of critical and interpretative content. Furthermore, Lowenthal's view that history is universal and universally accessible (p. 120) falls prey to narrow western prejudice. Nevertheless, his dichotomy might usefully be modified to represent the two poles of the broader historical urge.

The same line of argument applies to the notion that 'invented traditions' are somehow inferior to continuous ones. This attitude, to which even Eric Hobsbawm and Carl Dahlhaus are sometimes prone, raises again the chimera of 'authenticity', debunking it as a claim within the heritage industry but applying it to traditions in which the lines of practice are apparently unbroken. Of course, it is absolutely within the remit of critical scholarship to unmask claims that excellence resides in a tradition on account of its antiquity, by showing that much within the tradition is of remarkably recent vintage. A typical example of this is David Cannadine's study of the ceremonial of the British monarchy.[102]

Also extremely useful is Hobsbawm's observation that traditions are often invented at more or less the same time – such as during a particularly fertile period between 1870 and 1914 – and that such inventions are usually made when there is a public desire for the securities they offer (Hobsbawm, 'Mass-Producing Traditions', p. 263). Furthermore, such traditions – however archaic their practices or political colour – rely on the widespread progress of electoral democracy and mass politics (p. 267–8), and many of these have capitalised on the importance of 'irrational' elements in maintaining stability and order in an increasingly rationalised society.

But Hobsbawm seems to be making a dangerous and romantic distinction when he states that, 'the strength and adaptability of genuine traditions is not to be confused with the "invention of tradition". Where the old ways are alive, traditions need be neither revived nor invented' ('Introduction', p. 8). While there is an obvious conceptual difference between a traditional (especially non-western) culture and one that has been modelled on this in more recent times, there is surely no clear-cut practical distinction between the two. A continuous tradition might have undergone as many, if not more, modifications than one that is consciously invented. If Cannadine has made it more fashionable to ridicule the British monarchy on account of the relative novelty of so many of its traditions, this is not in fact in the debunking of an 'invented tradition' as such, rather – and perhaps much more potently – in the criticism of tradition *per se*, and its claims to legitimacy through continuity. In other words, *any* tradition, if it is to be successful, at least in the western world, has to reinvent itself on a regular basis if it is to survive at all.

Carl Dahlhaus, in examining the culture of restoration in nineteenth-century music, has suggested that any attempt at restoration will always contain traces of the original break in tradition, however strong the efforts to make that tradition appear 'natural'. Restoration is caught between Schiller's dialectic of the naive and the sentimental as nineteenth-century attempts at recovering the Palestrina idiom fail to avoid an element of longing and historical distance, and sixteenth-century modality unwittingly sounds as an 'other' within the context of romantic tonality, rather than as a universal norm.[103] All this is true enough, but it does not necessarily invalidate the attempts at restoration; indeed, by showing that these cannot escape the environment and attitudes of the present, Dahlhaus seems tacitly to justify them within the aesthetic of the new. However antiquarian the intentions of the restorers they cannot avoid sounding in some sense up-to-date, new or even exotic.

Dahlhaus's view that restoration can never cover its breaks in continuity implies that tradition 'proper' has a seamlessness, or at least a continuity, that is somehow more authentic than naked restoration. Yet one form of continuity can come with a radical break in some other regard; indeed, the very respectability of continuity can be used to disguise a departure. In sum then, neither tradition nor restoration guarantee continuity, nor is there any reason why they should be expected to do so. A conscious sense of tradition may conceal breaks and departures, just as restoration carries with it an inevitable sense of alterity or longing for the truly absent; furthermore, revolution itself may nourish hidden continuities of tradition and utopian notions of restoring an idealised historical past.

Just as restoration can never be entirely free of the attitudes of the modern age, the most consistent of continuities will never be immune from the changes surrounding it. In the context of twentieth-century HIP, the notion that HIP has destroyed a 'genuine' and 'single' tradition is increasingly implausible, especially in the light of closer examination of the diverse recorded evidence of pre-HIP performance in the twentieth century. Many features that we might otherwise have considered 'natural' to the mainstream tradition, such as continuous string vibrato, now appear to have been of very recent vintage. Moreover, it is clear that HIP has spawned many of its own traditions, which, however young, can lead to lively communities of performance. However much HIP may have originally eschewed 'tradition', it has automatically created traditions of its own. In short, tradition of any kind or age might be considered welcome evidence of human activity and interaction; but any claims that it gives an activity a quasi-genetic legitimacy or 'authenticity' are usually as flawed as they are dangerous.

HERITAGE AS REACTIONARY POLITICS

If the 'living museum' concept has animated the static objects of a traditional museum by putting them into some sort of wider context, HIP could claim to have done something similar within the musical field. Thus, while it has been a commonplace to assert that HIP imports a museum culture into music, it is rather more a question of music being transferred from one form of museum (i.e. the concert hall) to another (one more akin to the 'living museum'). Much of HIP, with its interest in broadening the context of the sound-related aspects of performance, does not concern itself with issues that are not palpably 'musical'.

But reconstructions of entire liturgies and complex court entertainments are also becoming increasingly common. Whatever direction these trends may be taking, the most important point is that as soon as context becomes an issue in the performance of music, the hermetic, antihistorical seal of the artwork is broken, and technically any historical element may become eligible for reconstruction.

Does this then mean that the original political context – and thus much of the social meaning – of the music becomes part of its restored form? To say that such implications are irrelevant not only returns the music to whatever ideology covertly accompanies the very concept of autonomous music, but it also stunts the activity of historical thinking that should surely be part of the very definition of HIP. Certainly HIP has been used in 'extra-musical' contexts, perhaps the most striking example being the burial ceremony held in 1984 for the English and (as it was presumed) American bones found on the Tudor wreck of the *Mary Rose* in Portsmouth. The entire service was done in period style (with simultaneous participation in Alabama), complete with Sarum Mass and reproduction coffin nails.[104] Clearly this was more than just an interesting experiment in historical reconstruction; the service must have served complex religious purposes, as if completing the unfinished business of five centuries before with a ritual the victims might have recognised. The period elements clearly also played on the sense of English and American cultural identity, by providing an historical grounding that was common to both cultures.

The concern for context is an essential part of the Heritage movement in general. Some of its more powerful origins may lie in the American living history installations beginning in the 1920s (see p. 180 above), but it became increasingly important after World War II. It was first articulated in British political circles as a response to the plight of country house owners facing crippling death duties and other high taxes in the aftermath of the war. The Gowers report of 1950 showed a move away from the pre-war argument that owners should be able to enjoy their private property in peace and security towards one based on context and the importance of the 'ensemble' to the cultural value of country houses. All aspects of the house, gardens, family and estate should be preserved as a 'way of life' in which the sum of its parts is more important than the individual elements.[105] Although the ensuing decade became the peak of country-house demolition, reducing the national stock by 10 per cent, the 'way of life' argument gradually gained ground in the 1960s and 70s (Mandler, 'Nationalising the Country House', pp. 108–10). Perhaps as a result of the very decline in the political power and perceived privilege of the aristocracy, the 'ensemble' concept became credible and it was possible to conceive of the aristocratic 'way of life' as a popular public 'property'. As Mandler has shown, the French chateaux tradition has had a more stable and secure history than the country house culture of Britain since the French owners have been accustomed to partial 'nationalisation' since the 1840s. By giving up at least some parts of the 'ensemble', the private owners in France have enjoyed more consistent public sympathy and support (p. 114). Yet the success has clearly also involved the owners continuing their occupancy, thus giving some authenticity to the surviving ensemble, albeit on considerably reduced terms.

The idea of restoring a context to make old artefacts 'work' might also evidence the influence of the nature conservation movement. The survival of many species of flora and fauna is dependent on returning them to their 'original habitat' (or something close), and it is not difficult to imagine how this scientific fact could influence our beliefs about artefacts from a disappearing human past. Reciprocally, the context thrives from the animating presence that has been restored to it: the countryside becomes fuller and richer with the 'correct' animals, the country house becomes more 'lived in' and, to circle back to HIP, seemingly obsolete instruments come back to life and forgotten repertories begin to speak to us.

Context has surfaced in another, more aesthetic, debate. As I outlined above, all European countries endured considerable modernisation during the 1950s and 60s, which involved the destruction of far more 'period' buildings than the war itself had wrought (at least outside Germany). Emblematic of this trend was the English city of Bath, which at the end of the war was one of the most complete 'period' cities in the world. The developers followed a policy which would seem to make sense according to traditional critical aesthetics: preserve the greater buildings, the 'set pieces', while replacing many of the lesser ones. Such practice is perfectly consonant with the 'canonic' arts which both allow lesser works to fall into oblivion and promote new developments (virtually in tandem).[106] Yet as Adam Fergusson made clear in his hysterical, yet pathbreaking, study The Sack of Bath, 1973,[107] removing the lesser buildings from the ensemble had rendered the city like a collection of 'mountains without foothills, like Old Masters without frames'.[108] His writing was one of the most influential articulations of the profound shift away from modernist conceptions of artistic progress.

While destruction and replacement throughout Europe had taken place on a modest scale during the last two centuries or so, the pace of change was slow, and regular enough to meet with little organised resistance. But the wholesale modernisation of the 1950s and sixties had engendered a complete change of attitude. Suddenly, context became of crucial importance, gaining a value that it had never had before. Thus, together with the historical 'ways of life' argument, the awareness of architectural context became the second important predisposition for the public enthusiasm for HIP. The example of Bath and other such cities was visible proof that the belief in individual, autonomous artworks – effortlessly transferable from one context to another – was simply inadequate in the situation of advanced modernity.

To the 'way of life' and 'aesthetic' concepts of context could be added a third, rather elusive sense of context, that I term 'homeopathic'. This involves importing something believed to be historically authentic (i.e. genuine) into the modern work or performance, in the belief that its influence will somehow spread throughout the whole and create a sense of authenticity. Lowenthal offers an extreme example, the filming of Waugh's *Brideshead Revisited*, in which the producers went to great lengths to secure the original sites used in the novel: Waugh's Oxford rooms, Castle Howard and Venice (Lowenthal, *The Past is a Foreign Country*, p. 231). The intention was to make the experience 'real for the actors', although Lowenthal claims that this 'degrades the novel's fantasy world by making it seem a slice of the actual past, with real rather than fictional events'. Yet it is surely the case that much of the power of fiction lies in its intersection with the 'real' and its articulation of possible worlds through the author's insights into actual experience. By believing that they were experiencing something that Waugh himself experienced the actors were not necessarily reducing his possible world to the actual but rather had the incentive to relive something of the author's own creative experience, thus making this a part of their own creative impulse. In sum, the 'homeopathic' notion of historical context, for all its vagaries, must be supremely important, since all forms of historical reconstruction work only with fragments from the past (regardless of the beliefs of the people concerned); a little bit of history usually has to go a very long way.

The argument against the preservation and recreation of context is based on two beliefs that can be held separately, but that – more often than not – intertwine. The first is the familiar modernist view that considers context to be irrelevant to art that is truly great, and the second is the view that the context brings with it the political implications of the original situation and thus evidences a reactionary stance and prolongs a backward political system. Not only can these views be used to support one another – e.g. we can appreciate the enlightened greatness of art precisely by peeling away the archaic context – but many still hold modernism in its original definition as a progressive movement that frees us from the injustices of the past. But, as Danto has observed, the history of modernism itself is one of 'purgation, or generic cleansing'. The political analogue of modernism was therefore not the specific politics of Left or Right but the concept of totalitarianism *per se*, 'with its ideas of racial purity and its agenda to drive out any perceived contaminant' (*After the End of Art*, p. 70).

Hewison, on the other hand, makes much of Roger Scruton's attack on modernism as the architecture of Leninism (*The Heritage Industry*, p. 76) and thus assumes that any antipathy to modernism is, by definition, the sign of a political reactionary. He notes that the *National Trust's* 'commitment to the continued occupation of houses for which it accepts responsibility by the families that formerly owned them has preserved a set of social values as well as dining chairs and family portraits' (p. 71). Furthermore, the attempt to underplay the museum quality of the exhibit reflects a refusal to interpret the historical evidence. The 'lived in' look of the houses negates, for Hewison, the idea of history as a process of development and change, and the private privilege represented by the houses 'becomes a question of national prestige'. A very similar view is presented by David Cannadine in a review of an exhibition in Washington of British country house treasures. To him, the exhibition presented not only the moveable treasures in a golden light, but also their houses and owners.[109] The real object of the exercise was not just the preservation of the 'ensemble' but also of the aristocratic system itself; the past activities of the noble class are idealised as a way of ensuring their protection in the future. In an elegant twist, he suggests that '[o]nce it was the country-house culture which was parasitic on the country-house élite; now it is the élite which is even more parasitic on the culture' (*The Pleasures of the Past*, p. 268). The answer, as Cannadine sees it, is to appreciate the great objects as art in galleries where they are accessible to all and shorn of the elitist connotations that inevitably accompany the cult of the country house. However, the idea of the museum as by nature a 'neutral' context is surely to miss the structures of power with which the museum itself may be associated. As Danto has observed, '[a]s long as the museums were represented as temples to truth-through-beauty, the realities of power were invisible' (*After the End of Art*, p. 182).[110] Moreover, even if the aims of those promoting the country-house exhibitions had been the specifically reactionary ones that Hewison and Cannadine assume, there is no certainty that the exhibitions would have been 'read' that way by the visitors. Indeed, there is mounting evidence that the public views museums and displays in startlingly diverse ways, many of which could not have been conceived by those who devise the exhibitions in the first place (Urry, in *Theorizing Museums*, pp. 53–4).

But it must be quite freely admitted that a concern for heritage and context *can* indeed support a reactionary view. The English architect, Quinlan Terry, is a fundamentalist Christian who builds houses in classical (or is it postmodern?) design using the Venetian 14-inch foot, in the belief that classical orders in architecture reflect and enhance the orders of God and society.[111] The tremendous growth in his trade during the Thatcher years nicely substantiates the view that would automatically associate Heritage, reactionary politics and new conservatism. Moreover, Cannadine's point about country house culture could be demonstrated by the case of the Tory MP (albeit 'wet'), Patrick Cormack, who was one of the most influential supporters of heritage in Britain in the late 1970s. His writing contains an *ad hominem* attack on those promoting the democratic, museum solution to country house treasures (*Heritage in Danger*, pp. 163–4), and his romantic view of the aristocratic collecting instinct and the concept of 'stewardship' entails assisting those who, through birth, 'have the duty of guarding much of a country's history and heritage' (p. 177). Here there is clear evidence of an association of class, tradition and national pride that goes well beyond the *National Trust's* policy of allowing the original owners to live on as tenants. The main question, then, is whether the latter policy – which gives emphasis to the concept of ensemble and the 'lived-in' quality of the whole – *necessarily* reduces to the notion that the aristocratic system itself should be propped up with tax cuts and other benefits.

Heritage movements themselves display extremely diverse political origins and appropriations. Back in the nineteenth century, the English gothic revival was basically a High Tory movement, hostile (unlike the modern Conservatives) to the industrial and capitalist world and thus much that was basically modern (Wiener, *English Culture*, p. 64). On the other hand, preservationism tended to challenge the rights of private property owners, running against traditional conservative values (p. 70). Morris's Arts and Crafts movement originated as a radical and socialist movement, but it attracted many who did not share Morris's politics, such as Tories who saw in Old England not an ideal egalitarian utopia untarnished by industrialisation but an organic social hierarchy.[112] Moreover, in its most direct American descendant, William Sumner Appleton Jr's *Society for the Preservation of New England Antiquities* (1910), Morris's movement was co-opted for overtly racist purposes.[113]

The growth of the early music movement under Arnold Dolmetsch clearly fitted Morris's Arts and Crafts ethos like a glove. Moreover, in its desire for pre-modern simplicity and social stability, it shared much with the growing folk movement (with figures such as R.R. Terry simultaneously spanning several restoration movements in music: plainsong, Renaissance polyphony and folksong).[114] Here again, the political mix is striking: for Hubert Parry, a high Tory, folksong provided a refuge from the commercialised present but also provided the authentic ground for national and racial identity. As Richard Luckett observes, only the slightest change of emphasis made the same arguments central to Cecil Sharp's Fabian determination to give native songs and dances back to the English people in their purest state. The movement 'proved equally attractive to reactionary traditionalists, to liberal-socialist waverers such as Rupert Brooke . . . and to dogmatic believers in the virtues of anything that appeared to emanate from the common people.'[115] What seems so striking about movements looking back to the lifestyle and cultural practices of past ages, then, is not that their politics are inessential but that the politics can be both so diverse and so extreme.

Another important stage in the nineteenth-century Heritage movement went hand-in-hand with the re-invention of monarchical tradition. The growing British enthusiasm for tradition was pursued in India from the 1860s, where the rulers attempted to preserve or reinstate traditions of Indian dress. As Lowenthal adds, early twentieth-century British attempts to reinstate tribal traditions in Africa clashed awkwardly with colonial assumptions about customary law and political structure (*The Past is a Foreign Country*, p. 337). Much of the British tradition for 'historical authenticity' in performance must lie in these tendencies within its colonial past, a communal desire to reverse the outward appearance of the modernising and colonising urge. But to condemn Heritage and HIP on the grounds of a colonial strand in its genealogy would also be to condemn most contemporary forms of anthropological study, not least ethnomusicology. As Lowenthal puts it, 'It is a common delusion that to retain any memory of a past iniquity serves to justify it' (*The Heritage Crusade*, p. 159).

While the large-scale European use of 'Heritage' stems from the European Architectural Heritage Year of 1975, the term had already been appropriated by the conservative *Heritage Foundation* in the US in

1973; furthermore, the *Heritage USA* themepark is associated with a fundamentalist Christian broadcasting network (Samuel, *Past and Present*, p.
289, Hewison, *The Heritage Industry*, p. 31). Yet in France the term had
been associated with the Left since the time of the Revolution. The concept of 'patrimoine' was part and parcel of Republican education and
thought and embraced all aspects of national heritage regardless of the
origins of the artefacts and buildings concerned (Samuel, *Past and Present*,
pp. 289–90). Conversely, national heritage in Germany (including a
flourishing early music movement, especially at the youth level) was appropriated by the Nazis during the 1930s, something which accounts
for the relative antipathy towards national heritage in Germany, even
into the 1960s (p. 290).[116] This might relate to the comparative slowness
of the post-war HIP movement in Germany compared with Holland,
Switzerland, Austria and America (a notable exception to this trend
being August Wenzinger's *Cappella Coloniensis*, founded in 1954). Prominent German intellectuals and composers, such as Theodor Adorno and
Ernst Krenek, condemned early music movements and neo-classicism
in compositional style on account of their resonance with the nauseating
dilution of art to craft, so characteristic of the Nazi youth movement (see
chapter 1, p. 6 above).[117]

The Collegium Musicum movement, meanwhile, flourished in the
United States where it was largely led by German and Jewish refugees
(including Hindemith himself) who could hardly have carried the stigma
of National Socialism. By the 1970s the younger generation in Germany
had simply forgotten these earlier associations and, like the other late-
comer to the Heritage movement, Britain, embraced it with particular
fervour. This was also, incidentally, the time that Green politics came to
the fore, another movement that had been appropriated, for its nature
and national mysticism, by the Nazis. Wiener notes a similar association of fascistic sentiments and rural myth in interwar England (Wiener,
English Culture, p. 107), but, given the comparative weakness of the fascist
wing and its disappearance during the course of the war, the association
presumably withered during the 1940s.

Several figures within HIP, as it stands at the beginning of the new
century, seem purposely or otherwise to embody the political context of
the music with which they are most closely associated: one hardly needs to
name conductors who are neo-aristocrats in the Netherlands and Austria,
absolute monarchists in France and self-proclaimed enlightened despots
in England. Nikolaus Harnoncourt is a particularly interesting figure in
this regard, someone who sees a general decline in music culture over

the last two centuries. Music has become less central to our lives and has therefore come to be seen as merely 'beautiful'. One of the major causes of this was the French Revolution and the institutionalisation of music within the new conservatoire system initiated by the revolution. The listener too 'is still suffering from the emasculation resulting from the French Revolution'.[118]

But, on the other hand, it is equally easy to find counter-cultural figures in early music, those who espouse environmental movements and those who see HIP as specifically the venue for democratised music-making, liberated from the hierarchical factory conditions of modern orchestral culture. Shelemay describes an American group that combined musical performance with yoga, meditation and general socialising; its repertory ranged from Medieval and Renaissance music to folk music of US and European provenance ('Towards an Ethnomusicology of the Early Music Movement', pp. 19–20). Ironically, the trend towards underplaying the role of the conductor (or, at least, the director with a single-minded inter- pretative stance to the music) often ignores the hierarchical structure of the music establishment originally associated with the music performed (see p. 9 above). Indeed, the road towards democratisation may be pre- cisely what is wrong with some forms of HIP, if we follow Taruskin in deploring the concept of neutralised performances, and the removal of individuality and character from musical interpretation. But the point begins to emerge that HIP may well be able to turn the autonomous mu- sical work into an 'ensemble' of historical elements without the original system of values *necessarily* emerging. Our bourgeois ability to abstract an artwork from its context thus still seems to work, even if a few aspects of that original context have been retroactively added to the field surround- ing the phenomenon identified as the work. The necessary rootlessness of HIP means that it does indeed present an opportunity to deploy a new politics of performance without necessarily negating the historicist basis of the exercise.

But, given that the concern for historical context seems more impor- tant in some periods than others, might there not be some underlying cultural (and thus political) reason for these changes of emphasis? Canna- dine associates the historical impulses towards Heritage and the simpler rural life in England with periods of economic depression: namely, the last quarter of the nineteenth century, the inter-war period and the slump of the mid-1970s (*The Pleasures of the Past*, p. 257). These periods of pes- simism and anxiety also coincide politically with shifts to the right, since depression tends to divide the left and open the field for conservatives.

Cannadine here makes his typical conflation of the conservative political scene with the nostalgic desire to preserve the artefacts of a past elite culture, attempting to refute the (to him) implausible claim that they really belong to everyone (p. 259).

Samuel also observes the coincidence of the historicist turns with moments of conservative political culture. But he explains the most recent coincidence (i.e. in the last two decades of the twentieth century) not as the symbiosis of Heritage and Reaction but as a result of some significant political and economic developments that were quite unlike anything that had happened before: this was the time at which traditional class divisions in society began to break down together with the barrier between 'high' and 'low' culture. The concept of the 'popular' was thus robbed of its subversive potential and could even itself be annexed to the conservative cause (*Past and Present*, pp. 163–4). On the other hand, many on the Left could not understand these fundamental shifts in meaning. Part of the traditional brief of British socialism had been the utopian transformation of housing with high-rise flats and the obliteration of the architectural legacy of Victorian industrialism. Thus the demolition of tower blocks and the rehabilitation of what had previously been considered 'slums' immediately seemed like the most pernicious form of reaction. But in other European countries, where considerations of housing style were merely secondary to the socialist cause, the housing of previous eras was not made to carry such devastating connotations. This in itself seems evidence enough for the seemingly uncontentious fact that historical artefacts can only carry the meanings that a broad consensus attributes to them.

When the term 'heritage' became used in Britain in the late 1970s it had a Conservative ring since it was often used as a stick to beat an inflexible Labour regime that threatened to tax owners of 'heritage' property almost out of existence. Patrick Wright perhaps gives one of the most detailed and subtle analyses of the strands comprising the British Heritage movement in the early 1980s. First, there is the 'complacent bourgeois alignment' which is essentially a reworking of the 'Whiggish' historical tradition, in which a complacent present looks narcissistically to the past to review the stages leading to its own more perfected state (*On Living in an Old Country*, pp. 147–8); secondly, the 'anxious aristocrat alignment' which, conversely, senses a betrayal and thwarting of historical promise and thus seeks to preserve whatever it can of a fragile past. Wright notes that these two strands can often align and thus give a particularly complex meaning to preservation movements (p. 149). But it is not clear how this means that preservation can thus 'be implicitly and in a dis-placed way about preserving those social relations which are taken for granted and legitimised by the public rendition of history as the national past'. This connection is rendered even more tenuous by Wright's next category that outlines the essentially anti-historicist bent of the Tories in the 1980s: the 'anti-traditional technicist alignment', epitomised by Margaret Thatcher's complaint that the miners' leader, Arthur Scargill, wished to plunge the country into a 'museum society' (pp. 150–1). The fact that Thatcher did, in fact, often present aspects of the past as a new future (p. 185) hardly substantiates the view that all forms of historicism are part of that same conservative impulse.

Wiener suggests that the anti-industrial, rural myth is essential to the Tory character right up to the beginning of the Thatcher years (the point at which he was writing). Moreover, he contends that English radical and socialist movements were conservative at heart since they tended 'to erect barriers to economic appetites and to sublimate their force in higher pursuits' (*English Culture*, p. 120).[19] But had Wiener been writing ten years later he might well have told a different story, and his view that the thwarting of economic appetite is conservative rings rather strangely in the wake of the free market policies of the Thatcher years. In short, the definitions of 'liberal' and 'conservative' have radically altered, and in many ways swapped, during the last twenty years of the twentieth century: liberalism, from the nineteenth century onwards, sponsored an unfettered market economy and modernisation, whilst pre-Thatcherite conservatism held such 'progressive' elements in disdain and tended to advocate a traditionalist and, literally, conservative society. Heritage and its associated movements (even including, perhaps, environmentalism) might be conservative in a traditional sense of the word that relates closely to the notion (and the related term) of 'conservation' but this hardly coincides with the changing political uses of the term.

By the end of the 1980s, heritage products and HIP recordings and performances were popular enough to render them economically vi-able and profitable, nicely thwarting the anti-modern motives of many within the movements. Thus Heritage became, by definition, an ele-ment of the new conservatism which espoused anything that made a profit in the free market. If it was more profitable to build in period styles and preserve older buildings, this was inevitably the direction in which property developers would go. To support the movement for its counter-cultural rejection of the present by buying its products was to make it ever more part of the present economic reality. In other words, it is the wider economic system, not a hidden reactionary elite, that lies behind the success of Heritage; the customer is as deeply implicated in the process as the producer. Most writers who nowadays automatically associate any form of conservation or heritage with conservatism are often employing an outdated definition of the term (as it is used politically) and assuming that Heritage conjures up the reactionary social system that the 'old' conservatism also entailed.

The fact that the second wave of Thatcherism in the 1980s attacked modernism as socialism's cultural form does not mean that the post- or anti-modern is going to be automatically reactionary.[120] Indeed, David Edgar notes that many of the complaints about modernism from the cultural Right are also echoed on the Left ('The New Nostalgia', pp. 31–3). Many of the more insidious forms of modernist architecture are the product of American capitalists and socialist countries have often demanded the most thorough preservation of their existing heritage (see also p. 177 above, for Bologna). Many of the 'new' conservatives make a conflation of Heritage and an archaic political order, just as do the critics on the left.[121] Samuel also senses a fundamental antipathy of conservative thought to Heritage, in that the latter will often reveal the grimy truth about a country's legendary moments (*Past and Present*, p. 164); moreover, it has the potential to dilute the 'great' events and figures in a welter of historical detail, just as HIP has threatened to do for musical masterworks.

Perhaps the most spectacular example of heritage-baiting from the Right is provided by Roger Scruton in his romantic polemic, *On Hunting*.[122] Heritage threatens his deep sense of rooted community by slowly emptying rural life 'of its entrails' and then preserving it as a 'varnished skin' (pp. 26–7). The rhetorical similarity with Hewison's view of the heritage industry is profound here, even though the political motivations are entirely different. Scruton's comment that heritage has 'packaged the remaining fragments of real life and sold them off . . . to be visited, gawped at and swallowed from the inside of a motor car' (p. 27) parallels directly his criticisms of HIP (see p. 13, above). His point of view does seem to confirm one thing, though: the fact that Heritage's work does *not* preserve the reality of earlier forms of life, that in its very act of preservation it cuts off some of its roots with the actual past. On the other hand, his very nostalgia for lost traditions is itself – parallel with the Heritage phenomenon – part of a complex reaction to 'detraditionalization'.[123] Moreover, he is absolutely correct in naming the motor industry as a principal cause of the heritage idea, 'driving highways hither and thither for no other purpose than to reach places rendered uniformly dull by the ease of reaching them', and such machines being 'not so much used as *consumed*'. Such technology relates to the Heritage phenomenon in exactly the same way as audio technology relates to HIP, something which 'drives highways' into parts of music history that would otherwise have been unimaginable.

For Samuel, Heritage, far from being the false prolongation of a past order, can actually be an escape from inherited class, just as environmentalism offers an alternative to the 'worn-out routines of party politics'. Consequently 'period' consistency replaces 'pedigree' in personal options (in architecture and design, for instance), one has a choice from the full range of historical styles regardless of one's background, and one can 'indulge in a romance of otherness' (*Past and Present*, p. 247). Lowenthal relates Heritage specifically to the decline of 'traditional heritage' so beloved of Scruton, which has succumbed to secularism, the terminal decline of inherited status and the rise of a populist nationalism that tends to exalt vernacular culture (*The Heritage Crusade*, pp. 61–3).[124]

If Heritage and HIP can legitimately be defended it is thus only in the context of a culture (the postmodern?) in which older meanings really have changed or been rendered unstable, and in which plurality is a fact of life. To support movements such as HIP is ultimately to believe that linear, teleological progress is no longer possible or desirable, and that values – however intensely they may be held – cannot automatically be applied outside one's own local context. Danto suggests that the notion of giving fresh meaning and identity to images with apparently stable meanings is the major creative development within the visual arts during the 1970s (*After the End of Art*, p. 15). But something of this was foretold by Nietzsche in *On the Genealogy of Morals*:[125] namely, that there is a world of difference between a thing's origins and its eventual uses, that everything is constantly reinterpreted by those with the power to do so, with fresh intentions. Much of this has been more recently developed in the claims of communitarian theorists who hold that social meanings are historical through and through and are entirely contingent on time and circumstance.[126]

To believe that older artworks, buildings and practices inevitably repeat or prolong past injustices is thus to take a monolithic view of meaning that is simply evaporating before our eyes. In architecture, the modern is perhaps more likely to hold connotations of elite financial institutions whilst older buildings and styles can lose their original oppressive significance and instead imply a depth of historical occupation over time, and a sense of belonging to all (Appleyard, *The Conservation of European*

Cities, p. 20). This is particularly evident in the case of colonial architecture that was once disdained by newly liberated nations. In economically prosperous Ireland, for instance, Georgian architecture is now preserved and held at a premium since the colonial power that created it no longer poses a threat. Such architecture thus acquires its meaning through its relation to a wider situation than through any inherent qualities. Connotation may arouse passions as high, if not higher than those of denotation, but there is nothing fixed or eternal about connotation. With a change of circumstances entirely unrelated to the material state of the artwork or building, the latter can acquire entirely new connotations. As Stephen Greenblatt puts it in relation to the use of western technology in far eastern countries:

I think it is important to resist what we may call *a priori* ideological determinism, that is, the notion that particular modes of representation are inherently and necessarily bound to a given culture or class or belief system, and that their effects are unidirectional.

The alternative is not to imagine that representational modes are neutral or even that they give themselves over . . . to whoever has embraced them, but to acknowledge that individuals and cultures tend to have fantastically powerful assimilative mechanisms, mechanisms that work like enzymes to change the ideological composition of foreign bodies. Those foreign bodies do not disappear altogether but they are drawn into . . . the zone of intersection in which all culturally determinate significations are called into question by an unresolved and unresolvable hybridity. Even representational technologies that require highly specialized equipment along with an infrastructure that includes electric generators, the accumulation of so-called hard currency, and the middlemen and customs bureaucracy . . . are not unequivocally and irreversibly the bearers of the capitalist ideology that was the determining condition of their original creation and their expansion throughout the world.[127]

The 'conspiracy theory' approach to Heritage, that there is some hidden central authority that governs the messages to be sent, and that the public media themselves conspire to reinforce such messages, simply belongs to a past world and ignores the sheer plurality of messages and forms of authority. As Eco suggests in the case of advertising, it is now impossible to trace authority to a single ideological source, since designers, manufacturers, advertisers and consumers all have a diversity of motives, interrelating and feeding back in numerous directions:

There is no longer Authority, all on its own (and how consoling it was!) . . . All are in it, and all are outside it: Power is elusive, and there is no longer any telling where the 'plan' comes from. Because there is, of course, a plan, but it is no longer intentional, and therefore it cannot be criticized with the traditional criticism of intentions. All the professors of theory of communications, trained by the texts of twenty years ago (this includes me), should be pensioned off.[128]

What has been so striking in so many of the examples covered in this study is that different commentators can look at what is essentially the same cultural phenomenon and draw extraordinarily contradictory conclusions. As Danto remarks in relation to the 1992 addition to the Jewish Museum in New York, which precisely duplicates the existing building: 'It was an architectural solution that had to have pleased the most conservative and nostalgic trustee, as well as the most avant-garde and contemporary one, but of course for quite different reasons' (Danto, *After the End of Art*, p. 15).

Much of this chapter has been aiming at an optimistic conception of Heritage and HIP. These movements arise from a contemporary need that is both real and vital. But, in the face of all the traditional epistemological objections to reconstructing the past 'as it really was', it is clear that they cannot return us to some prelapsarian state. Nevertheless, the notion of the uncomplicated restoration of past performance practice is paradoxically both erroneous and prodigiously productive. HIP serves to ground us in the present through renewed engagement with the past and in a way that has never been possible or necessary before. This involves a loosening of traditional categories and meanings and an accessibility to history and historical thought that is quite unparalleled in the past; in this sense, HIP can be justified precisely because the pasts to which it alludes are gone for ever. Whether this all reflects the 'democratisation of history' or the liberation of our thought from preconceived narratives about the past, I believe that the net benefit greatly outweighs the disadvantages.

Notes

PREFACE AND ACKNOWLEDGEMENTS

1 Friedrich Nietzsche, 'On the Uses and Disadvantages of History for Life' (1874), *Untimely Meditations*, trans. R. J. Hollingdale (Cambridge, 1983), p. 59.
2 Hermann Hesse, *The Glass Bead Game* (1943), trans. Richard and Clara Winston (Harmondsworth, England, 1972), p. 261.
3 See p. 7 below.
4 Lydia Goehr, *The Imaginary Museum of Musical Works* (Oxford, 1992), p. 284.
5 Copyright 2001 by the American Musicological Society. All rights reserved.

I JOINING THE HISTORICAL PERFORMANCE DEBATE

1 Paul Hindemith, *Johann Sebastian Bach* – a speech delivered on 12 September 1950 at the Bach commemoration of the city of Hamburg, Germany (New Haven, 1952), pp. 16–19.
2 Harry Haskell, *The Early Music Revival* (London, 1988), p. 145; Nikolaus Harnoncourt, *Baroque Music Today: Music as Speech*, ed. Reinhard G. Pauly, trans. Mary O'Neill (Portland, Oregon, 1988), pp. 111–12.
3 Harnoncourt, *Baroque Music Today*, esp. pp. 90–7, 129–36.
4 See Harnoncourt's sleeve-note to the first volume in the recording of the complete Bach cantatas, *Das Kantatenwerk*, vol. 1, Teldec, SKW 1/1–2, 1971, p. 8: 'We do not in the least regard this new interpretation as a return to something that has long since passed, but as an attempt at releasing this great old music from its historical amalgamation with the classical–symphonic sound and, by means of the transparent and characteristic selection of old instruments, at finding a truly modern interpretation.'
5 Theodor W. Adorno, 'Bach Defended against his Devotees' (1951), *Prisms*, trans. Samuel and Shierry Weber (Cambridge, Mass., 1981), p. 136.
6 For a quotation from Zukerman, see Bernard D. Sherman, *Inside Early Music* (New York and Oxford, 1997), p. 7. Many of Paul Henry Lang's writings on performance are found in *Musicology and Performance*, ed. Alfred Mann and George J. Buelow (New Haven, 1997), pp. 171–242. See also Editorial, *MQ*, 58 (1972), pp. 117–27.
7 Simon Jarvis, review of Peter Uwe Hohendahl, *Prismatic Thought. Theodor W. Adorno*, in *BJA*, 37 (1997), p. 90.

8 Theodor W. Adorno, *Introduction to the Sociology of Music* (*Einleitung in die Musiksoziologie*, Frankfurt, 1962), trans. E.B. Ashton (New York, 1976), pp. 9–12.

9 Theodor W. Adorno, 'Der mißbrauchte Barock', in *Ohne Leitbild* (Frankfurt, 1967), pp. 133–57.

10 Laurence Dreyfus, 'Early Music Defended against its Devotees: A Theory of Historical Performance in the Twentieth Century', *MQ*, 69 (1983), pp. 297–322.

11 As Kay Shelemay has recently suggested, the movement is less 'a bounded stream of musical discourse than a multi-faceted world of musical and cultural experience'. Kay Kaufman Shelemay, 'Toward an Ethnomusicology of the Early Music Movement: Thoughts on Bridging Disciplines and Musical Worlds', *Ethnomusicology*, 45 (2001), 1–29, see pp. 10–11.

12 Joseph Kerman, *Musicology* (London, 1985), p. 182. The identical book, published in America, is entitled *Contemplating Music*.

13 Introduction, *Rethinking Music*, ed. Nicholas Cook and Mark Everist (Oxford and New York, 1999), p. 12, note 5.

14 Dorottya Fabian notes several writers who perceived the 'pastness of the present and the presence of the past' and the twentieth-century nature of the HIP movement: Thurston Dart in 1954, Putnam Aldrich in 1957. See Fabian, 'J. S. Bach Recordings 1945–1975: *St Matthew* and *St John Passions, Brandenburg Concertos* and *Goldberg Variations* – A Study of Performance Practice in the Context of the Early Music Movement', 2 vols. (PhD Dissertation, University of New South Wales, 1998), vol. 1, pp. 27–32.

15 Robert P. Morgan, 'Tradition, Anxiety, and the Current Musical Scene', Nicholas Kenyon, ed., *Authenticity and Early Music* (Oxford, 1988), pp. 57–82.

16 *Baroque Music Today*, pp. 14–15.

17 Hermann Hesse, *The Glass Bead Game* (1943), trans. Richard and Clara Winston (Harmondsworth, England, 1972), p. 92.

18 The formulation David Lowenthal borrows from L. P. Hartley, see chapter 6, p. 168 below.

19 Daniel Leech-Wilkinson, 'Yearning for the Sound of Medieval Music', *Mittelalter-Sehnsucht?: Texte des interdisziplinären Symposions zur musikalischen Mittelalterrezeption an der Universität Heidelberg, April 1998*, ed. Annette Kreutziger-Herr and Dorothea Redepenning (Kiel, Vank, 2000), pp. 295–317.

20 Arthur C. Danto, *After the End of Art – Contemporary Art and the Pale of History* (Princeton, 1997).

21 Lydia Goehr, *The Imaginary Museum of Musical Works* (Oxford, 1992).

22 Roger Scruton, *The Aesthetics of Music* (Oxford, 1997), p. 448.

23 Richard Taruskin, *Text and Act* (New York and Oxford, 1995).

24 Richard Taruskin, Daniel Leech-Wilkinson, Nicholas Temperley, Robert Winter, 'The Limits of Authenticity: A Discussion', *EM*, 12 (1984), pp. 3–25; Nicholas Kenyon, ed., *Authenticity and Early Music* (Oxford, 1988).

25 E.g. Rudolph Kolisch, Erwin Stein, René Leibowitz, Theodor Adorno and Hans Swarowsky. As Walter Levin observes, the Kolisch Quartet (active in

the US during the 1930s) 'played with less rubato, tighter tempi, practically no portamenti, utmost dynamic contrast, a fierce fidelity to the score', coupled with a particular style of rhetorical expressiveness and disdain for beautiful tone. See Walter Levin, 'Immigrant Musicians and the American Chamber Music Scene, 1930–1950', *Driven into Paradise: The Musical Migration from Nazi Germany to the United States*, ed. Reinhold Brinkmann and Christoph Wolff (Berkeley and Los Angeles, 1999), p. 328. I am grateful to Daniel Leech-Wilkinson for pointing me to this reference.

26 David Lowenthal, *The Heritage Crusade and the Spoils of History* (Cambridge, 1998, originally published as *Possessed by the Past*, New York, 1996), p. 122.

27 Daniel Leech-Wilkinson, 'What We are Doing with Early Music is Genuinely Authentic to Such a Small Degree that the Word Loses Most of its Intended Meaning', *EM*, 12 (1984), pp. 13–16.

28 See Lowenthal, *The Heritage Crusade*, pp. 84–5.

29 Sherman, *Inside Early Music*, p. 21.

30 For an assessment of Nietzsche, see Hayden White, *Metahistory – The Historical Imagination in Nineteenth-Century Europe* (Baltimore and London, 1973), p. 332.

31 Indeed Reinhard Goebel, director of *Musica Antiqua Cologne*, is such a fundamentalist in his devotion to original sources, that I remember the *Guardian* once referring to him as 'the Ayatollah of the Baroque'.

32 Indeed, one of Harnoncourt's central points about the HIP movement is that it should counteract our enculturated view of music as 'merely' beautiful: 'In some contexts, only the "ugly" sound intended by the composer can render the truth of a musical statement.' *Baroque Music Today*, pp. 87–8.

33 Friedrich Nietzsche, 'On the Uses and Disadvantages of History for Life' (1874), *Untimely Meditations*, trans. R. J. Hollingdale (Cambridge, 1983), p. 67.

34 Karol Berger, *A Theory of Art* (New York and Oxford), pp. 60–2.

35 I am thinking here particularly of the exchange between Gary Tomlinson and Lawrence Kramer, in *CM*, 53 (1993).

36 At least as formulated by Lydia Goehr, *The Imaginary Museum of Musical Works* (Oxford, 1992).

37 Adorno, *Introduction to the Sociology of Music*, p. 12.

38 The turn away from master narratives is central to Jean-François Lyotard's *The Postmodern Condition: A Report on Knowledge* (1979), trans. G. Bennington and B. Massumi with a foreword by Frederic Jameson (Manchester, 1984).

39 José A. Bowen, 'Finding the Music in Musicology: Performance History and Musical Works', *Rethinking Music*, ed. Nicholas Cook and Mark Everist (Oxford and New York, 1999), pp. 424–51.

40 Patricia Waugh, ed., *Postmodernism: A Reader* (London, New York, Melbourne, Auckland, 1992), p. 113.

41 Christopher Norris, *The Truth about Postmodernism* (Oxford and Cambridge Mass., 1993), p. 17.

42 Habermas, in Waugh, *Postmodernism*, p. 169.

43 'Enlightenment is man's release from his self-incurred tutelage. Tutelage is man's inability to make use of his understanding without direction from another. It is self-incurred when its cause lies not in lack of understanding but

in lack of resolution and courage to use it without direction from another.'
Waugh, *Postmodernism*, p. 90.

44 Arthur C. Danto, *After the End of Art*, p. 5.

45 Peter Kivy, *Authenticities – Philosophical Reflections on Musical Performance* (Ithaca and London, 1995).

46 'Authenticity' could be considered offensive because it implies that anything else is inauthentic, not genuine or otherwise fraudulent.

47 For an intelligent survey of the possible terms, see Michelle Dulak, 'The Quiet Metamorphosis of "Early Music"', *Repercussions*, 2 (Fall 1993), pp. 31–61.

48 'Podiumdiskussion: Zur Situation der Aufführungspraxis Bachscher Werke', Reinhold Brinkmann: *Bachforschung und Bachinterpretation heute: Wissenschaftler und Praktiker im Dialog (Bericht über das Bachfest-Symposium 1978 der Philipps-Universität Marburg)*, Kassel, 1981, p. 187.

49 I use the term 'passive' here not to connote an irresponsible, indifferent form of listening, but rather in the sense that Karol Berger has recently borrowed from Besseler: 'The very distinction between subject and object in musical experience [after 1800] was challenged in favor of a primordial unity preceding the differentiation of the two. The listener was to become in some way identical with the music, experiencing it immediately, passively drowning in it.' Karol Berger, *A Theory of Art*, p. 200.

50 Dorottya Fabian traces the discussion, at least in the field of historical performance, back to Jacques Handschin in 1950, *Musica aeterna*, p. 126. See Fabian, 'J. S. Bach Recordings 1945–1975', vol. 1, p. 26.

51 Scruton, *The Aesthetics of Music*, p. 444.

52 Martin Elste, *Meilensteine der Bach-Interpretation 1750–2000 – Eine Werkgeschichte im Wandel* (Stuttgart, Weimar and Kassel, 2000), pp. 6–7.

53 See Bernard D. Sherman, *Inside Early Music – Conversations with Performers* (New York and Oxford, 1997), p. 18.

54 '. . . the effect [of HIP] has frequently been to cocoon the past in a wad of phoney scholarship, to elevate musicology over music, and to confine Bach and his contemporaries to an acoustic time-warp. The tired feeling which so many "authentic" performances induce can be compared to the atmosphere of a modern museum . . . [the works of early composers] are arranged behind the glass of authenticity, staring bleakly from the other side of an impassable screen.' Roger Scruton, *The Aesthetics of Music*, p. 448.

55 See Sherman, *Inside Early Music*, p. 19.

56 See also John Butt, 'Bach Recordings since 1980: A Mirror of Historical Performance', *Bach Perspectives*, 4, ed. David Schulenberg (Lincoln and London, 1999), pp. 192–3.

57 Michelle Dulak, who has much experience both in- and outside many American early music groups, notes that in the 1990s the only certainty about the movement was that it allowed players freedom from mainstream conventions, usually offering considerable latitude in how the historical evidence was used. See 'The Quiet Metamorphosis', and 'Early Music Circles Its Wagons Again', *The New York Times*, Sunday Arts and Leisure section, 11 June 1995, p. 40, also quoted in Sherman, *Inside Early Music*, p. 20.

58 Kerman, *Musicology*, p. 192.
59 Harnoncourt, *Baroque Music Today*, esp. pp. 72–3, 90–7.
60 In this point, Scruton's opinion coincides, almost directly, with Adorno's, in 'Der mißbrauchte Barock'.
61 Nietzsche, 'On the Uses and Disadvantages of History', p. 60.
62 Robert Philip, *Early Recordings and Musical Style* (Cambridge: Cambridge University Press, 1992), esp. pp. 208–12.
63 Jim Samson, 'The Practice of Early-Nineteenth-Century Pianism', *The Musical Work: Reality or Invention*, ed. Michael Talbot (Liverpool, 2000), pp. 110–27, esp. p. 126.
64 Martin Elste suggests that the fact that different people hear different things in the same performance is really the engine of stylistic change in the long run, *Meilensteine der Bach-Interpretation*, p. 6.
65 Carl Dahlhaus, *Foundations of Music History*, trans. J. B. Robinson (Cambridge, 1983), p. 156.
66 John Andrew Fisher and Jason Potter, 'Technology, Appreciation, and the Historical View of Art', *JAAC*, 55 (1997), pp. 169–85.
67 See Hillel Schwartz, *The Culture of the Copy – Striking Likenesses, Unreasonable Facsimiles* (New York, 1996).
68 Haskell notes that outrageous productions were coupled with Harnoncourt's Monteverdi cycle at the Zurich Opera during the 1970s, *The Early Music Revival*, p. 151. These may well mark the origin of the coupling of an HIP approach with a wildly modern production.
69 Michelle Dulak, 'The Quiet Metamorphosis of "Early Music"', p. 39.
70 *Ibid.*, pp. 51–2. *Suites for Violoncello Solo*, Anner Bylsma (cello), *Sony Classical*, S2K 48047 (1992). Dulak cites Nicholas Anderson's review, in *Gramophone*, 70 (January, 1993), p. 49.
71 Malcolm Boyd, in *EM*, 21 (1993), p. 319.
72 Dulak, 'The Quiet Metamorphosis', pp. 60–1.
73 Butt, 'Bach Recordings since 1980', pp. 184–6.
74 *Text and Act*, p. 194.
75 Dulak, 'Early Music Circles its Wagons Again', also quoted in Sherman, p. 20.
76 Laurence Dreyfus, 'Patterns of Authority in Musical Interpretation: Historical Performance at the Cross-Roads' (forthcoming).
77 'Toward an Ethnomusicology of the Early Music Movement', p. 9.
78 Kerman, *Musicology*, p. 191.
79 Christopher Page, 'The English *a cappella* Renaissance', *EM*, 21 (1993), pp. 453–71.
80 Page's intuitive, empathetic relation to the Middle Ages has drawn sharp criticism from Margaret Bent, who sees a greater sophistication in the Mediaeval mind. To her, the music contains many mysteries and puzzles which we can only just begin to understand. In some ways these two scholars represent the opposite poles of historiography: one sees the historical material as familiar, the other as remote. For a sensitive analysis of this dispute, and

the view that both scholars produce legitimate stories that basically serve different historical personalities, see Daniel Leech-Wilkinson, 'Translating Mediaeval Music' (in press).

81 Shai Burstyn, 'In Quest of the Period Ear', *EM*, 25 (1997), pp. 693-701, esp. pp. 694-5.

82 Peter Jeffery, *Re-Envisioning Past Musical Cultures: Ethnomusicology in the Study of Gregorian Chant* (Chicago and London, 1992), p. 124.

83 Danto, *After the End of Art*, p. 28.

84 Butt, 'Bach Recordings since 1980', pp. 193-4.

85 Kerman, *Musicology*, p. 196.

86 Jean Baudrillard, *Fatal Strategies* (New York, 1990), p. 13.

2 HISTORICAL PERFORMANCE AND 'TRUTH TO THE WORK': HISTORY AND THE SUBVERSION OF PLATONISM

1 Malcolm Bilson, 'The Viennese Fortepiano of the Late 18th Century', *EM*, 8 (1980), pp. 158–69, quotation on pp. 161–2.

2 Andrew Gurr, and John Orrell, *Rebuilding Shakespeare's Globe* (London, 1989), pp. 18–19.

3 For a perceptive introduction to the notion of 'period listening', see Shai Burstyn, 'In Quest of the Period Ear', *EM*, 25 (1997), pp. 693–701.

4 Bernard D. Sherman, *Inside Early Music – Conversations with Performers* (New York and Oxford, 1997), p. 305. As Bilson states in an article from the same year, it is not the notes that are sacrosanct but, as in a play, 'the *meaning of the words* in proper context'. 'The Future of Schubert Interpretation: What is Really Needed?', *EM*, 25 (1997), pp. 715–22, quotation p. 717.

5 Ludwig Finscher, 'Historisch getreue Interpretation – Möglichkeiten und Probleme', *Alte Musik in unsere Zeit* – Referate und Diskussionen der Kasseler Tagung 1967, ed. Walter Wiora (Kassel, 1968), pp. 25–34. Paul Henry Lang's notorious 'Editorial', *MQ*, 58 (1972), pp. 117–27, p. 127, makes a similar distinction between seeing the music 'as a personification of a historically determined style period, as a sort of document' and as 'a work of art in itself', again assuming a dichotomy between the two.

6 Most pervasive, is perhaps the attempt to see musical works as art objects in the same sense as painting and sculpture, and furthermore to see a person's interest in the arts in general as a guarantee of a particular quality and status. See R. A. Sharpe, 'Music, Platonism and Performance: Some Ontological Strains', *BJA*, 35 (1995), pp. 38–48. Lydia Goehr, in *The Imaginary Museum of Musical Works* (Oxford, 1992), shows the very complex origins and development of regulative and open concepts, specifically of the musical work.

7 Sharpe, 'Music, Platonism and Performance', pp. 41–2.

8 Jerrold Levinson, *Music, Art, and Metaphysics – Essays in Philosophical Aesthetics* (Ithaca and London, 1990), p. 249.

9 Peter Kivy, 'Orchestrating Platonism', *The Fine Art of Repetition – Essays in the Philosophy of Music* (Cambridge, 1993), pp. 75–94, see p. 85. Historical

evolution and improvement in performance is also assumed by James O. Young, 'The Concept of Authentic Performance', *BJA*, 28 (1988), pp. 228–38.

10 Lydia Goehr, *The Imaginary Museum of Musical Works* (Oxford, 1992), p. 47. Nicholas Wolterstorff, *Works and Worlds of Art* (Oxford, 1980), pp. 69–71.

11 Stephen Davies, 'General Theories of Art Versus Music', *BJA*, 34 (1994), pp. 315–25; see p. 316.

12 Stephen Davies, 'Authenticity in Musical Performance', *BJA*, 27 (1987), pp. 39–50, p. 40.

13 This is not to say that editing is any more an 'objective' office job. The role of the editor's critical faculties and interpretative imagination are increasingly being acknowledged. See, for instance, Philip Brett, 'Text, Context, and the Early Music Editor', *Authenticity and Early Music*, ed. Nicholas Kenyon (Oxford, 1988), pp. 83–114.

14 For an excellent summary and critique, see Goehr, *The Imaginary Museum*, pp. 21–43.

15 This regulative element for the performer is suggested in R. A. Sharpe's review of Goehr's *The Imaginary Museum of Musical Works*, *BJA*, 33 (1993), pp. 292–5.

16 Randall R. Dipert, 'The Composer's Intentions: An Examination of their Relevance for Performance', *MQ*, 66 (1980), pp. 205–18.

17 Kendall Walton, 'Style and the Products and Processes of Art', in *The Concept of Style*, revised and expanded edn, ed. Berel Lang (Ithaca and London, 1987), pp. 72–103, esp. p. 84.

18 Goehr, *The Imaginary Museum*, pp. 63, 74.

19 For an examination of issues of this kind, see Nicholas Cook, *Music, Imagination and Culture* (Oxford, 1990), esp. pp. 160–78.

20 Reinhard Strohm, *The Rise of European Music 1380–1500* (Cambridge, 1993). To Strohm, p. 2, the structural principles of fifteenth-century music 'are connected with the idea that music can convey meaning and emotion not only by reference to its generic form, text, performance circumstance – but directly, as it were by its *individually composed structures*'.

21 Strohm mounts a spirited defence of the work concept for much pre-nineteenth-century music in 'Looking Back at Ourselves: The Problem with the Musical Work-Concept', *The Musical Work: Reality or Invention*, ed. Michael Talbot (Liverpool, 2000), pp. 128–52.

22 Lydia Goehr, '"On the Problems of Dating" or "Looking Backwards and Forward with Strohm"', *The Musical Work*, pp. 231–46, esp. p. 238.

23 Karol Berger, *A Theory of Art* (New York and Oxford, 2000), p. 54. See also Michael Talbot, 'The Work-Concept and Composer-Centredness', *The Musical Work*, pp. 168–86, esp. p. 172. He suggests that the period 1780–1829 saw a shift in practice from a genre- and performer-centred culture to a composer-centred one.

24 Richard Taruskin, *Text and Act* (New York and Oxford, 1995), p. 240.

25 Theodor W. Adorno, 'Der mißbrauchte Barock', in *Ohne Leitbild* (Frankfurt, 1967), p. 151.

26 This point is made by Taruskin in his review of Norrington's recording of the first eight Beethoven symphonies, *Text and Act*, p. 231.

27 Dipert, 'The Composer's Intentions'.

28 Arthur C. Danto, *After the End of Art – Contemporary Art and the Pale of History* (Princeton, 1997), p. 198.

29 Young, 'The concept of authentic performance', pp. 232–3.

30 Stan Gotlovitch, 'Performance Authenticity – Possible, Practical, Virtuous', *Performance and Authenticity in the Arts*, ed. Salim Kemal and Ivan Gaskell (Cambridge, 1999), pp. 154–74.

31 Adorno, 'Der mißbrauchte Barock', pp. 151–2.

32 Burstyn, 'In Quest of the Period Ear', p. 697.

33 José A. Bowen, 'Finding the Music in Musicology: Performance History and Musical Works', in *Rethinking Music*, ed. Nicholas Cook and Mark Everist (Oxford and New York, 1999), p. 430.

34 Leo Treitler, *Music and the Historical Imagination* (Cambridge, Mass., 1989), p. 171.

35 See Derek Attridge, 'Language as History/History as Language: Saussure and the Romance of Etymology', *Post-Structuralism and the Question of History*, ed. Derek Attridge, Geoff Bennington and Robert Young (Cambridge, 1987), pp. 183–211, esp. p. 184.

36 See Jean-Jacques Nattiez, *Music and Discourse: Toward a Semiology of Music* (Princeton, 1990), p. 9: 'Now, musical meaning might be assigned some verbal translation . . . but it cannot be *limited* to that verbal translation. The temptation to do so is often difficult to resist, doubtless because we are never so *aware* of what the meaning of something in a nonlinguistic domain may be as when we attempt to explain that nonlinguistic domain in verbal terms.'

37 'Saussure's failed attempts to control folk etymology, spelling pronunciation, and prescriptive modification point the way towards a different view of history, one which will not simply reverse his privileging of synchrony over diachrony, but will encourage what Saussure tried to forbid: the entry of diachrony *into* synchrony – the entry of history into our current experience and current struggles' (Attridge, 'Language as History', p. 199).

38 Nattiez, *Music and Discourse*, pp. 75–7.

39 Goehr, *The Imaginary Museum*, p. 284.

40 Hermann Hesse, *The Glass Bead Game* (1943), trans. Richard and Clara Winston (Harmondsworth, England, 1972), see pp. 28–33.

3 HISTORICAL PERFORMANCE AND 'TRUTH TO THE COMPOSER': REHABILITATING INTENTION

1 Denis Stevens, 'Some Observations on Performance Practice', *CM*, 14 (1972), pp. 159–63, p. 159.

2 Laurence Dreyfus traces this tradition in music criticism, showing the subtle shifts in the meaning of the metaphor 'interpretation' from the time of Quantz onwards, 'Patterns of Authority in Musical Interpretation: Historical Performance at the Cross-Roads' (forthcoming).

3 *Ibid.*
4 Richard Taruskin, *Text and Act* (New York and Oxford, 1995), p. 97.
5 Peter Kivy, *Authenticities – Philosophical Reflections on Musical Performance* (Ithaca and London, 1995), p. 16.
6 Randall, R. Dipert, 'The Composer's Intentions: An Examination of their Relevance for Performance', *MQ,* 66 (1980), pp. 205–18, p. 212.
7 See Anthony Newcomb, 'Schumann and the Marketplace: From Butterflies to *Hausmusik*', *Nineteenth-Century Piano Music*, ed. R. Larry Todd (New York, 1990), pp. 258–315, esp. pp. 274–5.
8 Roger Scruton, *The Aesthetics of Music* (Oxford, 1997), p. 445.
9 See, for instance, Laurence Dreyfus's approach to Bach, *Bach and the Patterns of Invention* (Cambridge, Mass., 1996), p. 25, whose methods of analysis are designed to facilitate an understanding 'that is both more varied in scope and more vivid in its uncovering of human actions'.
10 Quotation commissioned by John Cage for *Notations* (New York, 1969).
11 W. K. Wimsatt and Monroe Beardsley, 'The Intentional Fallacy', *Sewanee Review*, 54 (1946), pp. 468–88. References here are to the reprint in *On Literary Intention*, ed. David Newton-de Molina (Edinburgh, 1976), pp. 1–13.
12 Monroe Beardsley, *Aesthetics – Problems in the Philosophy of Criticism* (New York, 1958), pp. 17–29; quote from p. 29.
13 Wimsatt and Beardsley, 'The Intentional Fallacy', p. 2.
14 George Watson, 'The Literary Past', *On Literary Intention*, ed. David Newton-de Molina (Edinburgh, 1976), pp. 158–73.
15 E. D. Hirsch Jr, 'In Defense of the Author', *On Literary Intention*, ed. David Newton-de Molina (Edinburgh, 1976), pp. 87–103, p. 87.
16 W. K. Wimsatt, 'Genesis: a Fallacy Revisited', *On Literary Intention*, ed. David Newton-de Molina (Edinburgh, 1976), pp. 116–38; see pp. 137–8: 'The words which the poet writes in a given passage depend for their meaning in one sense on the personal context and the author's intention (his word as *parole*), but they depend also, in a sense more important to the critic, on the wider context of the language (his words as *langue*) and culture.'
17 Karol Berger, *A Theory of Art* (New York and Oxford, 2000), pp. 217–19, 231–3.
18 For a critical assessment of Barthes's and Foucault's attack on the author, see Peter Lamarque, 'The Death of the Author: an Analytical Autopsy', *BJA*, 30 (1990), pp. 319–31.
19 'The Death of the Author', *Image, Music, Text – Roland Barthes*, Essays selected and translated by Stephen Heath (London, 1977), pp. 142–8.
20 Daniel C. Dennett, *The Intentional Stance* (Cambridge, Mass., 1987), p. 321.
21 Contemporary scholars often write about the 'unhealthy' cult of the composer as if this were a large-scale cultural phenomenon. In actual fact, I believe this to be mainly a 'malady' specific to scholars and certain performers, some of whom often try to elevate themselves with an element of 'crocodile humility'.

22 Brett, Philip, 'Text, Context, and the Early Music Editor', *Authenticity and Early Music*, ed. Nicholas Kenyon (Oxford, 1988), p. 110.

23 Jerome J. McGann, *The Textual Condition* (Princeton, 1991), esp. pp. 58–68.

24 For a general challenge to the position of Wimsatt and Beardsley, see *Intention and Interpretation*, ed. G. Isemiger (Philadelphia, 1992). For a defence of the original view, see, G. Dickie and W. Kent Wilson, ' The Intentional Fallacy: Defending Beardsley', *JAAC*, 53 (1995), pp. 233–50. A further discussion of both sides follows in *JAAC*, 55 (1997), pp. 305–12.

25 For a summary of Skinner's position, see Brian Rosebury, 'Irrecoverable Intentions and Literary Interpretation', *BJA*, 37 (1997), pp. 15–30, esp. pp. 17–18.

26 Jerrold Levinson, *The Pleasures of Aesthetics: Philosophical Essays* (Ithaca, 1996).

27 Susan R. Suleiman, 'Introduction: Varieties of Audience-Oriented Criticism', *The Reader in the Text*, ed. Susan R. Suleiman and Inge Crosman (Princeton, 1980), pp. 7–8.

28 Wayne Booth, *The Rhetoric of Fiction* (Chicago, 1961), p. 138; quoted in Suleiman, 'Introduction', p. 8.

29 Wimsatt and Beardsley, 'The Intentional Fallacy', p. 11.

30 Wimsatt, 'Genesis: a Fallacy Revisited', p. 129.

31 *Text and Act*, pp. 307–15.

32 Taruskin notes that Cone's question (posed in his monograph, *The Composer's Voice*) 'who is speaking?' yields only the answer, 'Not I' from modernist composers and performers. 'Put to any pre-modern composer, it would have elicited an unhesitating, if unreflective ... reply: "Why, I am, of course!"', *Ibid.*, p. 135.

33 Theodore Redpath, 'The Meaning of a Poem', *On Literary Intention*, ed. David Newton-de Molina (Edinburgh, 1976), pp. 20, 24.

34 Michael Baxandall, *Patterns of Intention – On the Historical Explanation of Pictures* (New Haven and London, 1985), pp. 41–2.

35 See also A. J. Close, '*Don Quixote* and the "Intentionalist fallacy" ', *On Literary Intention*, ed. David Newton-de Molina (Edinburgh, 1976), pp. 174–93, who suggests that we should reject the concept of intention as 'formal cause' and that we address more the question of the author's expectations of mutual recognition, the expected range of intended response. We may not discover intentions in the author's own terms, but should devise an 'explanatory grid' which fits over what he has written and to which he would assent (p. 189).

36 Richard Wollheim, *Painting as an Art* (Princeton, 1987), p. 21.

37 Roger Sessions, *The Musical Experience of Composer, Performer, Listener* (Princeton, 1950). This idea is developed by Jean-Jacques Nattiez within the context of 'inductive esthetics', the method by which we infer the historically 'correct' mode of listening appropriate to a piece by analysis of its style, *Music and Discourse: Toward a Semiology of Music* (Princeton, 1990), pp. 140–2. Rob C. Wegman draws attention to the potential risk of circularity in this type of approach, '"Das musikalische Hören" in the Middle Ages and Renaissance: Perspectives from Pre-War Germany', *MQ*, 82 (1998), pp. 434–54, p. 441.

38 'music involves *sounds* and, at least at first appearance, not how they are produced. Yet discussions of low-level intentions persist, even when these intentions do not result in any clear aural differences'. Dipert, 'The Composer's Intentions', p. 207.

39 This is suggested by Levinson, who considers the actual making of the sound to be essential to the experience of the music, even if there is no empirical difference in the sound itself; in other words, the beliefs of both player and audience play an important part in structuring the musical experience. See Levinson, *Music, Art, and Metaphysics*, pp. 394–5.

40 Stephen Davies, 'Authenticity in Musical Performance', *BJA*, 27 (1987), pp. 39–50; Levinson, *Music, Art, and Metaphysics*, p. 393.

41 E. D. Hirsch Jr, 'Objective Interpretation', 'In Defense of the Author', *On Literary Intention*, ed. David Newton-de Molina (Edinburgh, 1976), pp. 35–8, 102.

42 Paul Crowther, *Critical Aesthetics and Postmodernism* (Oxford, 1993), p. 43.

43 Benjamin Britten, *On Receiving the First Aspen Award* (London, 1964), p. 13.

44 Johann Mattheson, *Der vollkommene Capellmeister* (Hamburg, 1739), trans. Ernest C. Harriss (Ann Arbor, 1981), p. 294.

45 Kivy, *Authenticities*, p. 34.

46 This view is partly evident in Christopher Page's defence of the English choral tradition, 'The English *a cappella* Renaissance', *EM*, 21 (1993), pp. 453–71. See p. 43 above.

47 Johannes Manlius, *Locorum Communium Collectanea* (Basel, 1562), p. 542; quoted (p. 468) in Rob C. Wegman, 'From Maker to Composer: Improvisation and Musical Authorship in the Low Countries, 1450–1500', *JAMS*, 49 (1996), pp. 409–79.

48 Translation from Frederick Hammond, *Girolamo Frescobaldi – A Guide to Research* (New York, 1988), pp. 192–3.

49 Roger North, 'The Excellent Art of Voluntary', ed. John Wilson, *Roger North on Music* (London, 1959), pp. 133–45, p. 140.

50 John Butt, *Music Education and the Art of Performance in the German Baroque* (Cambridge, 1994), pp. 121–65.

51 David Fuller, '"Sous les doits de Chambonniere"', *EM*, 21 (1993), pp. 191–202.

52 See also José A. Bowen, 'Finding the Music in Musicology: Performance History and Musical Works', *Rethinking Music*, ed. Nicholas Cook and Mark Everist (Oxford and New York, 1999), p. 427.

53 Treitler usefully proposes that in cases where there are a variety of versions of the same piece, or rather a family of pieces linked by function, text or title, the scores are both functionally and ontologically parallel with performance. Leo Treitler, 'History and the Ontology of the Musical Work', *JAAC*, 51 (1993), pp. 483–97, p. 493.

54 Jim Samson, 'The Practice of Early-Nineteenth-Century Pianism', *The Musical Work: Reality or Invention?*, ed. Michael Talbot (Liverpool, 2000), pp. 110–27, esp. pp. 117–18.

55 This distinction is usefully made by Stephen Davies, 'The Aesthetic Relevance of Authors' and Painters' Intentions', *JAAC*, 41, (1982–3) pp. 65–76.

56 See also Paul Crowther, *Critical Aesthetics*, p. 109.

57 Kivy does briefly consider the issue of composers responding to the instrumental media at their disposal, quoting a perceptive passage by Aron Edidin (pp. 176–7). But he dismisses it on account of the fact that Edidin mentions no specific way in which a work might be better played on a period instrument than a modern one and that the argument is couched in terms of a 'possible' rather than actual outcome. But my approach obviates these objections by claiming that the hardware is of specific interest in the creative context of the music, but not that it is thus eternally fixed as the ideal medium for its future performance.

58 Fredric Jameson, *Postmodernism, or, The Cultural Logic of Late Capitalism* (Durham, NC, 1991), p. 220.

59 Hermann Hesse, *The Glass Bead Game* (1943), trans. Richard and Clara Winston (Harmondsworth, England, 1972), p. 261.

60 Crowther, *Critical Aesthetics*, p. 51.

4 NEGOTIATING BETWEEN WORK, COMPOSER AND PERFORMER: REWRITING THE STORY OF NOTATIONAL PROGRESS

1 Brian Ferneyhough, *Collected Writings*, ed. James Boros and Richard Toop, with a foreword by Jonathan Harvey (Amsterdam, 1995), p. 373.

2 This attitude is even more pronounced in early music vocal performance, particularly in England, where most singers are brought up in the Collegiate/Cathedral tradition and are thus accustomed to limited rehearsal time but maximal marking of the music.

3 Robert Philip, *Early Recordings and Musical Style* (Cambridge, 1992), p. 231.

4 Theodore W. Adorno, 'Über den Fetischcharakter in der Musik und die Regression des Hörens' (1938). Quoted from Max Paddison, *Adorno's Aesthetics of Music* (Cambridge, 1993), p. 200.

5 José A. Bowen, 'The Conductor and the Score: The Relationship between Interpreter and Text in the Generation of Mendelssohn, Berlioz and Wagner' (PhD Dissertation, Stanford University, 1993).

6 'But you must forgive a composer who would rather have heard a work performed exactly as written, however beautifully you played it in other respects', in William S. Newman, *Performance Practices in Beethoven's Piano Sonatas* (New York, 1971), p. 15.

7 Max Weber, *Die rationalen und sozialen Grundlagen der Musik*, appendix to *Wirtschaft und Gesellschaft* (written 1911, published Tübingen, 1921), trans. as *The Rational and Social Foundations of Music*, trans. and ed. Don Martindale, Johannes Riedel and Gertrude Neuwirth (Carbondale: Southern Illinois University Press, 1958).

8 Paddison, *Adorno's Aesthetics*, pp. 192–97, quotation on p. 195.

9 See John Butt, *Bach Interpretation* (Cambridge: Cambridge University Press, 1990), esp. pp. 81–3.

10 See Roger Parker, 'A Donizetti Critical Edition in the Postmodern World', *L'Opera Teatrale di Gaetano Donizetti – Proceedings of the International Conference on the Operas of Gaetano Donizetti, Bergamo, 1992*, ed. Francesco Bellotto (Bergamo, 1993), pp. 57–66; and especially Rebecca Harris-Warrick, 'The Parisian Sources of Donizetti's French Operas: The Case of *La Favorite*', in Bellotto, *L'Opera Teatrale*, pp. 77–90. Parker and Harris-Warrick suggest that singers in Donizetti did mark their parts with ornaments and cadenzas but that the instrumentalists marked nothing of musical importance.

11 Philip, *Early Recordings*, p. 180.

12 James Hepokoski, 'Overriding the Autograph Score: The Problem of Textual Authority in Verdi's "Falstaff"', *Studi Verdiani*, 8 (1992), pp. 13–51, quotation p. 15.

13 *Ibid.*, pp. 18–29.

14 Philip, *Early Recordings*, p. 33.

15 John Cage, *Notations* (New York, 1969).

16 Marc Treib, *Space Calculated in Seconds – the Philips Pavilion – Le Corbusier – Edgard Varèse* (Princeton, 1996), p. 176.

17 See Robert Rowe, *Interactive Music Systems: Machine Listening and Composing* (Cambridge Mass., 1993).

18 Umberto Eco, *Opera aperta* (Milan, 1962), trans., with additional chapters, by Anna Cancogni with an introduction by David Robey, as *The Open Work* (Cambridge, Mass., 1989), pp. 1–2.

19 Part 2 (1721) of *The Musical Guide*, trans. and ed. by Pamela L. Poulin and Irmgard C. Taylor (Oxford, 1989); see esp. pp. 155–78.

20 Reinhard Strohm, *The Rise of European Music 1380–1500* (Cambridge, 1993), esp. pp. 1–10.

21 Karol Berger, 'Musica ficta', *Performance Practice: Music Before 1600*, ed. Howard Mayer Brown and Stanley Sadie (New York and London, 1989), pp. 107–25, esp. pp. 107–8.

22 Anthony Newcomb, 'Unnotated Accidentals in the Music of the Post-Josquin Generation: Mainly on the Example of Gombert's First Book of Motets for Four Voices', *Music in Renaissance Cities and Courts: Studies in Honor of Lewis Lockwood*, ed. Jessie Ann Owens and Anthony M. Cummings (Michigan, 1997), pp. 215–25; quotation from p. 225.

23 Berger 'Musica ficta', pp. 110 and 121, n. 12.

24 Margaret Bent, 'Musica Recta and Musica Ficta', *Musica Disciplina*, 26 (1972), pp. 73–100, esp. p. 74.

25 See Ellen Rosand, *Opera in Seventeenth-Century Venice: The Creation of a Genre* (Berkeley and Los Angeles, 1991); and Philip Gossett, 'Gioachino Rossini and the Conventions of Composition', *Acta Musicologica*, 42 (1970), pp. 48–58.

26 Letter of 28 February 1778, quoted in Patricia Lewy Gidwitz, '"Ich bin die erste Sängerin": Vocal Profiles of Two Mozart Sopranos', *EM*, 19 (1991), pp. 565–79, quoted on p. 566.

27 *Ibid.*, p. 566.
28 Daniel Heartz, discussion (pp. 582–3) concluding Alessandra Campana, 'Mozart's Italian *buffo* singers', *EM*, 19 (1991), pp. 580–3.
29 See, for instance, Mary Ann Smart, 'The Lost Voice of Rosine Stoltz', *COJ*, 6 (1994), pp. 31–50; esp. pp. 48–50, where she suggests that something of Stoltz's voice remains in Donizetti's notation of her role in *La favorite*.
30 Parker, 'A Donizetti Critical Edition', p. 63.
31 *Ibid.*, p. 64.
32 C. Steven Larue, *Handel and his Singers: The Creation of the Royal Academy Operas, 1720–1728* (Oxford, 1995), esp. pp. 181–6.
33 Alan Armstrong, 'Gilbert-Louis Duprez and Gustave Roger in the Composition of Meyerbeer's *Le Prophète*', *COJ*, 8 (1996), pp. 147–65; p. 147.
34 José A. Bowen, 'Finding the Music in Musicology: Performance History and Musical Works', in Everest etc. pp. 425–7.
35 John Whenham, *Claudio Monteverdi – Orfeo* (Cambridge, 1986), p. 69. It may also be possible that Monteverdi was writing down what he recalled from Francesco Rasi's original performance of the role.
36 John Butt, *Music Education and the Art of Performance in the German Baroque* (Cambridge, 1994), p. 161. See also p. 153 for a similar case involving the Leipzig Kantor Tobias Michael.
37 See Neal Zaslaw, 'Ornaments for Corelli's Violin Sonatas, op. 5', *EM*, 24 (1996), pp. 95–115; and Robert E. Seletsky, '18th-Century Variations for Corelli's Sonatas, op. 5', *EM*, 24 (1996), pp. 119–30.
38 See John Butt, *Bach Interpretation* (Cambridge, 1990), p. 147, for the observation that Bach often seems to give no more care to the performance directives in prints than he does in manuscripts.
39 Peter Walls, 'Performing Corelli's Violin Sonatas, op. 5', *EM*, 24 (1996), pp. 133–42, see p. 138.
40 Robert D. Levin, 'Improvised Embellishments in Mozart's Keyboard Sonatas', *EM*, 20 (1993), pp. 221–33; quote from p. 221.
41 Wye J. Allenbrook, personal communication.
42 Walther Dürr, 'Schubert and Johann Michael Vogl: a Reappraisal', *19th-Century Music*, 3 (1979), pp. 126–40.
43 David Montgomery, 'Modern Schubert Interpretation in the Light of the Pedagogical Sources of His Day', *EM*, 25 (1997), pp. 101–18.
44 *Ibid.*, p. 104. He proceeds to give a detailed account of pedagogical sources of the time, and, while stressing that none of these has anything directly to do with Schubert, he tends to emphasise those that mention nothing about ornamentation or tempo fluctuation and explains away any that might suggest such freedoms. As Eric Van Tassel later suggests, Montgomery's very reading of sources that seem to support his viewpoint might be conditioned by the later nineteenth-century concept of *Werktreue* and that, in fact, even the seemingly conservative writers may have expected considerable licence. ' "Something Utterly New": Listening to Schubert Lieder', *EM*, 25 (1997), pp. 703–14, esp. p. 709. The same issue also contains dismayed responses to Montgomery from Malcolm Bilson and Robert Levin.

45 See Friedrich Neumann, *Ornamentation and Improvisation in Mozart* (Princeton, 1986), for one of the most extensive and forceful attempts to preserve Mozart from improvisatory indeterminacy.

46 Anthony Newcomb, 'Schumann and the Marketplace: From Butterflies to *Hausmusik*', *Nineteenth-Century Piano Music*, ed. R. Larry Todd (New York, 1990), pp. 258–315, esp. pp. 277–9.

47 See John Butt, 'Germany and the Netherlands', *Keyboard Music Before 1700*, ed. Alexander Silbiger (New York, 1995), pp. 147–52.

48 Bruce Gustafson, 'France', *Keyboard Music Before 1700*, ed. Alexander Silbiger (New York, 1995), p. 98.

49 Stanley Boorman, 'The Musical Text', *Rethinking Music*, ed. Nicholas Cook and Mark Everist (Oxford and New York, 1999), p. 408.

50 Claude Samuel, *Music and Color – Conversations with Claude Samuel / Olivier Messiaen* (1986), trans. E. Thomas Glasow (Portland, 1994), p. 25; see also p. 118.

51 Helmut Hucke, 'Towards a New Historical View of Gregorian Chant', *JAMS*, 33 (1980), pp. 437–67, p. 447.

52 Leo Treitler, 'The "Unwritten" and "Written" Transmission of Mediaeval Chant and the Start-up of Musical Notation', *JM*, 10 (1992), pp. 131–91.

53 Leo Treitler, 'The Early History of Music Writing in the West', *JAMS*, 35 (1982), pp. 237–79, p. 261.

54 Craig Wright, *Music and Ceremony at Notre Dame of Paris, 500–1550* (Cambridge, 1989), pp. 333–4.

55 Anna Maria Busse-Berger, 'Mnemotechnics and Notre Dame Polyphony', *JM*, 14 (1996), pp. 263–98, esp. 269; see also 'Die Rolle der Mündlichkeit in der Komposition der Notre Dame Polyphonie', *Das Mittelalter*, 1 (1998), pp. 127–43.

56 Rob C. Wegman, 'From Maker to Composer; Improvisation and Musical Authorship in the Low Countries, 1450–1500', *JAMS*, 49 (1996), pp. 409–79.

57 *Ibid.*, pp. 443–5. For more on Tinctoris's definition of the *res facta*, see Bonnie J. Blackburn, 'On Compositional Process in the Fifteenth Century', *JAMS*, 40 (1987), pp. 210–84, esp. pp. 247–54.

58 *Ibid.*, Wegman, pp. 451–2.

59 See Karol Berger, *A Theory of Art* (New York and Oxford, 2000), p. 28, who argues that while notation is in general a tool musicians use for performance and composition, 'this tool can acquire a life of its own and become indispensable to composers as they formulate ideas of unprecedented power, depth, and complexity'.

60 See Wright, *Music and Ceremony at Notre Dame*, p. 328, for a reference to memorisation at Notre Dame in 1662.

61 Anthony Newcomb, 'Schumann and the Marketplace', p. 259.

62 Wegman, 'From Maker to Composer', p. 450.

63 Michel Foucault, *The Order of Things: An Archaeology of the Human Sciences*, Translation of *Les Mots et les choses*, 1966 (New York, 1970), pp. 38–9.

64 Graham Dixon, 'The Performance of Palestrina: Some Questions, but Fewer Answers', *EM*, 22 (1994), pp. 667–75, esp. p. 672.

65 Giovanni Luca Conforti, *Breve et facile maniera d'essercitarsi* (Rome, 1593).
66 Noel O'Regan, 'The Performance of Palestrina: Some Further Observations', *EM*, 24 (1996), pp. 144–54, esp. p. 149.
67 Dixon, 'The Performance of Palestrina', p. 672.
68 Margaret Murata, ed., *Strunk's Source Readings in Music History – Revised Edition*, ed. Leo Treitler, vol. 4: The Baroque Era (New York and London, 1998), p. 24.
69 See Seletsky, '18th-Century Variations for Corelli's Sonatas'.
70 Quoted from Zaslaw, 'Ornaments for Corelli's Violin Sonatas', p. 103.
71 Bojan Bujic, 'Notation and Realization: Musical Performance in Historical Perspective', *The Interpretation of Music – Philosophical Essays*, ed. Michael Krausz (Oxford, 1993), pp. 129–40, quotation p. 137.
72 Newcomb, 'Schumann and the Marketplace', p. 280.
73 See Bernard D. Sherman, *Inside Early Music – Conversations with Performers* (New York and Oxford, 1997), p. 251; László Somfai, *Béla Bartók: Composition, Concepts, and Autograph Sources* (Berkeley and Los Angeles, 1996), pp. 279–95.
74 *Messiaen par lui-même*, EMI Classics CDZD 7 67400 2 (1992), *Messe de la Pentecôte*, recorded in 1950.
75 Brian Ferneyhough, *Collected Writings*, pp. 7–13, 70–1, 232–3, 369–78.

5 HISTORICAL PERFORMANCE AT THE CROSSROADS
OF MODERNISM AND POSTMODERNISM

1 Richard Taruskin, *Text and Act* (New York and Oxford, 1995), esp. 'The Pastness of the Present and the Presence of the Past', pp. 90–154.
2 Georgina Born, *Rationalizing Culture – IRCAM, Boulez, and the Institutionalization of the Musical Avant-Garde* (Berkeley and Los Angeles, 1995).
3 Arthur C. Danto, *After the End of Art – Contemporary Art and the Pale of History* (Princeton, 1997), p. 9.
4 Jean-François Lyotard, *The Postmodern Condition: A Report on Knowledge* (1979), trans. Geoff Bennington and Brian Massumi, with a foreword by Fredric Jameson (Manchester, 1984), Appendix 'Answering the Question: What is Postmodernism?' (1982), p. 79.
5 John Butt, 'Bach Recordings since 1980: A Mirror of Historical Performance', *Bach Perspectives*, 4, ed. David Schulenberg (Lincoln and London, 1999), pp. 181–98, esp. pp. 186–93.
6 See Taruskin, *Text and Act*, p. 93.
7 See Michelle Dulak, 'The Quiet Metamorphosis of "Early Music"', *Repercussions*, 2, (Fall 1993), pp. 31–61.
8 'Das ist ja der kleine Modernsky!', *Drei Satiren*, Op. 28, 1926.
9 T. J. Clark, *Farewell to an Idea – Episodes from a History of Modernism* (New Haven and London, 1999), p. 13.
10 For a brief summary of various viewpoints, see Margaret Rose, *The Post-Modern and the Post-Industrial* (Cambridge, 1991), pp. 14–16.

11 This is the point of view most closely associated with Jürgen Habermas; see Patricia Waugh, ed., *Postmodernism: A Reader* (London, New York, Melbourne, Auckland, 1992), pp. 160–70.

12 Danto, *After the End of Art*, p. 8.

13 Weber associated disenchantment with the process of 'rationalisation', one that – interestingly enough – included the rationalisation of keyboard temperaments. See Anthony J. Cascardi, *The Subject of Modernity* (Cambridge, 1992), pp. 16–71, esp. p. 17.

14 Indeed Clement Greenberg stresses the Modernism does not, in fact, mean a break with the past: 'It may mean a devolution, an unravelling, of tradition, but it also means its further evolution.' Greenberg, 'Modernist Painting' (Radio Lecture, 1961), reprinted in *Art in Modern Culture – An Anthology of Critical Texts*, ed. Francis Frascina and Jonathan Harris (London, 1992), p. 313.

15 Zygmunt Bauman, 'Parvenu and Pariah: Heroes and Victims of Modernity', *The Politics of Postmodernity*, ed. James Good and Irving Velody (Cambridge, 1998), pp. 23–35, see pp. 24–5.

16 Michael H. Levenson, *A Genealogy of Modernism – A Study of English Literary Doctrine 1908–1922* (Cambridge, 1984), p. ix.

17 James Longenbach, *Modernist Poetics of History – Pound, Eliot, and the Sense of the Past* (Princeton, 1987), pp. 6–7.

18 This point is reached forcefully by Taruskin, partly in response to José Bowen's contention that the 'modernist' stance has its roots in the nineteenth century, *Text and Act*, pp. 9–10.

19 'The Conductor and the Score: The Relationship between Interpreter and Text in the Generation of Mendelssohn, Berlioz and Wagner' (PhD Dissertation, Stanford University, 1993).

20 See also Hayden White, *Metahistory – The Historical Imagination in Nineteenth-Century Europe* (Baltimore and London, 1973), esp. pp. 331–425.

21 Richard Rorty, *Contingency, Irony, and Solidarity* (Cambridge, 1989).

22 Haskell, *The Early Music Revival* (London, 1988), p. 35. For Pound's modernist appreciation of Dolmetsch, see Taruskin, *Text and Act*, pp. 140–2.

23 All quotations and references are from the London edition of 1917.

24 Beverly Haviland, *Henry James's Last Romance – Making Sense of the Past and the American Scene* (Cambridge, 1997), p. 9.

25 Moreover, when Ralph finds himself plunged into a part of the house's history, it is not the point at which the house was built, but at a point *c.* 1820, between the building of the house and his own time.

26 Friedrich Nietzsche, 'On the Uses and Disadvantages of History for Life' (1874), *Untimely Meditations*, trans. R. J. Hollingdale (Cambridge, 1983), p. 74.

27 David Lowenthal, *The Past is a Foreign Country* (Cambridge, 1985), p. 30.

28 This should be distinguished from Hayden White's concept of the metonymical trope of history (*Metahistory*, pp. 31–4), since his is concerned with the historical description of any particular era (by relating a tangible part to an assumed whole), not with the metonymical connection between past and present.

29 See Rose, *The Post-Modern and the Post-Industrial*, p. 9, for Toynbee's use of the term to describe the age inaugurated by World War I; p. 13, for de Onis's dating back to 1905. See Lawrence Cahoone, ed., *From Modernism to Postmodernism – An Anthology* (Cambridge Mass. And Oxford, 1996), pp. 3–10 for a general history of the term.

30 Clark, *Farewell to an Idea*, p. 3.

31 Anthony Giddens, *Modernity and Self-Identity: Self and Society in the Late Modern Age* (Cambridge, 1991). Introduction reprinted in Frascina and Harris, *Art in Modern Culture*, p. 19.

32 See Clark, *Farewell to an Idea*, p. 8.

33 Eva Cockcroft, 'Abstract Expressionism, Weapon of the Cold War, *Artforum*, 15/10 (1974), pp. 39–41. Reprinted in Frascina and Harris, *Art in Modern Culture*, pp. 82–90; p. 86. See also Karol Berger, *A Theory of Art* (New York and Oxford, 2000), pp. 146–8, for references to modernist musical policy during the Cold War.

34 Danto, *After the End of Art*, 5, pp. 11–12.

35 Karol Berger, *A Theory of Art* (New York and Oxford, 2000).

36 Fredric Jameson, *The Cultural Turn – Selected Writings on the Postmodern* (London, New York, 1998), p. 49.

37 Summarised in Rose, *The Post-Modern and the Post-Industrial*, pp. 101–49. See also Perry Anderson, *The Origins of Postmodernity* (London, New York, 1998), p. 22.

38 *Text and Act*, p. 93. See also chapter 1, pp. 37 above.

39 Walter Benjamin, 'The Work of Art in the Age of Mechanical Reproduction' (1936), *Illuminations*, trans. Harry Zohn, ed., with an introduction by Hannah Ahrendt (New York, 1968), pp. 217–51, see p. 232.

40 Kay Kaufman Shelamay, 'Toward an Ethnomusicology of the Early Music Movement: Thoughts on Bridging Disciplines and Musical Worlds', *Ethnomusicology*, 45 (2001), pp. 11–12.

41 Butt, 'Bach Recordings since 1980', pp. 183–4.

42 See Anderson, *The Origins of Postmodernity*, pp. 30–1.

43 *The Postmodern Condition*, p. 67; see also Rose, *The Post-Modern and the Post-Industrial*, p. 57.

44 Bauman, 'Parvenu and Pariah', p. 31.

45 Waugh, *Postmodernism*, 113.

46 Fredric Jameson, *Postmodernism, or, The Cultural Logic of Late Capitalism* (Durham, NC, 1991), p. 320.

47 Terry Eagleton, 'Capitalism, Modernism and Postmodernism', *New Left Review*, 152 (1985), pp. 60–73; reprinted in Waugh, *Postmodernism*, pp. 152–9 and in Frascina and Harris, *Art in Modern Culture*, pp. 91–100; this quote p. 92.

48 Taruskin expresses optimism about the new-found freedom among the younger HIP performers, noting that they are 'thinking of themselves increasingly as normal rather than as deviant or alienated members of musical society', *Text and Act*, p. 194.

49 Lyotard, 'What is Postmodernism?', appendix (1982) to *The Postmodern Condition*, p. 81.

50 See Lydia Goehr, *The Imaginary Museum of Musical Works* (Oxford, 1992), and José A. Bowen, 'Finding the Music in Musicology: Performance History and Musical Works', *Rethinking Music*, ed. Nicholas Cook and Mark Everist (Oxford and New York, 1999), pp. 424–51.

51 See Rose, *The Post-Modern and the Post-Industrial*, pp. 21–39.

52 Benjamin, 'The Work of Art in the Age of Mechanical Reproduction', and Hillel Schwartz, *The Culture of the Copy – Striking Likenesses, Unreasonable Facsimiles* (New York, 1996), pp. 140–1.

53 Jean Baudrillard, 'The Year 2000 Will Not Take Place' (1987), quotation from Rex Butler, *The Defence of the Real* (London, 1999), p. 150.

54 Lyotard, 'What is Postmodernism?', appendix (1982) to *The Postmodern Condition*, p. 79.

55 David Lowenthal, *The Heritage Crusade and the Spoils of History* (Cambridge, 1998), p. 79.

56 Anthony Giddens, *Modernity and Self-Identity*, p. 18.

57 That which Baudrillard refers to as 'the hypertrophy of historical research, the frenzy to explain everything, attribute everything, footnote everything', see chapter 6, p. 170 below.

58 Nietzsche, 'On the Uses and Disadvantages of History for Life', p. 97.

59 As witnessed by the current (2001) rebuilding programme in Dresden.

6 'A REACTIONARY WOLF IN COUNTERCULTURAL SHEEP'S CLOTHING?' – HISTORICAL PERFORMANCE, THE HERITAGE INDUSTRY AND THE POLITICS OF REVIVAL

1 Lucy Lippiard's definition of 'retrochic', 1979, quoted in Raphael Samuel, *Theatres of Memory*, vol. 1: *Past and Present in Contemporary Culture* (London, 1994), p. 86.

2 Katherine Bergeron, *Decadent Enchantments – The Revival of Gregorian Chant at Solesmes* (Berkeley and Los Angeles, 1998), pp. 8–10.

3 Katherine Ellis, *Music Criticism in Nineteenth-Century France: La Revue et Gazette Musicale de Paris, 1834–80* (Cambridge, 1995), p. 13.

4 Richard Luckett shows quite a lively historicist scene in the eighteenth century: unpublished MS (1986), 'The Revival of Early Music and the Suppositions of Cultural History', II, pp. 1–4. See also Harry Haskell, *The Early Music Revival* (London, 1988), pp. 14–15.

5 Samuel, *Past and Present*, pp. 23, 139; Peter Borsay, *The Image of Georgian Bath, 1700–2000* (Oxford, 2000), p. 4. Moreover, figures within instrument conservation movements often see themselves as part of a wider community; see Jim Berrow (ed.), *Towards the Conservation and Restoration of Historic Organs* (London, 2000), esp. p. 2.

6 See Philip Brett, 'Text, Context, and the Early Music Editor', *Authenticity and Early Music*, ed. Nicholas Kenyon (Oxford, 1988), pp. 83–114.

7 Eric Hobsbawm, 'Mass-Producing Traditions: Europe, 1870–1914', *The Invention of Tradition*, ed. Eric Hobsbawm and Terence Ranger (Cambridge, 1983), pp. 263–307, quotation on p. 263.

8 Richard Taruskin, *Text and Act* (New York and Oxford, 1995), p. 64: 'The finger-in-the-dike mentality dies hard. In Britain it may never die'; p. 72: 'All too often the sound of a modern "authentic" performance of old music presents the aural equivalent of an Urtext score: the notes and rests are presented with complete accuracy and an equally complete neutrality (and this seems to be most characteristic – dare I say it? – of English performances)'; see also pp. 257–60 and p. 299.

9 David Lowenthal, *The Heritage Crusade and the Spoils of History* (Cambridge, 1998), p. 6.

10 David Lowenthal, *The Past is a Foreign Country* (Cambridge, 1985), p. 191. Lowenthal borrows the expression from L. P. Hartley.

11 See also Paul Crowther, *Critical Aesthetics and Postmodernism* (Oxford, 1993), p. 14, who describes pre-capitalist social formations as those in which '[t]he past and the domain of the other are both felt to be organically connected with the present experience of the individual. One feels oneself to be an active participant in an ongoing process of collective struggle and realization. One's choices and deeds, in other words, are meaningful beyond the immediate personal present.'

12 Of all the figures working within HIP, Harnoncourt is the one who speaks most of impending doom: 'There are many indications that we are heading toward a general cultural collapse', *Baroque Music Today: Music as Speech*, ed., Reinhard G. Pauly, trans. Mary O'Neill (Portland, Oregon, 1988), p. 19.

13 David Lowenthal and Marcus Binney (eds.), *Our Past Before Us – Why do we save it?* (London, 1981), Introduction, p. 11.

14 Gavin Stamp, 'The Art of Keeping one Jump Ahead: Conservation Societies in the Twentieth Century', *Preserving the Past: The Rise of Heritage in Modern Britain*, ed. Michael Hunter (Stroud, 1996), pp. 77–98, quotation from p. 98.

15 Luckett, 'The Revival of Early Music', II, p. 7, III, p. 2. Moreover, C. F. Zelter's performances of Bach choral works with the Berliner Singakademie in the first decades of the nineteenth century frequently used performance materials from the composer's own store.

16 Samuel, *Past and Present*, pp. 153–4.

17 Baudrillard, Jean, *The Consumer Society: Myths and Structures* (London, 1998), pp. 100–1.

18 Lowenthal and Binney, *Our Past Before Us*, Introduction, p. 11.

19 Samuel, *Past and Present*, pp. 157–8; Stamp, 'The Art of Keeping One Jump Ahead', p. 94.

20 Jean Baudrillard, *Fatal Strategies* (New York, 1990), p. 12.

21 Crowther, *Critical Aesthetics and Postmodernism*, p. 209.

22 Fredric Jameson, *The Cultural Turn – Selected Writings on the Postmodern* (London, New York, 1998), p. 54.

23 Michael Hunter, 'The Preconditions of Preservation: A Historical Perspective', *Our Past Before Us*, ed. Lowenthal and Binney, pp. 22–32, see p. 24.

24 See Lowenthal, *The Past is a Foreign Country*, p. 394 and Hunter, 'The Preconditions of Preservation', p. 24.

25 Patrick Cormack, *Heritage in Danger* (London, 1978), pp. 169ff; and Donald Appleyard (ed.), *The Conservation of European Cities* (Cambridge, Mass., 1979), p. 23.

26 Timothy Champion 'Protecting the Monuments: Archaeological Legislation from the 1882 Act to *PPG 16*,' *Preserving the Past*, ed. Hunter, pp. 38–56, see p. 40.

27 Hunter, 'The Preconditions of Preservation', p. 29; *Preserving the Past*, pp. 8–9; Champion, 'Protecting the Monuments', pp. 38–9.

28 Hunter, 'The Preconditions of Preservation', p. 24.

29 Andrew Saint, 'How Listing Happened', *Preserving the Past*, ed. Hunter, pp. 115–34, see p. 115.

30 Champion, 'Protecting the Monuments', p. 42.

31 John Earl, 'London Government: A Record of Custodianship', *Preserving the Past*, ed. Hunter, pp. 57–76, esp. pp. 59–64.

32 Haskell, *The Early Music Revival*, p. 100.

33 Beverly Haviland, *Henry James's Last Romance – Making Sense of the Past and the American Scene* (Cambridge, 1997), p. 2.

34 Saint, 'How Listing Happened', p. 124.

35 Appleyard, *The Conservation of European Cities*, p. 11.

36 Dorottya Fabian, 'J. S. Bach Recordings 1945–1975: *St Matthew* and *St John Passions, Brandenburg Concertos* and *Goldberg Variations* – A Study of Performance Practice in the Context of the Early Music Movement', 2 vols. (PhD Dissertation, University of New South Wales, 1998), vol. 1 pp. 93–4, notes the gradual adoption of HIP productions for quite major broadcasts in Germany and France during this period.

37 Appleyard, *The Conservation of European Cities*, pp. 10–11.

38 *Ibid.*, p. 19.

39 See Robert Hewison, *The Heritage Industry: Britain in a Climate of Decline* (London, 1987), p. 38.

40 Perry Anderson, *The Origins of Postmodernity* (London, New York, 1998), pp. 41–2.

41 *After the End of Art – Contemporary Art and the Pale of History* (Princeton, 1997), p. 13.

42 Maxwell Hutchinson, *The Prince of Wales: Right or Wrong? An Architect Replies* (London, 1989), p. 171.

43 Philippe Hoyau, 'Heritage and "The Conserver Society": The French Case', *The Museum Time-Machine*, R. Lumley, ed. (London, 1988), p. 28.

44 Patrick Wright, *On Living in an Old Country* (London, 1985), p. 22.

45 Samuel, *Past and Present*, p. 245.

46 Peter Mandler, 'Nationalising the Country House', *Preserving the Past*, pp. 99–114, see p. 108.

47 Quoted in Hewison, *The Heritage Industry*, p. 37.

48 Hutchinson, *The Prince of Wales: Right or Wrong?*, pp. 69ff.

49 See Sophie Andreae 'From Comprehensive Development to Conservation Areas', *Preserving the Past*, pp. 135–55, esp. pp. 144–5; Marcus Binney, *Our Vanishing Heritage* (London, 1984), pp. 10–11.

50 Wright, *On Living in an Old Country*, pp. 33–93.
51 Andreae, 'From Comprehensive Development', p. 148.
52 Haskell, *The Early Music Revival*, pp. 122–3.
53 Fabian, 'J. S. Bach Recordings 1945–1975', p. 78.
54 See also Samuel, *Past and Present*, p. 146.
55 *Ibid.*, p. 190.
56 Michael Stratton 'Open-air and Industrial Museums: Windows onto a Lost World or Graveyards for Unloved Buildings?', *Preserving the Past*, pp. 156–76, esp. 156–7.
57 Lowenthal, *The Past is a Foreign Country*, p. 299.
58 Julian Barnes, *England, England* (London, 1998), esp. pp. 207–13.
59 Umberto Eco, *Faith in Fakes*, trans. William Weaver (London, 1986), pp. 3–58.
60 *The Culture of the Copy – Striking Likenesses, Unreasonable Facsimiles* (New York, 1996), p. 279.
61 Baudrillard, *Fatal Strategies*, pp. 74–5.
62 Norman Foster, speaking in reaction to the excessive wobbling of the Millennium Bridge (Maev Kennedy, 'Designers back in step over bouncing millennium bridge', *The Guardian*, 29 June 2000, p. 1).
63 Joshua Rifkin, in conversation, May 2000.
64 Kay Kaufman Shelemay, 'Toward an Ethnomusicology of the Early Music Movement: Thoughts on Bridging Disciplines and Musical Worlds', *Ethnomusicology*, 45 (2001), pp. 10, 22.
65 Wiener, *English Culture and the Decline of the Industrial Spirit, 1850–1980* (Cambridge, 1981), pp. 69–70.
66 Chris Miele, 'The First Conservation Militants: William Morris and the Society for the Protection of Ancient Buildings', in Michael Hunter, ed., *Preserving the Past: The Rise of Heritage in Modern Britain* (Stroud, 1996), pp. 17–37; Hutchinson, *The Prince of Wales*, pp. 16–17.
67 Luckett, 'The Revival of Early Music', III, 14. For a brief sketch of the association between Dolmetsch and Morris, see Haskell, *The Early Music Revival*, pp. 29–30.
68 Lowenthal, 'Conclusion: Dilemmas of Preservation', *Our Past Before Us*, ed. Lowenthal and Binney, p. 227.
69 See also Strong's introduction to Cormack *Heritage in Danger*; and Hunter's concluding notes, *Preserving the Past*, p. 189.
70 Foreword to Hutchinson, *The Prince of Wales*, ix.
71 Danto, *After the End of Art*, p. 9.
72 Milton Babbitt, 'Who Cares if You Listen', *High Fidelity*, 8/2 (1958), pp. 38–40, 126–7. Babbitt's intended title was the much tamer 'The Composer as Specialist'.
73 Raymond Williams, 'When Was Modernism?', *New Left Review*, 175 (May/June, 1989), pp. 48–52. Reprinted in Francis Frascina, and Jonathan Harris, eds, *Art in Modern Culture – An Anthology of Critical Texts* (London, 1992), pp. 23–7, see esp. p. 25.
74 See Fabian, 'J. S. Bach Recordings 1945–1975', pp. 35, 41–3, 56.

75 Clement Greenberg, 'Modernist Painting' (Radio Lecture, 1961), reprinted in *Art in Modern Culture – An Anthology of Critical Texts*, ed. Francis Frascina and Jonathan Harris (London, 1992), pp. 308–14, quotation from p. 308.

76 'Top Dollar and Long Yen' becomes almost a mantra for the planners in Barnes's *England, England*.

77 Danto, *After the End of Art*, p. 5.

78 Stamp, 'The Art of Keeping one Jump Ahead', p. 88.

79 Fredric Jameson, *The Cultural Turn*, p. 7.

80 Chris Rojek, *Ways of Escape: Modern Transformations in Leisure and Travel* (London, 1993), p. 99.

81 Anthony Giddens, *Modernity and Self-Identity: Self and Society in the Late Modern Age* (Cambridge, 1991). Introduction, reprinted in Frascina and Harris, *Art in Modern Culture*, p. 19.

82 Rojek, *Ways of Escape*, p. 133. It is interesting to find Baudrillard himself described as 'not really working in academia but at the sharp end of the entertainment business', by Mark Gullick in a review of Floyd Merrell's *Semiotics in the Postmodern Age* (*BJA*, 36, 1996), p. 456.

83 Wright, *On Living in an Old Country*, p. 166.

84 See Wiener, *English Culture and the Decline of the Industrial Spirit*, p. 119.

85 John Urry 'How Societies Remember the Past', *Theorizing Museums: Representing Identity and Diversity in a Changing World*, ed. Sharon Macdonald and Gorden Fyfe (Oxford, 1996), pp. 45–64, esp. 59–60.

86 Hobsbawm, *The Invention of Tradition*, Introduction, pp. 5–6.

87 Schwartz, *The Culture of the Copy*, p. 276.

88 Rojek, *Ways of Escape*, p. 147.

89 Peter J. Fowler, *The Past in Contemporary Society: Then, Now* (London, 1992), p. 50.

90 It is highly significant that the Globe Theatre project was first formulated in the 1890s (Samuel, *Past and Present*, p. 247), precisely the same era in which Dolmetsch was first advocating the return to the original conditions of music making.

91 Andrew Gurr with John Orrell, *Rebuilding Shakespeare's Globe* (London, 1989), p. 163.

92 Walter Benjamin, 'The Work of Art in the Age of Mechanical Reproduction' (1936), *Illuminations*, trans. Harry Zohn, ed., with an introduction by Hannah Ahrendt (New York, 1968), pp. 217–51, see p. 221.

93 *Uppark – West Sussex* – National Trust Guide (1995), p. 45.

94 See Simon Jenkins, 'The Craftsman's Contract', *The Times*, 3 June, 1995, p. 18: 'the ageing and "distressing" went to astonishing lengths. The plaster was analysed and remixed from original paste strengthened with hair. If mistakes were found in the original woodwork, these were faithfully replicated . . . Wallpaper was printed to match exactly the fading of sunlight on each patch of wall, including bright colours behind pictures and fittings.'

95 Schwartz, *The Culture of the Copy*, p. 280.

96 Lowenthal, quoting Malraux, *The Past is a Foreign Country*, p. 172.

97 Stamp, 'The Art of Keeping One Jump Ahead', p. 93.
98 Laurence Dreyfus, 'Early Music Defended against its Devotees: A Theory of Historical Performance in the Twentieth Century', *MQ*, 69 (1983), pp. 297–322, see pp. 311–13.
99 See Brett, note 6 above.
100 Daniel Leech-Wilkinson, 'What We are Doing with Early Music is Genuinely Authentic to Such a Small Degree that the Word Loses Most of its Intended Meaning', *EM*, 12 (1984), pp. 13–16.
101 See Joseph Kerman, 'A profile for American Musicology', *JAMS*, 18 (1965), pp. 61–9, and Edward Lowinsky's response and Kerman's reply, *Ibid.*, 222–34; 426–7.
102 David Cannadine 'The Context, Performance and Meaning of Ritual: The British Monarchy and the "Invention of Tradition" ', *c*. 1820–1977', *The Invention of Tradition*, ed. Eric Hobsbawm and Terence Ranger (Cambridge, 1983), pp. 101–64.
103 Carl Dahlhaus, *Nineteenth-Century Music*, trans. J.B. Robinson (Berkeley and Los Angeles, 1989), pp. 28–9.
104 Wright, *On Living in an Old Country*, p. 169.
105 Mandler, 'Nationalising the Country House', p. 105.
106 This pattern was set in motion by German bombing raids, which took a heavy toll on the 'lesser' buildings, but left the 'classic' pieces essentially intact; see Borsay, *The Image of Georgian Bath*, pp. 172–3.
107 Adam Fergusson, *The Sack of Bath – and After: A Record and an Indictment* (1973, extended edition: Salisbury, 1989).
108 *Ibid.*, p. 12. See also Appleyard, *The Conservation of European Cities*, pp. 16, 77; Borsay, *The Image of Georgian Bath*, p. 196.
109 David Cannadine, *The Pleasures of the Past* (London, 1990), pp. 264–6.
110 See Tony Bennett, *The Birth of the Museum: History, Theory, Policy* (London, 1995).
111 Hewison, *The Heritage Industry*, p. 74; Wright, *On Living in an Old Country*, p. 23.
112 Peter Mandler, *The Fall and Rise of the Stately Home* (New Haven and London, 1997), p. 142.
113 Chris Miele, Review of James M. Lindgren, *Preserving Historic New England: Preservation, Progressivism and the Remaking of Memory* (New York and Oxford, 1995), *International Journal of Heritage Studies*, 3/2 (Summer, 1997), p. 124.
114 For a survey of Dolmetsch's interest in folk music and his friendship with Percy Grainger, see Haskell, *The Early Music Revival*, pp. 41–2.
115 Luckett, 'The Revival of Early Music', IV, pp. 5–6.
116 Haskell, *The Early Music Revival*, p. 64.
117 *Ibid.*, pp. 84–5.
118 Nikolaus Harnoncourt, *Baroque Music Today*, pp. 11–13, and quote on p. 24.
119 A similar view is expressed by Hewison, *The Heritage Industry*, p. 56, where he suggests that Ruskin's writings are 'deeply conservative in origin'.

120 David Edgar, 'The New Nostalgia', *Marxism Today* (March 1987), pp. 30–5, esp. p. 30.
121 E.g. Cannadine, in *Pleasures of the Past*, p. 270.
122 Roger Scruton, *On Hunting* (London, 1998). For the connection with Scruton's critique of HIP, see M. W. Rowe's review of Scruton's *The Aesthetics of Music*, in *BJA*, 39 (1999), p. 425.
123 See Barbara Adams, 'Detraditionalization and the Certainty of Uncertain Futures', *Detraditionalization: Critical Reflections on Authority and Identity*, ed. Paul Heelas, Scott Lash and Paul Morris (Oxford, 1996), pp. 134–48, esp. 139–40.
124 Samuel has been criticised for not mustering substantial evidence to support his case against heritage-baiters and for his drift towards uncritical populism. However, it is clear that he uncovers an elitist bias on the part of those who object to 'democratised heritage'. See Jim McGuigan, *Culture and the Public Sphere* (London and New York, 1996), pp. 124–8.
125 Friedrich Nietzsche, *On the Genealogy of Morals* (1887), trans. Douglas Smith (Oxford, 1996), p. 57.
126 Those working in the tradition of Wittgenstein, such as Richard Rorty.
127 Stephen Greenblatt, *Marvelous Possessions – The Wonder of the New World* (Oxford, 1991), p. 4.
128 *Faith in Fakes*, p. 149.

Bibliography

Adams, Barbara, 'Detraditionalization and the Certainty of Uncertain Futures',
  Detraditionalization: Critical Reflections on Authority and Identity, ed. Paul Heelas,
  Scott Lash and Paul Morris (Oxford, 1996), pp. 134–48
Adorno, Theodor W., 'Bach Defended against his Devotees' (1951), *Prisms*, trans.
  Samuel and Shierry Weber (Cambridge, Mass., 1981), pp. 133–46
  Introduction to the Sociology of Music (*Einleitung in die Musiksoziologie*, Frankfurt,
  1962), trans. E. B. Ashton (New York, 1976)
  'Der mißbrauchte Barock', *Ohne Leitbild* (Frankfurt, 1967), pp. 133–57
Anderson, Perry, *The Origins of Postmodernity* (London, New York, 1998)
Andreae, Sophie, 'From Comprehensive Development to Conservation Areas',
  Preserving the Past: The Rise of Heritage in Modern Britain, ed. Michael Hunter
  (Stroud, 1996), pp. 135–55
Appleyard, Donald (ed.), *The Conservation of European Cities* (Cambridge, Mass.,
  1979)
Armstrong, Alan, 'Gilbert-Louis Duprez and Gustave Roger in the Composition
  of Meyerbeer's *Le Prophète*', *COJ*, 8 (1996), pp. 147–65
Attridge, Derek, 'Language as History/History as Language: Saussure and the
  Romance of Etymology', *Post-Structuralism and the Question of History*, ed.
  Derek Attridge, Geoff Bennington and Robert Young (Cambridge, 1987),
  pp. 183–211
Barnes, Julian, *England, England* (London, 1998)
Barthes, Roland, 'The Death of the Author', *Image, Music, Text – Roland
  Barthes*, Essays selected and translated by Stephen Heath (London, 1977),
  pp. 142–8
Baudrillard, Jean, *Fatal Strategies* (New York, 1990)
  The Consumer Society: Myths and Structures (London, 1998)
Bauman, Zygmunt, 'Parvenu and Pariah: Heroes and Victims of Modernity',
  The Politics of Postmodernity, ed. James Good and Irving Velody (Cambridge,
  1998), pp. 23–35
Baxandall, Michael, *Patterns of Intention – On the Historical Explanation of Pictures*
  (New Haven and London, 1985)
Beardsley, Monroe, *Aesthetics – Problems in the Philosophy of Criticism* (New York,
  1958)

Benjamin, Walter, 'The Work of Art in the Age of Mechanical Reproduction' (1936), *Illuminations*, trans. Harry Zohn, ed., with an introduction by Hannah Arendt (New York, 1968), pp. 217–51

Bennett, Tony, *The Birth of the Museum: History, Theory, Policy* (London, 1995)

Bent, Margaret, 'Musica Recta and Musica Ficta', *Musica Disciplina*, 26 (1972), pp. 73–100

Berger, Karol, 'Musica ficta', *Performance Practice: Music Before 1600*, ed. Howard Mayer Brown and Stanley Sadie (New York and London, 1989), pp. 107–25

A Theory of Art (New York, Oxford, 2000)

Bergeron, Katherine, *Decadent Enchantments – The Revival of Gregorian Chant at Solesmes* (Berkeley and Los Angeles, 1998)

Berrow, Jim, (ed.), *Towards the Conservation and Restoration of Historic Organs* (London, 2000)

Bilson, Malcolm, 'The Viennese Fortepiano of the Late 18th Century', *EM*, 8 (1980), pp. 158–69

'The Future of Schubert Interpretation: What is Really Needed?', *EM*, 25 (1997), pp. 715–22

Binney, Marcus, *Our Vanishing Heritage* (London, 1984)

Blackburn, Bonnie J., 'On Compositional Process in the Fifteenth Century', *JAMS*, 40 (1987), pp. 210–84

Boorman, Stanley, 'The Musical Text', *Rethinking Music*, ed. Nicholas Cook and Mark Everist (Oxford and New York, 1999), pp. 403–23

Booth, Wayne, *The Rhetoric of Fiction* (Chicago, 1961)

Born, Georgina, *Rationalizing Culture – IRCAM, Boulez, and the Institutionalization of the Musical Avant-Garde* (Berkeley and Los Angeles, 1995)

Borsay, Peter, *The Image of Georgian Bath, 1700–2000* (Oxford, 2000)

Bowen, José A., 'The Conductor and the Score: The Relationship between Interpreter and Text in the Generation of Mendelssohn, Berlioz and Wagner' (PhD Dissertation, Stanford University, 1993)

'Finding the Music in Musicology: Performance History and Musical Works', *Rethinking Music*, ed. Nicholas Cook and Mark Everist (Oxford and New York, 1999), pp. 424–51

Brett, Philip, 'Text, Context, and the Early Music Editor', *Authenticity and Early Music*, ed. Nicholas Kenyon (Oxford, 1988), pp. 83–114

Britten, Benjamin, *On Receiving the First Aspen Award* (London, 1964)

Bujic, Bojan, 'Notation and Realization: Musical Performance in Historical Perspective', *The Interpretation of Music – Philosophical Essays*, ed. Michael Krausz (Oxford, 1993), pp. 129–40

Burstyn, Shai, 'In Quest of the Period Ear', *EM*, 25 (1997), pp. 693–701

Busse-Berger, Anna Maria, 'Mnemotechnics and Notre Dame Polyphony', *JM*, 14 (1996), pp. 263–98

'Die Rolle der Mündlichkeit in der Komposition der Notre Dame Polyphonie', *Das Mittelalter*, 1 (1998), pp. 127–43

Butler, Rex, *The Defence of the Real* (London, 1999)

Butt, John, *Bach Interpretation* (Cambridge, 1990)

Music Education and the Art of Performance in the German Baroque (Cambridge, 1994)
'Bach Recordings since 1980: A Mirror of Historical Performance', *Bach Perspectives*, 4, ed. David Schulenberg (Lincoln and London, 1999), pp. 181–98

Cage, John, *Notations* (New York, 1969)

Cahoone, Lawrence, (ed.), *From Modernism to Postmodernism – An Anthology* (Cambridge Mass. and Oxford, 1996)

Campana, Alessandra, 'Mozart's Italian *buffo* Singers', *EM*, 19 (1991), pp. 580–3

Cannadine, David, 'The Context, Performance and Meaning of Ritual: The British Monarchy and the "Invention of Tradition", *c.* 1820–1977', *The Invention of Tradition*, ed. Eric Hobsbawm and Terry Ranger (Cambridge, 1983), pp. 101–64

The Pleasures of the Past (London, 1990)

Cascardi, Anthony, J., *The Subject of Modernity* (Cambridge, 1992)

Champion, Timothy, 'Protecting the Monuments: Archaeological Legislation', *Preserving the Past: The Rise of Heritage in Modern Britain*, ed. Michael Hunter (Stroud, 1996), pp. 38–56

Clark, T. J., *Farewell to an Idea – Episodes from a History of Modernism* (New Haven and London, 1999)

Close, A. J., '*Don Quixote* and the "Intentionalist fallacy" ', *On Literary Intention*, ed. David Newton-de Molina (Edinburgh, 1976), pp. 174–93

Cockcroft, Eva, 'Abstract Expressionism, Weapon of the Cold War', *Artforum*, 15/10 (1974), pp. 39–41. Reprinted in Frascina and Harris, *Art in Modern Culture*, pp. 82–90

Conforti, Giovanni Luca, *Breve et facile maniera d'essercitarsi* (Rome, 1593)

Cook, Nicholas, *Music, Imagination and Culture* (Oxford, 1990)
(ed.), with Mark Everist, ed., *Rethinking Music*, (Oxford and New York, 1999)

Cormack, Patrick, *Heritage in Danger* (London, 1978)

Crowther, Paul, *Critical Aesthetics and Postmodernism* (Oxford, 1993)

Dahlhaus, Carl, *Foundations of Music History*, trans. J. B. Robinson (Cambridge, 1983)
The Idea of Absolute Music, trans. Roger Lustig (Chicago, 1989)
Nineteenth-Century Music, trans. J. B. Robinson (Berkeley and Los Angeles, 1989)

Danto, Arthur C., *After the End of Art – Contemporary Art and the Pale of History* (Princeton, 1997)

Davies, Stephen, 'The Aesthetic Relevance of Authors' and Painters' Intentions', *JAAC*, 41, (1982–3), pp. 65–76
'Authenticity in Musical Performance', *BJA*, 27 (1987), pp. 39–50
'General Theories of Art Versus Music', *BJA*, 34 (1994), pp. 315–25

Dennett, Daniel C., *The Intentional Stance* (Cambridge, Mass., 1987)

Dipert, Randall, R., 'The Composer's Intentions: An Examination of their Relevance for Performance', *MQ*, 66 (1980), pp. 205–18

Dixon, Graham, 'The Performance of Palestrina: Some Questions, but Fewer Answers', *EM*, 22 (1994), pp. 667–75

Dreyfus, Laurence, 'Early Music Defended against its Devotees: A Theory of Historical Performance in the Twentieth Century', *MQ*, 69 (1983), pp. 297–322

Bach and the Patterns of Invention (Cambridge, Mass., 1996)

'Patterns of Authority in Musical Interpretation: Historical Performance at the Cross-Roads' (forthcoming)

Dulak, Michelle, 'The Quiet Metamorphosis of "Early Music"', *Repercussions*, 2 (Fall 1993), pp. 31–61

Dürr, Walther, 'Schubert and Johann Michael Vogl: a Reappraisal', *19th-Century Music*, 3 (1979), pp. 126–40

Eagleton, Terry, 'Capitalism, Modernism and Postmodernism', *New Left Review*, 152 (1985), pp. 60–73; reprinted in Waugh, *Postmodernism*, pp. 152–9 and in Frascina and Harris, *Art in Modern Culture*, pp. 91–100

Earl, John, 'London Government: A Record of Custodianship', *Preserving the Past: The Rise of Heritage in Modern Britain*, ed. Michael Hunter (Stroud, 1996), pp. 57–76

Eco, Umberto, *Opera aperta* (Milan, 1962), trans., with additional chapters, by Anna Cancogni with an introduction by David Robey, as *The Open Work* (Cambridge, Mass., 1989)

Faith in Fakes, trans. William Weaver (London, 1986)

Edgar, David, 'The New Nostalgia', *Marxism Today* (March 1987), pp. 30–5

Ellis, Katherine, *Music Criticism in Nineteenth-Century France: La Revue et Gazette Musicale de Paris, 1834–80* (Cambridge, 1995)

Elste, Martin, *Meilensteine der Bach-Interpretation 1750–200– Eine Werkgeschichte im Wandel* (Stuttgart, Weimar and Kassel, 2000)

Fabian, Dorottya, ' J. S. Bach Recordings 1945–1975: *St Matthew* and *St John Passions, Brandenburg Concertos* and *Goldberg Variations* – A Study of Performance Practice in the Context of the Early Music Movement', 2 vols. (PhD. Dissertation, University of New South Wales, 1998)

Feagin, Susan, L., 'On Defining and Interpreting Art Intentionalistically', *BJA*, 22 (1982), pp. 65–77

Fergusson, Adam, *The Sack of Bath – and After: A Record and an Indictment* (1973, extended edition: Salisbury, 1989)

Ferneyhough, Brian, *Collected Writings*, ed. James Boros and Richard Toop, with a foreword by Jonathan Harvey (Amsterdam, 1995)

Finscher, Ludwig, 'Historisch getreue Interpretation – Möglichkeiten und Probleme', *Alte Musik in unsere Zeit* – Referate und Diskussionen der Kasseler Tagung 1967, ed. Walter Wiora (Kassel, 1968), pp. 25–34

Fisher, John Andrew, and Potter, Jason, 'Technology, Appreciation, and the Historical View of Art', *JAAC*, 55 (1997), pp. 169–85

Foucault, Michel, *The Order of Things: An Archaeology of the Human Sciences*, Translation of *Les Mots et les choses*, 1966 (New York, 1970)

Fowler, Peter, J., *The Past in Contemporary Society: Then, Now* (London, 1992)

Frascina, Francis, and Jonathan Harris, eds., *Art in Modern Culture – An Anthology of Critical Texts* (London, 1992)

Fuller, David, ' "Sous les doits de Chambonniere" ', *EM*, 21 (1993), pp. 191–202

Giddens, Anthony, *Modernity and Self-Identity: Self and Society in the Late Modern Age* (Cambridge, 1991)

Gidwitz, Patricia Lewy, ' "Ich bin die erste Sängerin": Vocal Profiles of Two Mozart Sopranos', *EM*, 19 (1991), pp. 565–79

Goehr, Lydia, *The Imaginary Museum of Musical Works* (Oxford, 1992)

' "On the Problems of Dating" or "Looking Backwards and Forward with Strohm" ', *The Musical Work: Reality or Invention*, ed. Michael Talbot (Liverpool, 2000), pp. 231–46

Gossett, Philip, 'Gioachino Rossini and the Conventions of Composition', *Acta Musicologica*, 42 (1970), pp. 48–58

Godlovitch, Stan, 'Performance Authenticity – Possible, Practical, Virtuous', *Performance and Authenticity in the Arts*, ed. Salim Kemal and Ivan Gaskell (Cambridge, 1999), pp. 154–74

Greenberg, Clement, 'Modernist Painting' (Radio Lecture, 1961), reprinted in *Art in Modern Culture – An Anthology of Critical Texts*, ed. Francis Frascina and Jonathan Harris (London, 1992), pp. 308–14

Greenblatt, Stephen, *Marvelous Possessions – The Wonder of the New World* (Oxford, 1991)

Gurr, Andrew with John Orrell, *Rebuilding Shakespeare's Globe* (London, 1989)

Harnoncourt, Nikolaus, *Baroque Music Today: Music as Speech*, ed. Reinhard G. Pauly, trans. Mary O'Neill (Portland, Oregon, 1988)

Harris-Warrick, Rebecca, 'The Parisian Sources of Donizetti's French Operas: The Case of *La Favorite*', *L'Opera Teatrale di Gaetano Donizetti – Proceedings of the International Conference on the Operas of Gaetano Donizetti, Bergamo, 1992*, ed. Francesco Bellotto (Bergamo, 1993), pp. 77–90

Haskell, Harry, *The Early Music Revival* (London, 1988)

Haviland, Beverly, *Henry James's Last Romance – Making Sense of the Past and the American Scene* (Cambridge, 1997)

Hepokoski, James, 'Overriding the Autograph Score: The Problem of Textual Authority in Verdi's "Falstaff" ', *Studi Verdiani*, 8 (1992), pp. 13–51

Hesse, Hermann, *The Glass Bead Game* (1943), trans. Richard and Clara Winston (Harmondsworth, England, 1972)

Hewison, Robert, *The Heritage Industry: Britain in a Climate of Decline* (London, 1987)

Hindemith, Paul, *Johann Sebastian Bach* – a speech delivered on 12 September, 1950 at the Bach commemoration of the city of Hamburg, Germany (New Haven, 1952)

Hobsbawm, Eric, 'Mass-Producing Traditions: Europe, 1870–1914', *The Invention of Tradition*, ed. Eric Hobsbawm and Terence Ranger (Cambridge, 1983), pp. 263–307

Hoyau, Philippe, 'Heritage and "The Conserver Society": The French Case', *The Museum Time-Machine*, ed. R. Lumley (London, 1988)

Hucke, Helmut, 'Towards a New Historical View of Gregorian Chant', *JAMS*, 33 (1980), pp. 437–67

Hunter, Michael, 'The Preconditions of Preservation: A Historical Perspective', *Our Past Before Us – Why Do We Save it?*, ed. David Lowenthal and Marcus Binney (London, 1981), pp. 22–32

(ed.) *Preserving the Past: The Rise of Heritage in Modern Britain* (Stroud, 1996)

Hutchinson, Maxwell, *The Prince of Wales: Right or Wrong? An Architect Replies* (London, 1989)

Isemiger, Gary (ed.), *Intention and Interpretation* (Philadelphia, 1992)

James, Henry, *The Sense of the Past* (London, 1917), unfinished novel with the author's notes for completion

Jameson, Fredric, *Postmodernism, or, The Cultural Logic of Late Capitalism* (Durham, NC, 1991)

The Cultural Turn – Selected Writings on the Postmodern (London, New York, 1998)

Jeffery, Peter, *Re-Envisioning Past Musical Cultures: Ethnomusicology in the Study of Gregorian Chant* (Chicago and London, 1992)

Kenyon, Nicholas, ed., *Authenticity and Early Music* (Oxford, 1988)

Kerman, Joseph, *Musicology* (London, 1985); US title: *Contemplating Music*

Kivy, Peter, *The Fine Art of Repetition – Essays in the Philosophy of Music* (Cambridge, 1993)

Authenticities – Philosophical Reflections on Musical Performance (Ithaca and London, 1995)

Lang, Paul Henry, Editorial, *MQ*, 58 (1972), pp. 117–27

Musicology and Performance, ed. Alfred Mann and George J. Buelow (New Haven, 1997)

Larue, C. Steven, *Handel and his Singers: The Creation of the Royal Academy Operas, 1720–1728* (Oxford, 1995)

Leech-Wilkinson, Daniel, 'What We are Doing with Early Music is Genuinely Authentic to Such a Small Degree that the Word Loses Most of its Intended Meaning', *EM*, 12 (1984), pp. 13–16

'Yearning for the Sound of Medieval Music' *Mittelalter-Sehnsucht?: Texte des interdisziplinären Symposions zur musikalischen Mittelalterrezeption an der Universität Heidelberg, April 1998*, ed. Annette Kreutziger-Herr and Dorothea Redepenning (Kiel, Vank, 2000), pp. 295–317

'Translating Medieval Music' (in press)

Levenson, Michael H., *A Genealogy of Modernism – A Study of English Literary Doctrine 1908–1922* (Cambridge, 1984)

Levin, Robert D., 'Improvised Embellishments in Mozart's Keyboard Sonatas', *EM*, 20 (1993), pp. 221–33

Levinson, Jerrold, *Music, Art, and Metaphysics – Essays in Philosophical Aesthetics* (Ithaca and London, 1990)

The Pleasures of Aesthetics: Philosophical Essays (Ithaca and London, 1996)

Longenbach, James, *Modernist Poetics of History – Pound, Eliot, and the Sense of the Past* (Princeton, 1987)

Lowenthal, David, *The Past is a Foreign Country* (Cambridge, 1985)

The Heritage Crusade and the Spoils of History (Cambridge, 1998); originally published as *Possessed by the Past* (New York, 1996)

Lowenthal, David, and Marcus Binney (eds.), *Our Past Before Us – Why do we save it?* (London, 1981)

Luckett, Richard, 'The Revival of Early Music and the Suppositions of Cultural History', unpublished MS (1986)

Lyotard, Jean-François, *The Postmodern Condition: A Report on Knowledge* (1979), trans. Geoff Bennington and Brian Massumi, with a foreword by Fredric Jameson (Manchester, 1984)

McGann, Jerome J., *The Textual Condition* (Princeton, 1991)

McGuigan, Jim, *Culture and the Public Sphere* (London and New York, 1996)

Mandler, Peter, 'Nationalising the Country House', *Preserving the Past: The Rise of Heritage in Modern Britain*, ed. Michael Hunter (Stroud, 1996), pp. 99–114
   The Fall and Rise of the Stately Home (New Haven and London, 1997)

Mattheson, Johann, *Der vollkommene Capellmeister* (Hamburg, 1739), trans. Ernest C. Harriss (Ann Arbor, 1981)

Molina, David Newton-de, ed., *On Literary Intention* (Edinburgh, 1976)

Montgomery, David, 'Modern Schubert Interpretation in the Light of the Pedagogical Sources of His Day', *EM*, 25 (1997), pp. 101–18

Morgan, Robert P., 'Tradition, Anxiety, and the Current Musical Scene', Nicholas Kenyon, ed., *Authenticity and Early Music* (Oxford, 1988), pp. 57–82

Murata, Margaret, (ed.), *Strunk's Source Readings in Music History – Revised Edition*, ed. Leo Treitler, vol. 4: The Baroque Era (New York and London, 1998)

Nattiez, Jean-Jacques, *Music and Discourse: Toward a Semiology of Music* (Princeton, 1990)

Newcomb, Anthony, 'Schumann and the Marketplace: From Butterflies to *Hausmusik*', *Nineteenth-Century Piano Music*, ed. R. Larry Todd (New York, 1990), pp. 258–315
   'Unnotated Accidentals in the Music of the Post-Josquin Generation: Mainly on the Example of Gombert's First Book of Motets for Four Voices', *Music in Renaissance Cities and Courts: Studies in Honor of Lewis Lockwood*, ed. Jessie Ann Owens and Anthony M. Cummings (Michigan, 1997), pp. 215–25

Niedt, Friedrich Erhard, *The Musical Guide*, Part 2 (1721), trans. and ed. by Pamela L. Poulin and Irmgard C. Taylor (Oxford, 1989)

Nietzsche, Friedrich, 'On the Uses and Disadvantages of History for Life' (1874), *Untimely Meditations*, trans. R. J. Hollingdale (Cambridge, 1983), pp. 57–123
   On the Genealogy of Morals (1887), trans. Douglas Smith (Oxford, 1996)

Norris, Christopher, *The Truth about Postmodernism* (Oxford and Cambridge Mass., 1993)

North, Roger, 'The Excellent Art of Voluntary', ed. John Wilson, *Roger North on Music* (London, 1959), pp. 133–45

O'Regan, Noel, 'The Performance of Palestrina: Some Further Observations', *EM*, 24 (1996), pp. 144–54

Paddison, Max, *Adorno's Aesthetics of Music* (Cambridge, 1993)

Page, Christopher, 'The English *a cappella* Renaissance', *EM*, 21 (1993), pp. 453–71

Parker, Roger, 'A Donizetti Critical Edition in the Postmodern World', *L'Opera Teatrale di Gaetano Donizetti – Proceedings of the International Conference on the Operas of Gaetano Donizetti, Bergamo, 1992*, ed. Francesco Bellotto (Bergamo, 1993), pp. 57–66

Philip, Robert, *Early Recordings and Musical Style* (Cambridge, 1992)

Rojek, Chris, *Ways of Escape: Modern Transformations in Leisure and Travel* (London, 1993)

Rorty, Richard, *Contingency, Irony, and Solidarity* (Cambridge, 1989)

Rosand, Ellen, *Opera in Seventeenth-Century Venice: The Creation of a Genre* (Berkeley and Los Angeles, 1991)

Rose, Margaret, *The Post-Modern and the Post-Industrial* (Cambridge, 1991)

Rosebury, Brian, 'Irrecoverable Intentions and Literary Interpretation', *BJA*, 37 (1997), pp. 15–30

Saint, Andrew, 'How Listing Happened', *Preserving the Past: The Rise of Heritage in Modern Britain*, ed. Michael Hunter (Stroud, 1996), pp. 115–34

Samson, Jim, 'The Practice of Early-Nineteenth-Century Pianism', *The Musical Work: Reality or Invention?*, ed. Michael Talbot (Liverpool, 2000), pp. 110–27

Samuel, Claude, *Music and Color – Conversations with Claude Samuel / Olivier Messiaen* (1986), trans. E. Thomas Glasow (Portland, 1994)

Samuel, Raphael, *Theatres of Memory*, vol. 1: *Past and Present in Contemporary Culture* (London, 1994)

Schwartz, Hillel, *The Culture of the Copy – Striking Likenesses, Unreasonable Facsimiles* (New York, 1996)

Scruton, Roger, *The Aesthetics of Music* (Oxford, 1997)
  On Hunting (London, 1998)

Seletsky, Robert E., '18ᵗʰ-Century Variations for Corelli's Sonatas, op. 5', *EM*, 24 (1996), pp. 119–30

Sessions, Roger, *The Musical Experience of Composer, Performer, Listener* (Princeton, 1950)

Sharpe, R. A., 'Music, Platonism and Performance: Some Ontological Strains', *BJA*, 35 (1995), pp. 38–48

Shelemay, Kay Kaufman, 'Toward an Ethnomusicology of the early music Movement: Thoughts on Bridging Disciplines and Musical Worlds', *Ethnomusicology*, 45 (2001), 1–29

Sherman, Bernard D., *Inside Early Music – Conversations with Performers* (New York and Oxford, 1997)

Silbiger, Alexander, ed., *Keyboard Music Before 1700* (New York, 1995)

Smart, Mary Ann, 'The Lost Voice of Rosine Stoltz', *COJ*, 6 (1994), pp. 31–50

Somfai, László, *Béla Bartók: Composition, Concepts, and Autograph Sources* (Berkeley and Los Angeles, 1996)

Stamp, Gavin, 'The Art of Keeping one Jump Ahead: Conservation Societies in the Twentieth Century', *Preserving the Past: The Rise of Heritage in Modern Britain*, ed. Michael Hunter (Stroud, 1996), pp. 77–98

Stevens, Denis, 'Some Observations on Performance Practice', *CM*, 14 (1972), pp. 159–63

Stratton, Michael, 'Open-air and Industrial Museums: Windows onto a Lost World or Graveyards for Unloved Buildings?', *Preserving the Past: The Rise of Heritage in Modern Britain*, ed. Michael Hunter (Stroud, 1996), pp. 156–76

Strohm, Reinhard, *The Rise of European Music 1380–1500* (Cambridge, 1993)
'Looking Back at Ourselves: The Problem with the Musical Work-Concept', *The Musical Work: Reality or Invention?*, ed. Michael Talbot (Liverpool, 2000), pp. 128–52

Suleiman, Susan R., and Inge Crosman (eds.), *The Reader in the Text*, (Princeton, 1980)

Talbot, Michael, 'The Work-Concept and Composer-Centredness', *The Musical Work: Reality or Invention?*, ed. Michael Talbot (Liverpool, 2000), pp. 168–86

Taruskin, Richard, *Text and Act* (New York and Oxford, 1995)

Treib, Marc, *Space Calculated in Seconds – the Philips Pavilion – Le Corbusier – Edgard Varèse* (Princeton, 1996)

Treitler, Leo, 'The Early History of Music Writing in the West', *JAMS*, 35 (1982), pp. 237–79
Music and the Historical Imagination (Cambridge, Mass., 1989)
'The "Unwritten" and "Written" Transmission of Medieval Chant and the Start-up of Musical Notation', *JM*, 10 (1992), pp. 131–91
'History and the Ontology of the Musical Work', *JAAC*, 51 (1993), pp. 483–97

Urry, John, 'How Societies Remember the Past', *Theorizing Museums: Representing Identity and Diversity in a Changing World*, ed. Sharon Macdonald and Gordan Fyfe (Oxford, 1996), pp. 45–64, esp. 59–60

Van Tassel, Eric, ' "Something Utterly New": Listening to Schubert Lieder', *EM*, 25 (1997), pp. 703–14

Walls, Peter, 'Performing Corelli's Violin Sonatas, op. 5', *EM*, 24 (1996), pp. 133–42

Waugh, Patricia, ed., *Postmodernism: A Reader* (London, New York, Melbourne, Auckland, 1992)

Weber, Max, *Die rationalen und sozialen Grundlagen der Musik*, appendix to *Wirtschaft und Gesellschaft* (written 1911, published Tübingen, 1921), trans. as *The Rational and Social Foundations of Music*, trans. and ed. Don Martindale, Johannes Riedel and Gertrude Neuwirth (Carbondale: Southern Illinois University Press, 1958)

Wegman, Rob C., 'From Maker to Composer; Improvisation and Musical Authorship in the Low Countries, 1450–1500', *JAMS*, 49 (1996), pp. 409–79
' "Das musikalische Hören" in the Middle Ages and Renaissance: Perspectives from Pre-War Germany', *MQ*, 82 (1998), pp. 434–54

Whenham, John, *Claudio Monteverdi – Orfeo* (Cambridge, 1986)

White, Hayden, *Metahistory – The Historical Imagination in Nineteenth-Century Europe* (Baltimore and London, 1973)

Wiener, Martin J., *English Culture and the Decline of the Industrial Spirit 1850–1980* (Cambridge, 1981)

Williams, Raymond, 'When Was Modernism?', *New Left Review*, 175 (May/June, 1989), pp. 48–52. Reprinted in Francis Frascina, and Jonathan Harris, eds., *Art in Modern Culture – An Anthology of Critical Texts* (London, 1992), pp. 23–7

Wimsatt, W. K., 'Genesis: a Fallacy Revisited', *On Literary Intention*, ed. David Newton-de Molina (Edinburgh, 1976), pp. 116–38

Wimsatt, W. K., and Monroe Beardsley, 'The Intentional Fallacy', *Sewanee Review*, 54 (1946), pp. 468–88; Reprinted in *On Literary Intention*, ed. David Newton-de Molina (Edinburgh, 1976), pp. 1–13

Wollheim, Richard, *Painting as an Art* (Princeton, 1987)

Wright, Craig, *Music and Ceremony at Notre Dame of Paris, 500–1550* (Cambridge, 1989)

Wright, Patrick, *On Living in an Old Country* (London, 1985)

Young, James, O., 'The Concept of Authentic Performance', *BJA*, 28 (1988), pp. 228–38

Zaslaw, Neal, 'Ornaments for Corelli's Violin Sonatas, op. 5', *EM*, 24 (1996), pp. 95–115

Index